I take great pleasure in applauding the advent of the Ubu Repertory Theater Publications. Devoted to bringing English versions of important contemporary dramatic works from French-speaking countries, this program could not be more important or timely when institutions such as the Eugene O'Neill Theater Center and the Milwaukee Repertory Theater have begun to embrace and espouse the cause of this key element of cultural exchange.

It is particularly important to realize that the plays chosen for translation and publication are not part of any specific genre, but rather are eclectic and are selected to inform the English-speaking public of the scope and richness of present-day French-speaking playwrights.

I cherish the hope that this marvelous project will spark a renaissance in professional collaboration between our French and English-speaking theaters and foster greater understanding between diverse national groups.

George C. White, President
Eugene O'Neill Memorial Theater Center

UBU REPERTORY THEATER PUBLICATIONS

ANTHOLOGIES:

PREFACE

This collection presents the works of five outstanding playwrights from France, Quebec, the United States and Belgium. Among these works are two plays by the late Argentine-French writer Copi that were previously unavailable in English: the outrageous black comedy **A Tower Near Paris,** about a troubled young woman and the disastrous consequences of her impossible love for a gay man, and the farce **Grand Finale,** a remarkable sendup of his illness and impending death which Copi wrote while he was dying of AIDS in a Paris hospital. We believe these plays are a tribute to his extraordinary talent.

In grouping six very different works under the heading "Gay Plays," we were guided by the definition put forth by William M. Hoffman in the first published anthology of this kind: "I define a 'gay play' as one whose central figure or figures are homosexual or one in which homosexuality is a main theme. A gay play is not necessarily written by a homosexual or for homosexuals." Readers will doubtless feel, as we do, that for plays as diverse in style and content as the ones presented her, all labels—including Hoffman's loose definition—are strikingly inadequate. The fact that these plays are "gay" is not necessarily their most distinctive feature. **The Function,** by the young French playwright Jean-Marie Besset, sheds new light on power, masculinity and procreation by setting up a very modern triangle between two men and a woman. In **The Return of the Young Hippolytus,** Quebecois playwright Hervé Dupuis dramatizes an emotional encounter between a gay man and the eighteen-year-old son he hasn't seen in six years. Jean-Claude van Itallie's **Ancient Boys** is a moving "requiem" for a talented young set designer who comes vividly to life as four bereaved friends take turns reenacting scenes from the recent past. In **The Lives and Deaths of Miss Shakespeare,** the Belgian playwright Liliane Wouters uses satire, theatricality and a colorful cast of characters to unmask social convention, accepted clichés and sexual stereotypes. Grouped together, these plays embrace an unusually wide range of issues, including some that happen to be extremely timely—AIDS, child abuse, surrogate motherhood, drugs, incest—but they also evoke themes as eternal as death and bereavement, friendship, sexual attraction, rebellion, ambition and the search for identity.

Catherine Temerson
Françoise Kourilsky

Besset/Copi/Dupuis/van Itallie/Wouters

GAY

plays

an

international

anthology

Ubu Repertory Theater Publications
Françoise Kourilsky
Catherine Temerson
General Editors

Printed in the United States of America
1989
Library of Congress Catalog Card Number: 89-051446
ISBN 0-913745-31-6

CONTENTS

Jean-Marie Besset

THE FUNCTION

Translated from the French by Richard Miller

For Hal J. Witt

The Function was given its first public reading at Ubu Repertory Theater on April 8 1986, with the following cast:

ROBERT ADAMSON   **Christopher Stockton**
EVELYN CHEEK   **Tracy Poust**
HENRY EDEN   **Robert O'Neill**
Directed by **Jane I. Roth**

JEAN-MARIE BESSET was born in Carcassonne, in Southwest France, in 1959. He presently divides his time between Paris and New York. A recipient of grants for playwriting from the French government (1987) and the Fondation Beaumarchais (1989), Besset's plays include *Villa Luco* (1984), *La Fonction* (1985), *Fête Foreign* (1986), *Ce qui arrive et ce qu'on attend* (1988), and the French translations of Michael Frayn's *Benefactors (Les Bienfaiteurs,*1988) and David Hare's *A Secret Rapture (Le Ravissement,* 1989). *Villa Luco,* directed by Jacques Lassalle, was premiered in May and June, 1989, at the Théâtre National de Strasbourg. The production is moving to Paris, where it will be performed at the Théâtre Paris Villette from November 24, 1989, to February 3, 1990; it will tour throughout Europe in the spring of 1990. *La Fonction (The Function)* will be produced at the Studio des Champs-Elysées in Paris in the fall of 1990. Besset's plays have been broadcast on Swiss Radio (RTSR) and on French National Radio (France-Culture). They are published in France by Actes Sud-Papiers. The English translation of *Villa Luco,* by Donald Watson, was given staged readings in London (1986) and in New York as part of Ubu Repertory Theater's 1988 Festival "The Second World War Revisited." *The Function* was given its first staged reading in English at Ubu Repertory Theater in April 1986, and it was given subsequent readings at Staret and as part of Ubu's 1987 "Festival of Gay Plays in Twentieth-Century France."

RICHARD MILLER has translated many literary works of fiction and nonfiction, including several books by Brassaï and Roland Barthes. He has translated four other plays published by Ubu Repertory Theater: Aimé Césaire's *A Tempest*; Reine Bartève's *A Man With Women*; Sony Labou Tansi's *The Second Ark*, included in the anthology *Afrique*; and Michèle Fabien's *Jocasta*, included in the anthology *Plays by Women*. He also translated Jean-Marie Apostolidès's *Waiting for Beckett* and other plays by Jean-Marie Besset, as well as Michel Deutsch's *Thermidor* and Claire Etcherelli's *Germinal, Year III* for Ubu's 1989 Festival "Homage to the Revolution."

CHARACTERS

ROBERT ADAMSON, *a young man*
EVELYN CHEEK, *a young woman*
HENRY EDEN, *a man*

(The action takes place in the living room of a luxury apartment. The room is in white and gray tones; it is functional and austere. It is large and sparsely furnished, with high columned walls. At left is a two-cushioned sofa, elegant but not obviously designed for comfort. On the right is an Eames chair. Some abstract painting is on the back wall, a Hartung, perhaps, or a Kline. An elegant halogen lamp is the only other furnishing. A door, left, gives onto the entry. Another door, right, leads to the rest of the apartment. The room is underfurnished for its size, filled with a very white light, giving the impression of order, emptiness, and sophistication.)

ACT ONE

(Nine in the morning. Adamson enters, right, from the bedroom. He is buttoning his shirt. He looks around the room, searching for something that belongs to him. He gets down on his knees to look under the couch. Miss Cheek enters, right. She seems somewhat surprised to see him.)

CHEEK: Good morning.

ADAMSON: *(getting quickly to his feet)* Oh, ... good morning. I ... I was getting my things together, ... you know.... And then I'm going.... I don't want to.... You wouldn't happen to have found ... to have found a shoe, by any chance?

CHEEK: A shoe?

ADAMSON: A man's shoe.

CHEEK: What kind of shoe?

ADAMSON: *(holding up his shoe)* One like this. They come in pairs, you know.

CHEEK: Did you look in the bedroom?

ADAMSON: Yes. Do you think I should look again?

CHEEK: As a matter of fact, I did find a shoe earlier this morning, ... but it was in the kitchen. It looked something like yours....

ADAMSON: In the kitchen?

CHEEK: Yes.... Over by the sink. Silly, isn't it? It couldn't have been yours.

ADAMSON: Can I see it?

CHEEK: Of course. Would you like some coffee?

ADAMSON: I don't want you to ... I mean, ... it's a lot of trouble. But thank you....

CHEEK: I've just made it ... fresh coffee. You're sure you won't have a cup?

ADAMSON: Why not. You're sure there's enough? I mean, for me?

CHEEK: If there weren't enough, would I be asking you if you wanted some?

ADAMSON: No, of course not. It's just ... in case you might want more later.

CHEEK: Well, if I want a cup later, I can always make some more, can't I?

ADAMSON: Of course. Thank you.

CHEEK: I don't often drink more than one. Maybe later, after lunch, during the one o'clock news.... I'll get you a cup.

ADAMSON: What's that noise?

CHEEK: Noise?

ADAMSON: Yes, that humming sound? Do you hear it?

CHEEK: You mean the air conditioning?

ADAMSON: Oh, ... yes, the air conditioning.

CHEEK: I can turn it off if you like.

ADAMSON: Is it that hot outdoors? I didn't know.

CHEEK: It's always the same temperature in here. The thermostat's built in.

ADAMSON: Doesn't it make the air very dry?

CHEEK: I beg your pardon?

ADAMSON: They say it makes the air very dry.

CHEEK: Dry, . . . yes. I'll turn it off.

ADAMSON: No, don't do that . . . . I don't want to . . . .

CHEEK: Really, it's easy to turn it down. So. You will have a cup?

ADAMSON: Yes, thank you.

(She exits. Adamson sits down gingerly on the edge of the sofa; he does not seem very comfortable. Miss Cheek returns with a glass of water and a cup on a tray. She pours him some coffee and hands him a shoe.)

ADAMSON: Thanks. That's my shoe. It *is* mine, you see; they're exactly alike. They're a pair.

CHEEK: Odd, isn't it, it's being in the kitchen?

ADAMSON: I must have . . . . I don't know.

CHEEK: Are you staying?

ADAMSON: I was going to leave . . . . I should go.

CHEEK: Oh, that's not what I meant. I meant, today.

ADAMSON: Oh, today? No, I have things to do, a couple of errands . . . . I have to do some shopping.

CHEEK: You wouldn't be going downtown, by any chance?

ADAMSON: I wasn't going to, but if you . . . .

CHEEK: Oh, no. I don't want you to go out of your way. It's just that the stores are so crowded on Saturdays.

ADAMSON: You're not . . . sick?

CHEEK: No, I'm just . . . . *(She looks down at her stomach.)*

ADAMSON: Sorry! I always forget . . . .

CHEEK: I'm in my seventh month, and he doesn't like me to leave the house too often. He says it's dangerous. *(Pause. She takes a pill and a sip of water.)* He doesn't want to leave anything to chance. I suppose he's right. When you see the things they have on television . . . . He's right, of course.

ADAMSON: Of course.

CHEEK: Would you leave things like that to chance if you were he?

ADAMSON: No.

CHEEK: When you think of the danger . . . .

ADAMSON: Absolutely . . . .

CHEEK: Do you have any children?

ADAMSON: Well, ...as a matter of fact . . . .

CHEEK: I don't mean to embarrass you or be indiscreet, or....

ADAMSON: As a matter of fact, no.

CHEEK: So I wasn't being indiscreet?

ADAMSON: No, not at all.

(Pause)

CHEEK: So.... Do you?

ADAMSON: No, no. That's what I was saying. I don't have any.

CHEEK: It's my first.

ADAMSON: What's it like?

CHEEK: I've gotten used to it now. It's my seventh month.

ADAMSON: Your husband must be pleased.

CHEEK: Oh, yes, very.

ADAMSON: He's away....

CHEEK: Yes.... He's gone.... Only for a few days..... A business trip, you know....

ADAMSON: Oh? Your husband is in business. That's nice.

CHEEK: What do you do?

ADAMSON: I'm in statistics.

CHEEK: You mean figures, things like that?

ADAMSON: Yes; figures, data, that kind of thing.

CHEEK: You're a sort of accountant, then?

ADAMSON: No, not exactly. I'm more of a . . . statistician.

CHEEK: A statistician?

ADAMSON: Because I deal with statistics, you know. Well, that is, for the most part . . . .

CHEEK: Do you have a car?

ADAMSON: I don't need a car.

CHEEK: You live downtown, do you?

ADAMSON: Well, not too far.

CHEEK: Do you live near your work?

ADAMSON: I can walk to the office . . . . It's only forty minutes, very convenient.

CHEEK: That *is* convenient. Forty minutes is quite a walk, though. The last time I worked . . . . The last job I had, I used to try to walk too. But sometimes I'd have to stay late, and walking home, especially in the wintertime . . . . It gets dark so early, in the winter. And walking home at night . . . .with all you read . . . . It's like committing suicide, really.

ADAMSON: It's not as nice in the wintertime; that's true.

CHEEK: Especially last winter. It was so cold, last winter.

ADAMSON: I wasn't here, last winter.

CHEEK: It was unbelievably cold.

ADAMSON: I heard about it. It sounded very bad, actually.

CHEEK: It was awful, I can tell you. Late in January the sidewalks were covered with ice for three weeks. It wouldn't melt. You can't believe . . . .

ADAMSON: It never got that cold where I was.

CHEEK: You weren't here?

ADAMSON: I was in the south.

CHEEK: It's always much warmer in the south, isn't it?

ADAMSON: Not that much. Last winter it was pretty cold there, too.

CHEEK: Yes, but you didn't get any ice, did you?

ADAMSON: Oh, no, of course not.

CHEEK: That's what I said. It's much warmer in the south. It's the same everywhere, though, isn't it? It gets warmer as you go south. Everything in the world. All souths are alike.

ADAMSON: But only in the northern hemisphere.

CHEEK: What do you mean?

ADAMSON: What you said about the south—it only goes for the northern hemisphere.

CHEEK: Oh, because of the equator and all that?

ADAMSON: Yes. In the southern hemisphere, it's the other way around.

CHEEK: Is it?

ADAMSON: It's colder in the south.

CHEEK: I never thought of that.

ADAMSON: The closer you get to the poles, the colder it gets.

CHEEK: Well, that I did know. I mean, ...obviously I knew that. It's just it's one of those things you never think about.

ADAMSON: My parents live down there.

CHEEK: You mean . . . .near the poles?

ADAMSON: No, no. They live in the south. That's where I was, last winter.

CHEEK: Your parents live in the south. You mean, ...that's where you're from?

ADAMSON: Yes. I grew up there, in the south.

CHEEK: And you were born there too?

ADAMSON: Yes. What about you?

CHEEK: Isn't that incredible? I'm from the south too. I was born and raised there. I'm always meeting people who were born in the south. Yesterday, sitting on a bench, there was a woman from there, from not far from where I'm from. You'd think everyone was from the south . . . .Of course, you'll tell me it's just my impression . . . . I know. You don't need to say it. It *is* only an impression because of course everyone can't be from the south. I mean, people are born in the north too. Only you don't notice it, when you're from the south. You don't pay attention when people say they're from the north. You only listen when they talk about the south.... You feel closer to them....

(Pause)

ADAMSON: Is he from the south too?

CHEEK: Who?

ADAMSON: Henry.

CHEEK: Mr. Eden.... Now, that's a good question. I'm not sure. I don't know where he's from. Really, I've no idea whether he's from the south or from the north.

ADAMSON: Maybe he was born here. Anyway, you could never tell from his accent.

CHEEK: I'm sure he's traveled a lot.

ADAMSON: You don't lose your accent by traveling.

CHEEK: How did you lose yours?

ADAMSON: He doesn't have any accent at all. It's almost frightening, his having no accent at all. He must have been born here, in a good neighborhood.

CHEEK: Why don't you have an accent?

ADAMSON: I've got more of an accent than he has.

CHEEK: But you were born in the south.

ADAMSON: Do you think he lost his accent traveling?

CHEEK: I don't even know that he *has* traveled.

ADAMSON: But you just said . . . .

CHEEK: I said?

ADAMSON: You said you were sure he had.

CHEEK: I said . . . . I just said that. I mean, I'm sure he's traveled. He must have traveled. For a man of his class, educated as he is, with good manners, he must have traveled.
It's just . . . just a supposition, you know. He really must
have traveled. I don't know how he could help from having
traveled . . . .

ADAMSON: You don't need to travel to be well educated. You
can find everything in books, after all. Everything. However, it is possible that he's traveled . . . .

CHEEK: That's what I meant.

ADAMSON: And yet you're not sure. How come you don't
know?

CHEEK: He's never said anything to me about it.

ADAMSON: Never? He seems to be a very secretive man. Because you really ought to know. You would know, if he
weren't so secretive.

CHEEK: Yes, I should.

ADAMSON: So, then, it's possible he's never traveled at all.
The fact is that you can't tell from his accent.

CHEEK: But *you* don't have much of an accent.

ADAMSON: You can't tell anything from *your* accent either.

CHEEK: That's because I've lived here for a long time. It's normal.

ADAMSON: Normal? Did you know that "normal" is a statistical term?

CHEEK: And you? You were still in the south up until last winter. . . .

ADAMSON: How do you know?

CHEEK: You told me so yourself.

ADAMSON: I said I was *in* the south. I didn't say I was still in the south.

CHEEK: Maybe you didn't.

ADAMSON: But you're right. I'd never left the south. How did you know?

CHEEK: It was just a guess.

ADAMSON: Did he tell you so? *(Pause)* What else did he tell you about me? Does he often talk about me?

CHEEK: No. He's never mentioned your name. He never talks about you.

ADAMSON: And you knew that I'd never left the south. How did you know that?

CHEEK: I don't know. Your accent, probably.

ADAMSON: You said I didn't have one.

CHEEK: I said you had a little accent.

ADAMSON: Because if he talks about me, you may as well tell me. I mean, whatever he says, what difference does it make to you? You might as well tell me. I won't tell him that you've told me. I give you my word. You can trust me.

CHEEK: I do trust you. *(A fairly long pause)* How do you happen to have so little, by the way?

ADAMSON: Huh?

CHEEK: Accent. So little accent?

ADAMSON: It's my business, you know. It's because of my job.

CHEEK: Statistics?

ADAMSON: Well, it depends on how ambitious you are. But if you want people to respect you, I mean, if you want to have some authority over them . . . .

CHEEK: I see what you mean.

ADAMSON: Can you imagine taking orders from someone with a strong southern accent? Oh, it happens, of course. But people always smile. You have the feeling people are making fun of you behind your back. You can't maintain any authority. Not that I'm so important, or anything . . . . I'm only starting out.

CHEEK: You purposely tried?

ADAMSON: No, ...it's just . . . .it's just that I adapt easily. It's just a question of listening and mimicking. I'm a good mimic. I could imitate Henry if you'd like . . . .

CHEEK: Mr. Eden? Oh, I don't think that would be very fitting.

ADAMSON: I think I could. I could try, anyhow.

CHEEK: I really don't think it would be fitting. What about your father?

ADAMSON: What about him?

CHEEK: I'll bet he has a very strong southern accent. Am I right? Can you imitate your father?

ADAMSON: I could, but . . . .

CHEEK: Oh, yes, why not? Why not imitate your father for me? It's been years since I've heard a southern accent.

ADAMSON: It's not a nice thing to do, making fun of your father's accent . . . . I suppose I could do it, though . . . .

CHEEK: Of course you could! I'm sure you can. Oh, you could make it sound so funny! Oh, please!

ADAMSON: What makes you think it'd be funny? Do you want me to make fun of my father? Would you like that? What makes you think it would be so funny? Why should I do that for you? No, come on! I hardly know you! I don't even know your name!

CHEEK: Miss Cheek. My name is Evelyn Cheek.

ADAMSON: Well, Miss Cheek, tell me why you want me to make fun of my father.

CHEEK: You misunderstood.... I didn't mean....

ADAMSON: Oh, what did you mean, then? Are you that bored? You said it would be funny. I heard you say it. Maybe it would be funny for you! Yes, my father had a strong southern accent. But it wasn't funny. He never meant to be funny.

CHEEK: You mean he's....

ADAMSON: That's right! I no longer have a father. Not that I miss him, but all the same.... There are limits!

CHEEK: I'm sorry. I didn't know.

ADAMSON: And how come you're called "Miss"? You're married; you're pregnant....

CHEEK: Oh, you mean.... Well, in fact it's....it's Mr. Eden's idea. He says...he says that "Mrs." puts you in a certain category,....something to do with age, I guess. He says that I don't look at all like a "Mrs." He calls me "Miss Cheek." It's his idea. But I....

ADAMSON: I'd like to know what your husband says about that. I'll bet he doesn't even know. Right? Does he know?

CHEEK: Well,....no, he doesn't!

ADAMSON: Of course he doesn't *(He sinks into the chair at the right, as if exhausted. A long silence ensues.)*

CHEEK: Don't be angry. I'm really sorry. I didn't know, ...how could I have? I didn't mean that your father was funny. I only thought that your imitation of him might be. My father had a strong accent too. I really didn't know,

...how could I have? And earlier, you did say that you'd spent the winter in the south, at your parents'.... So I thought.... I just supposed you had both parents, do you see....? That's why I thought....

ADAMSON: I didn't mean to get angry. I don't know what came over me.... Of course, you couldn't have known. I did say "my parents." I meant my mother, my uncles, my family. It's all my fault. Forgive me.

CHEEK: Well, we won't talk about it anymore. Would you like some more coffee?

ADAMSON: No, thank you. It's very nice of you. You *are* very nice. Can I call you Evelyn? And you'll call me Bob.

CHEEK: All right.

ADAMSON: Let's shake hands...as a sign of peace. Will you shake hands with me, Evelyn?

CHEEK: It wasn't really important.

ADAMSON: Let's shake hands anyway.

(She shakes his hand.)

I'm glad I met you, Evelyn.

CHEEK: Thank you.

ADAMSON: Please. Call me Bob.

CHEEK: Thank you, Bob.

(Pause)

ADAMSON: Does Henry call you Miss Cheek? Shouldn't he

call you Evelyn? After all, you're very close, aren't you? He's a very secretive man, Evelyn; don't you think so? He's so secretive it's almost frightening.

CHEEK: Have you known him for long?

ADAMSON: Not too long, as a matter of fact. And yet I . . . .

CHEEK: Is this the first time you've been here?

ADAMSON: Here? Yes, this is the first time, here. But you should know. If I'd been here before, you'd surely remember it.

CHEEK: Sometimes I sleep late. I mean, especially nowadays. I've been very tired lately. I only seem to sleep well in the morning. I'm not always awake when Mr. Eden leaves. He doesn't always allow his friends to stay on after he's left. In fact, this is the first time. It's the first time such a thing has happened. I'd remember it.

ADAMSON: You mean the first time for a long time?

CHEEK: No, no: the very first time. Otherwise, I'd remember. Mr. Eden is very strict about that. He doesn't trust people that easily. It takes time for him to. It takes all the time it takes, as he says. He's right. You never know. It's rare for him to allow people to stay on in the apartment after he's left. And when I say rare, I mean, I should really say never. It's never happened before, as far as I can remember.

ADAMSON: But he hasn't really left, has he?

CHEEK: As far as I know, he has.

ADAMSON: No; I mean, he hasn't gone for the day. It's Saturday.

CHEEK: Sometimes Mr. Eden works on Saturdays. In fact, he often works on Saturdays. He works on Sundays too, sometimes. He could be gone the whole weekend.

ADAMSON: But you suggested I stay and wait for him.

CHEEK: That's not what I said. I offered you some coffee. You said you were going to leave. I was surprised to find you here at all.

ADAMSON: You didn't seem surprised.

CHEEK: Because obviously it was all right with Mr. Eden for you to be here after he'd gone. Otherwise, you'd have left with him.

ADAMSON: But...you think he's coming back soon.

CHEEK: I don't think anything. It's your idea. It's none of my business.

ADAMSON: Why?

CHEEK: At first, I used to wonder when he would be back. I used to wait. I'd set the table. He never came when I expected him to. He's not that kind of man.

ADAMSON: Still, you must have some idea. For example, from the way he's dressed.

CHEEK: What do you mean?

ADAMSON: If he's wearing a suit and tie, that means...it might mean that he's going to work. What was he wearing this morning?

CHEEK: This morning?

ADAMSON: When he left. How was he dressed?

CHEEK: I didn't see him this morning. What about you?

ADAMSON: I didn't see him either.

CHEEK: How could you not have seen him?

ADAMSON: I was asleep. I didn't pay attention.... I don't even remember hearing anything.

CHEEK: Anyway, it wouldn't prove anything.

ADAMSON: Why do you keep saying that? If he went out wearing a suit and tie....

CHEEK: That wouldn't prove anything at all.

ADAMSON: If he was wearing a suit, a tie....

CHEEK: He could be going to an early lunch, or to a sale, or to his office. He could also just as well be going to his gym before a meeting in town.

ADAMSON: Then he would have taken his gym gear. There you are! All we have to do is see if his gym bag is in his room.

CHEEK: Mr. Eden doesn't carry a gym bag. He has his own locker, at his club.

ADAMSON: And his briefcase? Let's see if he took that with him....

CHEEK: He hasn't got one. He stopped carrying around things like that when he was twelve years old.

ADAMSON: Did he say that?

CHEEK: Yes.

ADAMSON: You said he never let people stay here if he wasn't here. So, if he let me sleep this morning, that must mean something.... It must mean that he wants me to wait for him, that he'll be back soon. That's what it must mean. Don't you think so?

CHEEK: Well, ... he didn't wake you. That's unusual. But it might not mean anything. Maybe he only meant to let you sleep on, if you were sleeping so soundly, and maybe he expected you to leave as soon as you got up. That may be what he meant. That's what you were going to do, isn't it? Drink your coffee and leave.

ADAMSON: I'd just gotten up. But now, now it's clearer to me, what he meant. I'll wait for him.

CHEEK: But you can't.

ADAMSON: I'll help you with whatever you have to do, in the meantime.

CHEEK: I haven't got anything to do. Just shopping. I can't leave you here on your own.

ADAMSON: Why not? He left me sleeping, didn't he?

CHEEK: Yes, but ....

ADAMSON: He didn't see you before he left. You weren't even up. He didn't know whether you were here or not.

CHEEK: He knew I was here.

ADAMSON: But he wasn't sure.

CHEEK: He was pretty sure.

ADAMSON: Your husband could have come back last night, unexpectedly. He could have taken you out to dinner. You might have not slept here, last night. He'd never have known.

CHEEK: He could have checked to see if I was asleep in my room.

ADAMSON: He didn't do it last night.

CHEEK: What about this morning?

ADAMSON: Evelyn, you're just arguing.

CHEEK: Mr. Eden knew I was here this morning.

ADAMSON: He wasn't sure of it.

CHEEK: He *was* sure of it.

ADAMSON: What makes you think Henry trusts you more than he trusts me?

   (Pause)

CHEEK: That's not the point.

ADAMSON: But he let me sleep . . . .

CHEEK: Anyway, I can't leave you the keys.

ADAMSON: I can pull the door shut after me.

CHEEK: Then the alarm won't be set.

ADAMSON: But I told you: I'll wait until he gets back. Which means I'll be here until he returns. I won't even need to pull the door shut. I won't need the keys. We won't need the alarm. I'll just sit here and wait for him.

CHEEK: Very well. Wait for him.

ADAMSON: Thank you, Evelyn.

(Miss Cheek exits, right, and returns with a mini cassette-recorder. She turns it on.)

CHEEK: *(recording)* Good morning, Mr. Eden. Miss Cheek speaking. Your friend is up, but he does not want to leave. He wishes to remain here and await your return. I am going shopping. I will be back soon. *(She shuts off the recorder. To Adamson)* Won't you be bored?

ADAMSON: I'm happy here.

(Blackout)

ACT TWO

(Noon of the same day. Adamson is sitting on the floor—he seems to have been there for some time. His appearance is sloppy, his shirt untucked. He is toying with an empty coffee cup. A mini cassette-recorder is on the floor near him. Suddenly, he sets the cup back on its saucer and picks up the recorder. He takes a deep breath, smiles, and begins to speak.)

ADAMSON: Henry, it's me, Robert. *(He stops, rewinds, and begins again.)* Henry, it's Bob. I waited for you but it's getting late. I didn't want to leave without speaking to you. I'll pull the door closed after me. Don't be angry with Evelyn. If the alarm isn't on when you get back, it's my fault.... *(Pause.)* You left so early. I hope you won't be too tired when you come back. I hope that your day hasn't been too difficult. ... I stayed here to wait for you. The room is so large; it's strange, it almost seems to have an echo. There isn't a single trace of you here. None. Nothing to indicate your presence. Unless the whole thing is you.... That must be it. Yes. This room *is* you, Henry. I'm really sorry I was still asleep when you left. I just wanted to tell you.... I just wanted you to know that.... I know. You'll think this weird; you'll think I don't mean it, that I'm being phony, like you said the last time.... I always seem to say things I shouldn't, but....

(The sound of the outside door opening. Adamson quickly shuts off the recorder. He stands, rewinds the cassette, and presses the "Erase" button. Eden enters.)

EDEN: Oh, hello.

ADAMSON: I just thought it would be all right if I waited here.

EDEN: What are you doing?

ADAMSON: I was waiting for you.

EDEN: What are you doing with that?

ADAMSON: What do you mean? What do you *think* I was doing?

EDEN: Well, then what *were* you up to?

ADAMSON: You think I was . . . is that it? I mean, . . . you really don't believe I was trying to. . . . What do you think I am? I waited for you . . . .

EDEN: What were you doing?

ADAMSON: I was . . . . It didn't look like you were coming back, so I decided . . . I decided I'd leave you a message . . . .

EDEN: Let me hear it.

ADAMSON: I've just erased it. I erased it when I heard you come in. It's silly, if you're here. . . . It doesn't make any difference, now. I mean, I can say it to you . . . .

EDEN: Where is Miss Cheek?

ADAMSON: She's out shopping.

EDEN: She left you the keys?

ADAMSON: I told her I'd shut the door behind me when I left.

EDEN: So you have been alone here, all this time . . . .

ADAMSON: It hasn't seemed that long. She only left a little while ago. We talked.

EDEN: I nearly didn't come back here at all.

ADAMSON: That's what she said.

EDEN: What she said? You spoke to her? What did you talk about?

ADAMSON: Nothing, just things.... She has theories, ideas....

EDEN: What "theories"?

ADAMSON: Oh, theories like.... Well, for example, she says, "All souths are alike."

EDEN: All souths are alike?

ADAMSON: Yes. But only in the northern hemisphere, of course....

EDEN: That is an erroneous theory.

ADAMSON: In the northern hemisphere it's true that the South is less developed, there's no industry, the people are more....

EDEN: And England?

ADAMSON: It's.... You're right. England. I forgot about that.

EDEN: Is that all you did, expound some erroneous theories?

ADAMSON: The girl has lots of theories about you, Henry.

EDEN: Really?

ADAMSON: Yes, really. She's nice, isn't she?

EDEN: I shall have to go soon. I have an appointment. I left the address on my desk and.... Anyway, no matter.... I shall have to go soon.

ADAMSON: All right, Henry.

EDEN: And how long would you have stayed, if I hadn't come back at all?

ADAMSON: I'd have left in a little while.

EDEN: A little while?

ADAMSON: Never mind.... How could you think I was...? I mean the recorder. That lousy tape recorder.... You weren't being serious. Were you?

EDEN: Come now, Bob. It was a joke.

ADAMSON: Oh,... I *thought* you were just teasing me.... Was it really a joke? You fooled me. You're very good at that.

(Eden has poured himself a drink and offers one to Adamson.)

Thanks. So you've got to leave soon?

EDEN: I'm afraid so.

ADAMSON: Could you drop me off somewhere?

EDEN: Where are you going?

ADAMSON: Nowhere in particular.... I like to just wander around on Saturdays....

EDEN: Is that all?

ADAMSON: Yes....

EDEN: Then why not just start "wandering around" from here?

ADAMSON: Why not drop me off somewhere?

EDEN: Where, for instance?

ADAMSON: Well, near the park, or....

EDEN: That is not really on my way.

ADAMSON: Well, anywhere that *is* on your way.... It doesn't make any difference to me, really.

EDEN: I do not want to take you with me.

ADAMSON: Oh.... All right.... You didn't have to put it so....

EDEN: No?

ADAMSON: It's just that.... But I.... You're right, Henry. I'll just start from here. Actually, it's best. I was very happy to wake up this morning in this part of town.

EDEN: Most people do like this part of town.

ADAMSON: Oh, it's not because of... because of the elegant houses or what people think are....

EDEN: No?

ADAMSON: It's quiet here.... And the trees.... Just to walk under the trees, especially when it's hot, like yesterday....

The trees on this street make a kind of canopy.... It must be nice....

EDEN: It cools off very quickly in the late afternoon. It is deceptive.

ADAMSON: And all the leaves seem to dampen the sound. It's quiet.

EDEN: It is quite noisy during the week.

ADAMSON: Oh? Well, at least it's quiet on the weekend. You really can't hear a thing.

EDEN: That's because of the double windows, and the walls are fairly thick.

ADAMSON: I was really awfully glad to find myself here this morning. Today's Saturday.

EDEN: Indeed.

ADAMSON: Oh, no.... I don't mean.... Do you know what today is?

EDEN: Today? Is there anything special about today?

ADAMSON: The game. The finals are today, at three.

EDEN: You sound like a TV guide, Adamson.

ADAMSON: Did you know there was a game?

EDEN: I am vice-president of the league. But I cannot attend the game. I have a meeting later. I would have given you my tickets, but they are in the VIP box.

ADAMSON: Thanks anyway, but I'm not really all that interested.

EDEN: No?

ADAMSON: I don't really keep up with it. I'm not a fan.

EDEN: You, a fan? That would never have occurred to me.

ADAMSON: Well, I *do* keep up.... Like everyone. I know who's won,... usually. It's hard not to.... You look surprised....

EDEN: You said: it's Saturday,... the game. It did seem to indicate that you were interested in it.

ADAMSON: I mentioned the game because it's so quiet here.

EDEN: I don't follow you.

ADAMSON: You've been to my place....

EDEN: Your place?

ADAMSON: You've gone by the stadium. On the left, two blocks before my place, you cross the street to the stadium.

EDEN: You live near the stadium.

ADAMSON: That's why, on Saturdays....

EDEN: But not every Saturday....

ADAMSON: Well, every other Saturday....

EDEN: Not quite. And the stadium gives you some greenery. You mentioned trees. At least you have some grass. And you can go running in the stadium too, without having to drive for miles. Think of all the people who have to take a car to get to their clubs. Frankly, I do not see what you have to complain about.

ADAMSON: I'm not complaining. Just about Saturdays. And today is the final.

EDEN: So, it livens things up.

ADAMSON: But all the cars . . . for miles . . . in every direction. The streets are all blocked. People park anywhere, on both sides, on the sidewalks. You have to walk in the middle of the street. And when the game is over you have two hours of horns blowing, traffic jams and people arguing. And greasy paper and discarded food for days . . . .

EDEN: Bread and circuses, Adamson. . . . Would you deny the people its harmless diversions?

ADAMSON: Well, maybe in the VIP box . . . .

EDEN: What do you mean?

(Pause)

ADAMSON: When I first came in here, I was struck by something.

EDEN: The difference between your place and mine?

ADAMSON: In a way.

EDEN: Yes. There can be no question about that.

ADAMSON: Not that way, . . . not in the way you think.

EDEN: And what way might that be?

ADAMSON: You think in terms of money.

EDEN: Not at the moment, no.

ADAMSON: Really?

EDEN: Not in the least.

ADAMSON: About what, then?

EDEN: About taste. The difference between your taste and mine, your apartment and mine. So different.

ADAMSON: Taste is all a question of money.

EDEN: Not in the final analysis.

ADAMSON: To start with.

EDEN: Perhaps to start with.

ADAMSON: To start with and in the final analysis. Always.

EDEN: All right. What are you getting at?

ADAMSON: The first time I came here I felt as if I were entering the room of some pharaoh.

EDEN: Have you been to Egypt?

ADAMSON: I've been to the British Museum.

EDEN: The Rameses Exhibit?

ADAMSON: No, the permanent collection.

EDEN: It has been a long time since I was there.

ADAMSON: Me too. But the impression I got was so strong, unforgettable.

EDEN: Is that so? Well, there are no frescoes in my bedroom.

ADAMSON: Your two TV sets, your VCRs, your video camera, your stereo, a whole wall of video cassettes and answering machines and your closed-circuit TV at the entrance; . . . what don't you have? Aren't those your frescoes?

EDEN: I like gadgets. I'm fond of them . . . .

ADAMSON: You can't listen to all of them or watch all of them at the same time.

EDEN: No, but one at a time I can.

ADAMSON: All those . . . devices . . . all turned off, silent. Those screens were like dead worlds.

EDEN: You're extrapolating.

ADAMSON: The apartment is so full, so empty, so neat, so clean, so big, so comfortable!

EDEN: Just comfortable! A nice snug place to live. "Be it ever so humble"—you know.

ADAMSON: Henry, you seem nervous.

EDEN: The quickest way to make someone nervous is to tell them they are.

ADAMSON: So, you *are* nervous.

EDEN: I am tired.

ADAMSON: And me?

EDEN: You?

ADAMSON: I'm tired too.

EDEN: From sleeping late? From sitting here doing nothing?

ADAMSON: From waiting.

EDEN: Who asked you to wait?

ADAMSON: Oh, what am I doing here?

EDEN: Indeed, I was wondering that myself. Things are happening. The world wakes up early. And you are sleepy. You are tired from waiting!

ADAMSON: Listen, . . . I *came* here.

EDEN: Yesterday. Today is another day.

(Pause)

ADAMSON: So, . . . what then?

EDEN: What? *(Pause)* You don't get it.

ADAMSON: Get what?

EDEN: It isn't a criticism.

ADAMSON: No?

EDEN: It is only a simple statement of fact.

ADAMSON: Don't get what?

EDEN: It.

ADAMSON: You mean you, right? You think I don't understand what you're saying. You're so sure it's way over my head.

EDEN: Quite the contrary. I do not underestimate you. But such false humility! The way you say "What?" instead of.... In any event, you are off the mark. Remember with whom you are dealing!

ADAMSON: And Evelyn? I suppose she gets it?

EDEN: What do you mean by that?

ADAMSON: Well, if "getting it" means anything, it seems to me that....

EDEN: It seems to you? *(Pause)* Miss Cheek is carrying my child.

ADAMSON: I beg your pardon?

EDEN: The child she is carrying is mine.

ADAMSON: What about her husband?

EDEN: Miss Cheek has no husband. That is the story for public consumption.

ADAMSON: I see.... It is your child?

EDEN: Whose did you think it was?

ADAMSON: I don't know.... I thought she was a relative or....

EDEN: I do not see why I should discuss it with you. Especially with you.

ADAMSON: Why?

EDEN: You have no children, right?

ADAMSON: I could have.

EDEN: You could?

(Pause)

ADAMSON: So, you're involved with Evelyn....

EDEN: Not at all.

ADAMSON: It *is* an involvement.

EDEN: Call it what you like! I do not believe such things exist. People... people are prone to promiscuity. And even if it did exist....

ADAMSON: If it did exist?

EDEN: You are confusing involvements with attachments, Adamson. My nights and your mornings.

ADAMSON: But that woman....

EDEN: She is carrying my child. That is a fact.

ADAMSON: Why did you have to get her pregnant?

EDEN: Have you ever heard of the desire to reproduce?

ADAMSON: Reproduce?

EDEN: Yes, Adamson. The function of reproduction. Heard of it? Has it never occurred to you that a person might have a function? That is what I am doing, Adamson. Reproducing myself....

ADAMSON: What will you do with Evelyn?

EDEN: What do you mean, what will I *do* with Evelyn?

ADAMSON: Afterwards.

EDEN: Oh, *after*wards? After the child is born? After a healthy child is born?

ADAMSON: Yes. What will you do with her?

EDEN: She will care for the child.

ADAMSON: Will she remain with you?

EDEN: Not *with* me. She will remain in this apartment. She will live here, yes, for a little while.

ADAMSON: And if she doesn't stay?

EDEN: She will stay.

ADAMSON: Yes, but if she . . . .

EDEN: Frankly, I do not believe she will find better accommodations elsewhere.

ADAMSON: Evelyn has feelings.

EDEN: A deal is a deal.

ADAMSON: You made love to her. You call that a deal?

EDEN: I did not make love to her.

ADAMSON: But . . . you said it was your child.

EDEN: Have you ever heard of *in vitro* fertilization, Adamson? No? Well, then, now you have. That is what we did. It is more than an agreement. It is a valid medical and legal contract in due form, the terms of which—I might add—are extremely favorable to her.

ADAMSON: Medical?

EDEN: Yes.

ADAMSON: You aren't husband and wife.

EDEN: We signed a commonlaw agreement. I agree with you that the term is repugnant.... However, it even has some tax benefits.

ADAMSON: It's immoral.

EDEN: That's a strange word, coming from you.

ADAMSON: I meant it.

EDEN: I see. You believe in God?

ADAMSON: I don't know, but....

EDEN: You do not know whether or not you believe in God and you set yourself up as a judge! *I*, on the other hand, am sharing my home with a woman who is carrying my son!

ADAMSON: A woman you're paying to do so.

EDEN: And what do the majority of husbands do, if not pay their wives?

ADAMSON: You don't love her.

EDEN: How naive you are! Marriage *is* reproduction. At the French court the Church used to permit annulment on the grounds of sterility. Love? What about repudiated women who still continued to love their husbands?

ADAMSON: It wasn't justice.

EDEN: It was justice enough for the Pope to be in favor of it. Who are you to judge such things?

ADAMSON: We're not at the French court.

EDEN: No? Where are we? What do you suggest? Love? Great romance? Right? A relationship, any relationship, if I understand you correctly....

ADAMSON: You despise her.

EDEN: What makes you think that?

ADAMSON: You've reduced her to some bodily function.

EDEN: Not at all. It just happens that, with her, I don't....

ADAMSON: That's what I mean. She deserves better than that.

EDEN: Perhaps. In meantime, she did sign the agreement. Of her own free will. She is here.

ADAMSON: She might find someone who loves her.

EDEN: In any event, there are precedents. Many precedents.

ADAMSON: What?

EDEN: Ancient Rome, for example. The woman's role in the Roman citizen's family....

ADAMSON: What role?

EDEN: Reproduction. While the husbands sought their

pleasure with slaves . . . .

(Pause)

ADAMSON: The Romans were different. That's different. . . .

EDEN: I am just trying to find an example you might understand. However, if you want others, I can cite them, famous
ones. *(laughing)* You only have to think of our own civiliza-
tion, Adamson: the Virgin Mary was a surrogate mother!

ADAMSON: That's . . . that's just a myth . . . .

EDEN: A myth that has formed the basis of Western civiliza-
tion, Adamson. Of which, whether you like it or not, you
are a part.

ADAMSON: Don't tell me what I'm a part of! Don't tell me
what I think!

EDEN: You are part of nothing! *(Pause)* As a matter of
fact . . . .

ADAMSON: Yet I'm here. Even if. . . .

EDEN: Yes. *(He pours himself a drink. Pause.)* You are good at
math.

ADAMSON: Statistics.

EDEN: Isn't it the same thing?

ADAMSON: It's not that I'm good at it. I haven't got any
choice.

EDEN: What do you mean?

ADAMSON: Statistics are my job.

EDEN: What about school? You must have been good in math to go on to study statistics. You had good enough grades, did you not, at school?

ADAMSON: Fairly good.

EDEN: As I said. Good in math.

ADAMSON: So?

EDEN: Good in math. How exciting. A statistician. I had forgotten. And yet, you must have told me. You did tell me, did you not? I rarely meet people who are good in math. Were you good in literature too?

ADAMSON: Not as good.

EDEN: You were not good?

ADAMSON: Frankly, not very good.

EDEN: But not bad, right?

ADAMSON: Let's say fairly weak.

EDEN: Perfect! Really, how exciting! Don't you think it is? "Good" in mathematics and "fairly weak" in literature. So many people are just the opposite. I would even say, most people.

(Pause)

ADAMSON: And you?

EDEN: What about me?

ADAMSON: Were you like me?

(Pause)

EDEN: What do you mean?

ADAMSON: Good in math.

EDEN: I was good in everything.

ADAMSON: At gymnastics?

EDEN: I loved sports.

ADAMSON: Which?

EDEN: Football.

ADAMSON: Football? Were you good?

EDEN: I was on the team. We won a lot of games. We were champions.

(Pause)

ADAMSON: You're good at everything. . . .

EDEN: Why do you say that?

ADAMSON: No reason. . . . For no particular reason.

EDEN: Oh, no? You just asked if I were like you!

ADAMSON: I asked that?

EDEN: I am not like you, Adamson.

ADAMSON: No?

EDEN: No.

ADAMSON: Why?

EDEN: Because I understand everything.

ADAMSON: Oh?

EDEN: Yes. And you are wasting my time.

ADAMSON: I guess . . . I guess I'd better be going.

(A long pause. Neither of them moves. Then Adamson begins to tuck his shirt into his trousers. He goes slowly to the entry door and turns towards Eden.)

EDEN: How much do you earn, as a statistician?

ADAMSON: Well, . . . it's my first job, and . . . .

EDEN: You don't earn peanuts.

ADAMSON: It's . . . its a good starting salary.

EDEN: Not a good salary.

ADAMSON: Not bad, for a beginner.

EDEN: But a bad salary.

ADAMSON: It could be worse.

EDEN: And it could be better.

ADAMSON: Of course it could be better. Like everything.

EDEN: Would you be willing to work for me?

ADAMSON: Here?

EDEN: Here? Why here? Do you like it here?

ADAMSON: Yes, I like it here.

EDEN: I thought you would be bored to death.

ADAMSON: It's one of those places you get used to.

EDEN: And what kind of place might that be?

ADAMSON: The kind of place you get used to.

EDEN: You said it was like a tomb. That was your word.

ADAMSON: Well, I don't think so anymore.

EDEN: What happened?

ADAMSON: Nothing. I got used to it.

EDEN: Or perhaps you died without anyone's noticing. You died while we were talking, and now you like your tomb.

ADAMSON: It's the kind of place you get attached to.

EDEN: And just what would you do here? I've no need for a manservant. The maid comes in every day during the week. Miss Cheek does things for me—not that I ask her to, but she says it keeps her from being bored. I have no need of you, here.

ADAMSON: You suggested I work for you. There *is* no work, here.

EDEN: Not here. Would you work for me somewhere else, not here?

ADAMSON: Where, somewhere else?

EDEN: Somewhere else.

ADAMSON: Is it far from here?

EDEN: Is distance a problem?

ADAMSON: I don't have a car. If it's not downtown, I . . . .

EDEN: What makes you think it isn't downtown?

ADAMSON: Companies often have offices away from downtown.

EDEN: Why is that?

ADAMSON: The rent, I guess.

EDEN: Rent?

ADAMSON: Rents are so high downtown . . . .

EDEN: And you think that the company I work for is unable to afford a high rent? Is that what you are trying to say?

ADAMSON: A lot of industries are in the suburbs.

EDEN: Do you think I'm involved in mass production?

ADAMSON: A lot of companies are out in the suburbs too.

EDEN: Is your company in the suburbs?

ADAMSON: No.

EDEN: Well, neither is mine! What is your company called, Adamson?

ADAMSON: M.F.L., Inc.

EDEN: And what might that be?

ADAMSON: Metropolitan Fiat Lux, Incorporated.

EDEN: Never heard of it.

ADAMSON: You haven't?

EDEN: What does it make?

ADAMSON: Neon lights.

EDEN: Neon?

ADAMSON: Actually, we don't make them. We shape them.

EDEN: You shape neon lights? Is it a large factory?

ADAMSON: There are twenty-nine employees.

EDEN: Twenty-nine? You might as well clerk in a store, Adamson. I'm saving you from the world of small business!

(Pause)

ADAMSON: What kind of work would it be?

EDEN: Statistics.

ADAMSON: How much?

EDEN: A great many of them.

ADAMSON: No; I mean, what's the salary?

EDEN: We would have to set up a new scale for you.

ADAMSON: You don't already have one?

EDEN: We had a statistician working for us, a very old man.

ADAMSON: Did he die?

EDEN: He retired last week. We're looking for someone.

ADAMSON: How much did he make?

EDEN: He was a drain on our budget. A heavy one. That is why we will have to work out some new arrangement. On a solid basis. You would not be eligible for his benefits.

ADAMSON: I wouldn't?

EDEN: There would be a new scale.

   (Pause)

ADAMSON: So, it isn't too far from here?

EDEN: It is downtown. Very convenient.

ADAMSON: Your company?

EDEN: We are not a company. We are a government agency.

ADAMSON: What's your agency called?

EDEN: Before giving you that information I shall have to have your agreement and your signature. Basic security requirements, you understand. I am sure that you do understand. Well, think about it. Take your time. Take all the time you need. Let me know when you have made up your mind.

   (Pause)

ADAMSON: Is that why you were so pleased that I was good at math? I understand, now. You needed someone and I was your man.

EDEN: Actually, the two aren't connected. How can you confuse our little chat with a serious job offer? Your logic is extremely limited.

ADAMSON: How did you get the job?

EDEN: I told you. The post became open about a week ago.

ADAMSON: No, I meant your own job. How did you get it?

EDEN: I have had it for some time.

ADAMSON: How long a time?

EDEN: Long enough. Oh, and by the way: if you should take the job, you would have to speak to me differently. And you couldn't come here, either.

ADAMSON: Why?

EDEN: We do not approve of out-of-the-office relationships. Our organizational guidelines are very strict on that point.

ADAMSON: Oh?

EDEN: It was my idea.

   (Pause)

ADAMSON: In that case, I can't take the job.

EDEN: You can't?

ADAMSON: I'm happy here.

EDEN: I cannot guarantee that you will be coming back here, in any event.

ADAMSON: But I don't think I can take the job. . . .

EDEN: Either way, I do not see why you should be allowed to come and go here as you please.

ADAMSON: There's something different about here.

EDEN: Well, then, enjoy it while you can.

(The doorbell rings.)

ADAMSON: That must be Evelyn.

EDEN: Miss Cheek does not ring. She has keys. It must be the plumber. They said they would send him around at lunchtime. Would you get it, please? I'll be back in a moment.

(Eden exits, right. Adamson looks around the room and in the direction Eden has gone. The bell rings again. Adamson goes out, left. Eden returns, moves to the back wall, and presses a panel that opens to reveal a television screen and a VCR. He pushes the rewind button. He closes the panel. Adamson reenters, alone.)

EDEN: It wasn't the plumber?

ADAMSON: Yes, it was.

EDEN: Well, where is he?

ADAMSON: I told him he'd made a mistake, that we didn't need a plumber here.

EDEN: What!?

ADAMSON: I'll fix the pipe.

EDEN: Do you know how long it took to get him to come? Miss Cheek told me she had to call him hundreds of times. The man has been paid for the work in advance.

ADAMSON: I'll fix the pipe.

EDEN: You don't know how.

ADAMSON: I'll fix it.

EDEN: It's a sink, not a pipe. It's a very complicated repair job. It requires a trained man. Professional skill.

ADAMSON: I'll fix the damned sink!

EDEN: I'm late. I can't leave you here.

ADAMSON: You would have left the plumber.

EDEN: The plumber is a professional. You are totally unskilled.

ADAMSON: Trust me. I'll fix the sink.

EDEN: Out of the question.

ADAMSON: I won't steal anything. Trust me.

EDEN: I do *not* trust you, Adamson.

ADAMSON: Henry, don't call me Adamson....

EDEN: Get out.

ADAMSON: But why...?

EDEN: Get out. Out of the house where my son is to be born! Don't look around! You haven't forgotten anything! You didn't even have a jacket! Now, out! Out!

(Eden takes hold of Adamson and they go out, left. Adamson does not resist. Eden returns alone. He goes to the wall at the back and reopens the panel. He presses a button; Cheek and Adamson appear on the screen, filmed in the living room. We hear a snatch of their earlier conversation.)

CHEEK: It's always warmer in the south, isn't it?

ADAMSON: Not that much. Last winter it was pretty cold there too.

CHEEK: Yes, but you didn't get any ice, did you?

ADAMSON: Oh, no, of course not.

(The alarm bell at the front door suddenly rings and then stops. Eden quickly turns off the VCR and closes the panel. Miss Cheek enters, left.)

EDEN: Good afternoon, Miss Cheek.

CHEEK: Mr. Eden? Hello. . . . Did you see your friend?

EDEN: I did, thank you.

CHEEK: I tried to keep him from staying, but . . . .

EDEN: It's unimportant, actually. You did your best. There was no problem.

CHEEK: Oh? All right . . . .

EDEN: However, you had better call the plumber again. He didn't come.

CHEEK: But they promised . . . .

EDEN: Well, he hasn't come. It's really too much.

CHEEK: He may still come. . . .

EDEN: I doubt it. It's already past lunchtime.

CHEEK: It's unbelievable!

EDEN: They may have got the address wrong or something! In any case, they can't be trusted. I did tell you so, didn't I?

CHEEK: I'll try someone else.

EDEN: I think you should. Only if you want to, of course.

CHEEK: Oh, please! I haven't anything else to do.

EDEN: You keep saying that. It's becoming a bit boring.

CHEEK: Sorry.

EDEN: And of course, you don't really mean it, do you?

CHEEK: No, of course I don't.

EDEN: In any event, it isn't true. You do know that, don't you?

CHEEK: I'm sorry, really. I didn't mean it that way.

EDEN: You have something to do, Miss Cheek. You are carrying my child. That is a full-time occupation.

CHEEK: And I'm doing it . . . you know that . . . all the time.

EDEN: It's part of the agreement, right?

CHEEK: Every second, sir. All the time.

EDEN: All the time, is it? Well put. You're right. All the time it is.

CHEEK: There's a lot to do, Mr. Eden. A lot, all the time. I won't forget.

   (Pause)

EDEN: I intend to take you to dinner this evening, Miss Cheek.

CHEEK: What's the occasion?

EDEN: I had a meeting with the chairman this morning.

CHEEK: The chairman?

EDEN: I have been given a promotion.

CHEEK: How wonderful!

EDEN: They are very pleased with what I have been doing.

CHEEK: I'm sure they must be. You work so hard!

EDEN: Excellent results, the chairman said.

CHEEK: Excellent results?

EDEN: Those were his words.

CHEEK: The chairman said that?

EDEN: Exceptional, he said.

CHEEK: I'm so happy for you! How should I dress?

EDEN: I beg your pardon?

CHEEK: *(speaking softly)* How should I dress for dinner this evening?

EDEN: That's a rather inane question, isn't it?

CHEEK: I just ....

EDEN: Yes?

CHEEK: Nothing, sir.

EDEN: Come on, out with it. You began to say something; let's hear it.

CHEEK: The last time, the chairman complimented me on my suit.

EDEN: He thought you had attractive legs.

CHEEK: He liked my smile and ... my eyes ....

EDEN: The best legs in town, according to him.

CHEEK: And my suit was just right.

EDEN: It certainly showed off your legs to advantage.

CHEEK: I can't wear the same suit.

EDEN: The chairman is a great administrator. But he is getting old and a little senile, and lately the expression in his eyes has occasionally betrayed a certain interest in ... shall we say "the bawdy"? Something that would never have happened five years ago. In those days, his expression was perfect, controlled, flawless. However, he has begun to show his age.

CHEEK: The chairman is still an attractive man.

EDEN: And one without worldly cares. As soon as he settles down in a plane he sleeps like a baby. That's an indication. The chairman likes to think of himself as a ladies' man; his flattery is just a reflex. It was just his way of finding something to say to you. He didn't really see your eyes, your smile, your good taste or your suit. He saw your legs and he said something to you.

CHEEK: What should I wear this evening, sir?

EDEN: Wear whatever you like. You do have excellent taste.

CHEEK: I'll wear a dress with a full skirt. I really can't wear suits anymore. The chairman may enjoy seeing a young pregnant woman.

(Pause.)

EDEN: Where have you been? Did you go out?

CHEEK: I went shopping.

EDEN: What for?

CHEEK: The stores were having sales today.

EDEN: Are you out of your mind? The Saturday sales? The crowds must have been terrible! Don't you think that was a bit risky?

CHEEK: I bought something for the baby.

EDEN: Was that necessary?

CHEEK: They had wonderful toys, on sale.

EDEN: You bought a toy?

CHEEK: I bought a pacifier... for when he's teething.

EDEN: A pacifier?

CHEEK: A rubber one. So he can chew on it. It helps during teething. And it strengthens the jaw muscles. You wouldn't want your child to have a weak jaw, would you?

EDEN: You didn't by any chance pick up a newspaper on your way back, did you?

CHEEK: I did buy a paper, but I read it in the park.

EDEN: The park?

CHEEK: I was in the park for awhile. It was so nice out.

EDEN: You didn't sit in the sun, did you?

CHEEK: I found a bench in the shade.

EDEN: You mean in the shade of a tree?

CHEEK: In a cool spot, on a bench, under a tree.

EDEN: Do you realize how dangerous the shade of a tree can be? I hope it wasn't a willow tre.

CHEEK: I think it was a chestnut tree.

EDEN: Are you certain?

CHEEK: I think so. I'm not very good with trees. As a matter of fact, the only trees I know are chestnut trees, because of the chestnuts. . . .

EDEN: I should hope so. Be careful the next time. You've no idea what the shadow of a willow tree can be like. You don't have a slight headache?

CHEEK: Not really, but I'm a little tired. From having read the paper, and the outdoors and the sun . . . .

EDEN: You read the paper in the park? Anything special?

CHEEK: If I'd known, I'd have brought it back.

EDEN: But you didn't read anything that seemed particularly interesting?

CHEEK: You mean the thing about babies in the twenty-first century?

EDEN: Did you read it?

CHEEK: About babies being born outside the womb? I read it.

EDEN: What did you think about it?

CHEEK: It made me think that newspapers will print anything. . . .

EDEN: It was a statement issued by the Chairman of the Ethics Committee.

CHEEK: I didn't know that. You mean, it's true?

EDEN: Is what true?

CHEEK: That babies won't need a mother's womb anymore?

EDEN: They are working on it. No more risk. No more discomfort. No more anxiety, Miss Cheek.

(Pause)

CHEEK: The child will be fine, sir. I won't go to the sales anymore. I won't sit in the park anymore. I'll stay here. I promise. I won't go out to dinner tonight. I'm tired. I'll stay here. I won't subject the baby to any more risks. It's only for two more months. I'll behave.

EDEN: Have you watched the tapes I gave you?

CHEEK: Yes, sir, several times. I . . . .

EDEN: Sometimes I wonder if your lack of education isn't a drawback. . . .

CHEEK: I didn't go to college, . . . it's true I'm not educated, but I do know one thing, and that is that I will know how to raise this child. That, I know.

EDEN: You know?

CHEEK: I think . . . . Yes, I'll know. I'm pregnant; that's not easy. And then there's the birth. That's what all the suffering is for. For that day. Birth. After that, everything will seem easy.

EDEN: How do you know such things?

CHEEK: A friend . . . . I mean, there's this woman I've been talking to, in the park. . . . That's what she said. She said that on that day all the pain just disappears. Afterwards, it's all easy. She said you can't imagine it. And I tried to imagine.

EDEN: Tried. You don't know. Every case is unique.

CHEEK: It'll all be easy.

EDEN: Those are just words. You're trying to convince yourself.

CHEEK: It'll all be easy. I know it will.

EDEN: You know nothing about it! Some other woman's experience! On a park bench. And you think you know it all! In the meantime, you sit around under trees, you traipse around in crowded stores! You know nothing now and you think you're going to know anything later?

CHEEK: I.... Now, it's discomfort. Nervousness. I don't know what.... But afterwards, I swear....

EDEN: You swear?

CHEEK: It'll all be easy. She told me, and I can feel that it's true. That I could stay. That I'd be a good mother. Under the terms of the contract, of course, under the terms of the contract.

EDEN: We can only hope so. I would be extremely sorry if I were forced to part from you after the birth merely because you had broken our agreement.

CHEEK: The agreement won't be broken. I'll watch the tapes again.

EDEN: I must go. I hope you won't make any more mistakes.

CHEEK: No.

   (Pause)

EDEN: Would you get me the envelope I left on my desk,

please? It's addressed, but there's no stamp on it. The one without a stamp.

(Cheek exits, right.)

Thank you.

(Alone, Eden goes to the back wall, opens the panel, and pushes the "Record" button. He shuts the panel. Cheek returns with an envelope.)

EDEN: That's the one. Thank you.

CHEEK: You're welcome.

EDEN: So, until later.

CHEEK: Until later.

(Eden exits, left. Cheek remains standing, looking after him. Then she lowers her eyes and looks down at her belly. Black-out.)

ACT THREE

(A few minutes later. Same setting, the same atmosphere. Nothing has changed. Miss Cheek enters from the kitchen, right. She is holding a container of yogurt and a small spoon. She sits down on the sofa and opens the yogurt. The doorbell rings. She exits, left, and returns, talking to Adamson.)

ADAMSON: I'm really sorry to be bothering you again.

CHEEK: Not at all. You must have just missed him. He's only been gone for a few minutes.

ADAMSON: It's better this way. I wouldn't have wanted to bother him for such a little.... I must have dropped it in the bedroom.

CHEEK: I didn't see anything. What does it look like?

ADAMSON: It's gold-plated. It was a gift. That's why I came back.

CHEEK: Go take a look.

(Adamson exits, right, and returns holding a cigarette lighter. Cheek watches.)

ADAMSON: Got it. I knew it was there. It had fallen down by the bed.

CHEEK: I'm glad you found it. Are you going to stay?

ADAMSON: A while ago, you wanted me to leave....

CHEEK: You were right. Mr. Eden wasn't even angry that I'd let you wait for him.

ADAMSON: He wasn't?

CHEEK: He said I'd done the right thing. So I guess you're welcome to stay. I'm not going out. You can keep me company. Would you like a yogurt?

ADAMSON: Yes. What flavor?

CHEEK: Plain. I only have plain yogurt. The others are full of chemicals and preservatives and food coloring, ... even the expensive brands. You can't trust them anymore. Do you want sugar?

ADAMSON: Yes, please.

CHEEK: A spoonful?

ADAMSON: Yes, a spoonful.

(Cheek exits, right, and returns with another container of yogurt. They sit down on the sofa and begin to eat.)

CHEEK: I put in one and a half. *(Pause. They eat in silence.)* The problem is that ... when you put in sugar, you've got to stir it. It makes it lumpy unless you stir it really hard until it gets smooth. But you can't do that when you're out in public. It's really bad manners. ... I like mine solid, like eating ice. You can make like a hole in the middle and the sides will stay firm. Like making cliffs, see? And then I eat the cliffs. I just read an article about it in the newspaper, but they didn't describe my method. Do you think I should write them about it?

ADAMSON: They must get lots of letters.

CHEEK: Well, then maybe I won't write.

(Pause)

ADAMSON: How did the shopping go?

CHEEK: It was a mob scene. The stores are always so crowded on Saturdays.

ADAMSON: Why can't you do it some other day?

CHEEK: I could. But I always end up going on Saturdays. I think they restock the shelves with new things on Friday evening.

ADAMSON: I'd have thought they'd do that on Mondays....

CHEEK: And leave it like that all week?

ADAMSON: People shop during the week.

CHEEK: Not as many. I'm telling you. The stores are always crowded on Saturdays.

ADAMSON: Have you ever gone on Tuesday during lunch hour? It's a mob scene then.

CHEEK: Over the lunch hour, maybe. But that's only an hour, isn't it? While on Saturdays....

ADAMSON: You didn't tell me it was his child.

(Pause)

CHEEK: What child?

ADAMSON: Your child. You didn't tell me he was the father.

CHEEK: It isn't my child.

ADAMSON: How can you say that?

CHEEK: I'm only carrying it for him.

ADAMSON: You were hiding it from me, that he was the father.

CHEEK: I thought...I thought it was obvious.

ADAMSON: Sure. And that story about your husband on a business trip and all that?

CHEEK: Mr. Eden gave very strict instructions.

ADAMSON: The version for public consumption, is that it? To think you fed me all that nonsense!

CHEEK: You don't believe me? You don't believe that I had my orders?

ADAMSON: Orders? Sure. In the meantime, *he* told me.

CHEEK: That's his business.

ADAMSON: But you...you didn't trust me.

CHEEK: I...I do trust you.

ADAMSON: Oh, do you? Then why didn't you tell me?

CHEEK: I trust you when it's something that's got to do with me.

ADAMSON: And this hasn't got anything to do with you?

CHEEK: What do you want me to do?

ADAMSON: Nothing. I ought to have known better.

CHEEK: Did I ask you what *you* were doing, last night?

ADAMSON: You could have.... It all seems like such ancient history, now....

CHEEK: It was only yesterday evening....

(Pause)

ADAMSON: Evelyn, what kind of man is he?

CHEEK: To begin with, I shouldn't have let you call me by my first name. Miss Cheek was just fine.

ADAMSON: It's one of those things . . . .

CHEEK: And that gold-plated lighter you "lost"? Of course that was a lie, wasn't it?

ADAMSON: It's something that once you've done it, you can't go back. . . .

CHEEK: It was in your pocket all the time, wasn't it? Answer me. . . .

ADAMSON: Once you've been friends with someone, once you've called them by their first name, you can't go back. . . . Even if you become enemies, even if you hate each other or want to kill each other, you still call each other by your first names. Always.

CHEEK: Not Mr. Eden.

ADAMSON: Why do you say that?

CHEEK: He does what he pleases. He calls you what he wants to. He maintains the distances between people.

ADAMSON: Is that so?

CHEEK: Mr. Eden pays attention to things like that.

ADAMSON: To distance?

CHEEK: As far as I'm concerned, I'd rather we went back to where we were, Mr. Adamson.

ADAMSON: How do you know my name?

CHEEK: You left your wallet on the table last night.

ADAMSON: You looked in it?

CHEEK: I wanted to see.

ADAMSON: Were you looking for money?

CHEEK: Mr Eden gives me all I need. What do you think I am?

ADAMSON: So why did you look?

CHEEK: I was checking.

ADAMSON: Checking on me? Why?

CHEEK: To find out what kind of person you are.

ADAMSON: What kind of information did you expect to find in a wallet?

CHEEK: It was quite useful, as a matter of fact. Robert Adamson, 25 years of age, green eyes, almost no money. But a credit card, and valid ID. A public library card.

ADAMSON: Proving that I know how to read.

CHEEK: I didn't feel safe. You never know.

ADAMSON: Was it because of me or because of him, that you didn't feel safe?

CHEEK: Of him . . . ?

ADAMSON: I suppose you feel safe with Henry?

CHEEK: How can you say a thing like that? He's a man who.... He's not like you....

ADAMSON: He keeps you locked up here.

CHEEK: He doesn't keep me locked up. I'm free to come and go.

ADAMSON: You are?

CHEEK: Yes. You don't know anything about it. You can't understand.

ADAMSON: Understand what?

CHEEK: The kind of man he is. You don't realize. He... He's there. I'm never afraid with him, never.

ADAMSON: And with me, you are?

CHEEK: You don't realize. He's a man...a man who has *lived*.

ADAMSON: Lived! That's what you say!

CHEEK: It's true; where he's concerned, it's true.

ADAMSON: What do you know about it?

CHEEK: He's a man.... Well, for example, he's a man who leaves no clues.... You can look. Aside from his electronics equipment, there's nothing. Not a book, not a letter, not a picture. No one ever calls him. There's nothing about him.

ADAMSON: And then suddenly, there's me. Me here.

CHEEK: But before you, nothing. Not a clue. So it's obvious that up until now he hasn't wanted there to be any. But there must have been some, once.

ADAMSON: Once?

CHEEK: Earlier, before you, before me, before everything. He must have had some kind of life, another life, photographs, letters, phone calls. Life. And then something must have happened. Too many clues to life. And then none at all.

ADAMSON: You're imagining things. Did he tell you about his life?

CHEEK: He told me about someone.

ADAMSON: Someone?

CHEEK: A few months ago.

ADAMSON: There you are: that's a clue, isn't it?

CHEEK: He just mentioned it in passing: "I used to live with someone." Once. In all this time. And he never talked about it again.

ADAMSON: Did he mention a name?

CHEEK: No. Just "someone."

ADAMSON: A man?

CHEEK: Why do you ask that?

ADAMSON: Did he mention a woman?

CHEEK: He said "someone."

ADAMSON: Well, "someone" could mean anything.

CHEEK: Not a man.

ADAMSON: No?

CHEEK: That's my impression.

ADAMSON: Exactly!

CHEEK: And what if it was a man? Anyway, it wasn't you. It was before.

ADAMSON: Well, "someone," then. He lived with someone. So what? Why act like it was such a mystery? "I don't realize"! What don't I realize? That's all you've got. Time alone here. Nothing.

CHEEK: It was someone who mattered. Not like us.

ADAMSON: What?

CHEEK: Yes, someone who mattered. Not like us.

ADAMSON: Speak for yourself.

(Pause)

CHEEK: Do *you* matter?

ADAMSON: Too early to tell.

CHEEK: Too early? I can tell you. . . . I've been living here for seven months. . . .

ADAMSON: So you live here. So what?

CHEEK: I share Mr. Eden's life.

ADAMSON: Share? That's not what he told me.

CHEEK: He didn't tell you anything. If you think that Mr. Eden feels about you any. . . .

ADAMSON: What?

CHEEK: Nothing.

ADAMSON: And for you? What does he feel for you? Well? "Share" his life! Is that how you describe it? Just because he had you made pregnant? Yes, you see, . . . he *did* talk to me about you. . . .

CHEEK: I'm carrying his son.

ADAMSON: *In vitro* fertilization! And you're sharing his life! I'll bet that he just wanted to be sure that he would really be the father.

CHEEK: What do you mean?

ADAMSON: Artificial. The egg fertilized by clearly identified sperm. The whole process was done by doctors. He wanted to be sure he was really the father.

CHEEK: What difference does that make?

ADAMSON: What other proof could he have had? What proof that it wasn't some other guy's baby?

CHEEK: What other guy?

ADAMSON: Some guy you might have slept with. Someone on the side. He didn't trust you; that's the truth.

CHEEK: He trusted me enough to choose me to be the mother of his child.

ADAMSON: You're really proud of that, aren't you?

CHEEK: And why shouldn't I be? You just wish you were in my place. . . .

   (Pause)

ADAMSON: I could kill you for saying that.

CHEEK: *(quietly)* I'll bet you could.

   (Pause)

ADAMSON: When the baby's born, Henry can send me a card.

CHEEK: I don't suppose there'll be any.

ADAMSON: You plan to keep it a big secret?

CHEEK: Mr. Eden doesn't believe in sending cards.

ADAMSON: Doesn't he?

CHEEK: Mr. Eden says that cards are for people who don't know very many other people. He said that when you know a lot of people, you put an announcement in the evening paper. You'll just have to read your favorite paper.

ADAMSON: Why do you talk to me like that?

CHEEK: How am I talking to you?

ADAMSON: You should really learn to control yourself. Henry warned me about you. . . .

CHEEK: What do you mean?

ADAMSON: Henry told me, he told me about how moody you are, how unpredictable. . . .

CHEEK: Unpredictable? Mr. Eden told you I was unpredictable? That's not like him. When did he tell you that?

ADAMSON: Last night.

CHEEK: The fact is that I'm not a bit unpredictable. I'm very even-tempered. Mr. Eden couldn't have told you such a thing because he's very fair.

ADAMSON: Maybe he didn't mean it to be unkind.

CHEEK: He didn't say it.

ADAMSON: It's not that terrible a thing to say.

CHEEK: Why would he have told you that about me?

ADAMSON: For the same reason he told me you were carrying his child. He trusts me. As you were saying a while ago, he likes me. We're friends. . . . Friends tell each other a lot of things. . . . Friends share things. We trust each other completely, he and I.

CHEEK: And . . . did he say why he thought I was unpredictable?

ADAMSON: He said that he had had plenty of time to observe you, over the last seven months. He said that you were moody. He said that the seven months had seemed longer than he'd expected, sharing his apartment with you. And he said you were thoughtless.

CHEEK: Thoughtless?

ADAMSON: He couldn't believe you'd gone out shopping on a Saturday. He said it was very careless of you. He didn't think you realized the dangers you were exposing the child to. It's the word he used. "In short," he said, "she's a bit thoughtless."

CHEEK: We talked about that a while ago. Mr. Eden brought it up. He talked about it. He forgave me. It was a misunderstanding.

ADAMSON: Fine, if that's what you think. If that makes you happy, then everything's fine. I mean, if you can't see the difference between today's little incident and a general observation based on months of consideration, then that's your fault. Those were his very words: "In short, she's thoughtless." Now, that's what *he* thinks. That's *his* opinion of you.

CHEEK: *(her features working, extremely agitated)* You said ... you said "*a bit* thoughtless."

ADAMSON: Does that make a difference? Do you know what "a bit" means? "A bit" means that you're polite, that you're not *totally* uneducated. "A bit" means that you don't want to be too blunt about it. That's all "a bit" means. And are you sure he really said "a bit"? Are you sure about that?

CHEEK: But you.... He said, "In short, she's ...."

ADAMSON: I said what he said, okay? Maybe he didn't say that exactly. Maybe I don't remember exactly what he said. All I remember is the impression. The meaning. What counts is the idea. And that, I recall, perfectly. Because I was surprised at what he said about you. His thinking you were careless.

CHEEK: Maybe he said it without thinking it.

ADAMSON: Is Henry the kind of man to speak carelessly? Is that how you think of him, Evelyn?

CHEEK: But he forgave me. By the time he left, it had all been forgotten.

ADAMSON: Of course he *forgave* you. You've still got two months to go, right? So you'll be forgiven for two months. He's relying on you. He hasn't got any choice. He's got to go on pretending for two months. But then, then you'll remember what I've told you today.

CHEEK: If I live up to the agreement, so will he. Mr. Eden is an honest man.

ADAMSON: Excepting that he doesn't think you *have* been living up to it. That's the problem. Deep down, he believes you haven't. He thinks you're careless. He thinks your carelessness is damaging the child.

CHEEK: *(on the verge of tears)* How do you know what he thinks? Mr. Eden keeps his feelings to himself. It's impossible to know him.

ADAMSON: For *you*, maybe . . . .

CHEEK: Mr. Eden would never do anything dishonest. You don't know him any better than I do.

ADAMSON: I know him in a different way. You know his house; you share it with him. But I know his heart. And *there,* I know how he feels. He feels betrayed.

CHEEK: Betrayed?

ADAMSON: Betrayed by a careless woman whose morals are . . . loose.

CHEEK: You're lying! He couldn't have said that about me!

ADAMSON: So maybe he didn't, Evelyn; maybe he didn't say it.

CHEEK: He didn't.

ADAMSON: No? Well, he not only said it, but he obviously meant it. You still don't see, do you? Artificial. He was the only possible father. He knew you were ... that you were having relations with other men.

CHEEK: No! No!

ADAMSON: That's what he thinks. He must have some reason for it. He said that that was why he picked you. Because it would be easier to get rid of you, afterwards. He has a whole file on you. He said that your past is more than enough to condemn you. Loose morals. A careless child producer, ... that's what he called you.

CHEEK: He couldn't have said that. He picked me out of a whole lot of others. More than a hundred, and he picked me.

ADAMSON: From a personal ad? A personal ad in the classified section? Is that how he picked you? Of course it was! Doesn't it all come clear to you now? Remember the ad? Remember the first words? You must remember that. What were they; come on, tell me. Wealthy man? Gentleman, well off? How did it go? You haven't forgotten; you can't have forgotten. Tell me!

CHEEK: *(staring)* It said ... it just said ....

ADAMSON: *What* did it say? Eh?

CHEEK: "You shall be the mother of my child."

ADAMSON: "You shall be the mother of my child"? Is that what it said? What else?

CHEEK: Nothing.

ADAMSON: Nothing.

CHEEK: Nothing else. Just . . . the box number.

ADAMSON: How very clever! How tremendously clever! "You shall be the mother of my child." Now do you understand? See how obvious it is? A man like him, putting an ad in the paper! All of it must have disgusted him from the very beginning. Then he picked you. He must have sensed something in your reply. Something must have attracted him. Something that appealed to him. He must have sensed something. Loose morals—that's what he sensed. "Loose morals" would have made the whole thing seem doable. Simple, even! He'd only been daydreaming about it, before. He'd been daydreaming when he wrote the ad. He must have been daydreaming when he asked his secretary to send it to the paper. And then comes your letter. Then, he *knew*. He knew you were the one. Now do you see? Contempt. Contempt and disgust. You won't be allowed to raise the child. You can be sure of that!

CHEEK: *(expressionless)* We have an agreement. I'm not worried.

ADAMSON: Oh? Not worried about what? What rights do you think you've got?

CHEEK: The law. . . .

ADAMSON: The law? Oh, then of course you're in a really strong position! The law is on your side. The men who *make* laws are on Henry's side. Henry has men on his side who are *above* the law. Henry has men on his side who see to it that laws are *enforced*. Henry can throw you out any time he feels like it. He'll keep the child and he'll throw you out. If you try to make trouble, Henry will destroy you. Henry loathes and despises you. He thinks you're nothing but a careless woman with loose morals.

(Miss Cheek begins to sob and runs toward the bedroom, right. She slams and locks the door behind her. Pause. Adamson runs after her, but the door is locked.)

ADAMSON: Evelyn? Open the door, Evelyn! I was only trying to help you. I was only trying to make you see, Evelyn! Come with me. Evelyn?

(We hear the front door open. The alarm goes off, then stops. Eden enters.)

EDEN: Why have you come back again, Adamson? What are you doing here? Where is Miss Cheek? Why did she let you in? Where is she?

ADAMSON: She's ... she's .... It's nothing. She's just locked herself in there.

EDEN: What do you mean?

ADAMSON: Evelyn ... Miss Cheek, I mean, ... she's ... she's locked herself in.

EDEN: When?

ADAMSON: Just now. A moment ago.

EDEN: Why?

ADAMSON: She ... she was very nervous. She went and locked herself in.

EDEN: *(facing the bedroom door)* Miss Cheek? Miss Cheek? Open the door. It's me. Henry Eden. You can unlock the door; I'm here. Henry Eden. Would you please open the door? Please? It's me. It's Henry Eden. Evelyn? *(There is no response. A long pause.)* Very well. Adamson, break down the door. Break it down now!

(Adamson tries the doorknob again and then throws himself against the door. Just as he is about to do so again, the door opens. Miss Cheek enters.)

EDEN: Evelyn! Sit down.... Why didn't you answer? Here, sit down....

CHEEK: I don't want to sit down.

EDEN: Are you all right? You locked yourself in....

CHEEK: Yes, I locked myself in.

EDEN: Why...? Because of him?

CHEEK: Him?

EDEN: Did he do something to you?

CHEEK: Him? No.... Just talked. I couldn't keep him from talking. He kept on talking. He didn't stop.

ADAMSON: You're lying. You were glad to see me! To keep you company. You said you never saw anyone.

CHEEK: I said .... Yes, I did say that. I was glad to see you, at first. But afterwards....

ADAMSON: Afterwards? Wasn't I polite?

CHEEK: Polite? You, polite to me?

ADAMSON: I didn't do anything....

CHEEK: You told me.... You said I was a....

ADAMSON: I just explained a few things to you that....

EDEN: What right have you to explain things, Adamson? And what things were you going to explain? What did you come back here for? You knew I wasn't here. You knew I had absolutely no desire to see you, that there was no reason to wait for me.

ADAMSON: You realize what you're doing, Henry?

EDEN: The time for guessing games is over! What are you doing here?

ADAMSON: You're taking her side against me.

EDEN: (sarcastic, with a harsh laugh) Taking her side? Against you? Who are you, that I should take sides against you?

ADAMSON: I'm Bob, Henry. I.... You and I.... Something ...more than you....

EDEN: More than I can imagine? Oh, yes! A great deal more! But I imagine nothing, absolutely nothing; don't you realize that? (Pause) What did you do to her? What did you come back for? You knew I had gone out, didn't you? That she was alone? An easy victim for a big, strong man like you! For revenge! To worm your way in here! That's it, isn't it? You don't want to admit it? All right, then, let's have a look. Watch!

(He goes to the back wall, opens the panel, and starts the VCR.

ADAMSON and CHEEK appear on the screen, in the preceding scene.)

ADAMSON: *Wealthy man? Gentleman, well off? How did it go? You haven't forgotten; you can't have forgotten. Tell me!*

CHEEK: *(staring) It said . . . it just said . . . .*

ADAMSON: What *did it say? Eh?*

CHEEK: *"You shall be the mother. . . ."*

(Cheek moves to Eden and depresses the "Stop" button on the VCR.)

CHEEK: That's enough. It's a good thing he came back. He made me realize . . . . I'm the one who's going to leave.

EDEN: Leave? To go where?

CHEEK: I'm leaving.

EDEN: Where will you go?

CHEEK: To a hotel. With the last installment.

EDEN: You're breaking the agreement, Evelyn Cheek. Don't go too far, or. . . .

CHEEK: Or?

EDEN: You will not be the mother of my child.

CHEEK: And who'll stop me?

EDEN: I will.

CHEEK: You? And who says you *are* the child's father. . . .

EDEN: What do you mean?

CHEEK: Other men! Wasn't that it, other men? Well, I'll have other men, and then some!

EDEN: What do you mean, other men?

ADAMSON: I don't know, Henry.

EDEN: But what does that mean, "other men"? What are you talking about? What did he say to you? *(to Adamson)* Are you fond of pregnant women, Adamson?

(Pause)

CHEEK: No. It's not.... But he did say.... He's right. Other men until I find one to be the father of my child!

EDEN: Your child? How dare you say such a thing! You signed.

CHEEK: I signed a piece of paper.

EDEN: A contract. For a large sum of money we had agreed on.

CHEEK: You've got the paper and I've got the child. And if I left now....

EDEN: Where would you go? To a hotel? Your money would run out in a few weeks. And you'd have a baby....

CHEEK: I'd have a baby.... Or maybe....

EDEN: Shut up! You're talking nonsense! I forbid you to say such things. You signed. For a great deal of money.

CHEEK: Yes, for a great deal of money.

EDEN: So, what has changed? I was wrong to let him sleep here; I admit it.

CHEEK: That.... I don't care about that. It's a good thing he did stay, that he came back. I was the one who was asleep. He woke me up, your friend.

EDEN: "My friend"? "Woke up"? "Other men"? You must be mad! Nothing has happened to change anything. We have an agreement. Think of the money involved. That hasn't changed. There's still just as much.

CHEEK: It's true I signed it for the money.

ADAMSON: One always signs for the money.

EDEN: *(to Cheek)* I've respected the agreement. You've wanted for nothing. You'll have the money, as soon as the child is born, if you like; you don't even have to stay with it. The conditions are exactly the same. Nothing has changed.

CHEEK: Nothing, no. Except for me. I've changed. There's the contract, there's the money, but there's me, too.

EDEN: There's the function. And you've been free to come and go as you pleased...so long as your comings and goings haven't been damaging to the function and to the child.

CHEEK: I've told you: there's me!

EDEN: How can you say such things! We have a contract. There are papers. Insemination. Cohabitation. There are lawyers, doctors, authorities! It's my son, understand? My son!

(He moves towards her, threateningly.)

CHEEK: What are you doing?

(Eden stops short, alarmed at his own violence. Pause.)

EDEN: *(more softly)* I don't understand you. It's a lot of money, Evelyn. You know that.

CHEEK: I signed it for the money.

EDEN: You'll get it.

CHEEK: For the money; but there was something more, too.

EDEN: Do you want more?

CHEEK: More?

EDEN: More money!

CHEEK: No.

EDEN: You said "something more."

CHEEK: Yes, something more than money. There was you. Me with you. There was here, too, in a way....

EDEN: When you signed, you had never been here.

CHEEK: But I'd seen you. I'd seen you talk, smile, persuade. I imagined that where you lived would be a special place, ...like you. So I agreed. Because it was you.

ADAMSON: Listen to her, Henry! Do you hear that! Miss Cheek is getting all sentimental!

EDEN: *(to Cheek)* He's right, isn't he? Because it was me? You want more money, say so. Don't be ashamed. We'll talk about it. The boy wasn't part of the contract. No provision was made for this kind of... setback. I'm prepared to renegotiate. Let's talk about it. How much do you want?

CHEEK: Nothing. I assure you.

ADAMSON: She wants it *all*, Henry. Everything.

EDEN: Everything?

CHEEK: No! I don't want money. I don't want anything. I want to go.

ADAMSON: She's blackmailing you. Sentimental blackmail.

EDEN: *(turning on Adamson, furious)* That's enough! Sentiment! What do you know about sentiment? You've got the mind of a teenage girl, Adamson! You get your feelings out of cheap romantic novels. Your ideas of love are as suburban as the neighborhood where you live, out there by the stadium! You act like a hurt child, but you're worse than all the rest. You're cheap stuff. If people didn't watch out, you might really be able to make them believe that your petty behavior was just naivefe, that your aggressiveness was just youth, that your puny schemes were just honest ambition, that your tawdry emotions were true love, that your weakness of character was detachment, that your passive servility was really enthusiasm—if people didn't watch out, they could really be mistaken about you! But not me. You haven't fooled me! Elope! True romance! Marriage! You're one of those people who really believe that people *do* elope. Elope from yourself! Go on, run off. Escape from yourself, if you can. I'm not going along,... not with you, not against you, not because of you! Go! Don't come back. Don't ever come back here again. Never.

(Pause. Adamson exits, in a frozen silence. We hear the front door slam. A long pause.)

EDEN: There. That takes care of him.

(Pause)

CHEEK: I shouldn't have let him back in.

(Pause)

EDEN: I'd like you to call me Henry.

CHEEK: You've been calling me Evelyn.

(Pause)

EDEN: You aren't upset with me?

(Pause)

CHEEK: You'll have your child, your son. I'm going to lie down now. Good night.

EDEN: Good night.

(Blackout)

ک

Copi

A TOWER NEAR PARIS

Translated from the French by Mark O'Donnell

This English translation of *A Tower Near Paris* was given its first public reading at Ubu Repertory Theater during Ubu's "Festival of Gay Plays in Twentieth-Century France" on May 4 1987, with the following cast:

JEAN	**Reed Birney**
LUC	**Stephen Bogardus**
DAPHNEE	**Patricia Clarkson**
MICHELINE	**David Saint**
AHMED	**Anjul Nigam**
JOHN	**Lawrence O'Donnell**

Directed by **Mark O'Donnell**

COPI, whose real name was Raul Damonte, was born in Buenos Aires in 1939. He moved to Paris in 1963 and was already well-known as a designer and cartoonist when he started to write for the stage. His plays were very successful and he rapidly became one of the most talked-about playwrights in Paris. Copi himself acted in some of the productions of his plays, which were often directed by French-Argentine directors such as Jorge Lavelli, Alfredo Arias, and Jérôme Savary. He wrote a total of fifteen plays; among his best known ones are *Eva Peron* (1969), *The Homosexual or the Difficulty of Sexpressing Oneself* (1971), *The Four Twins* (1973), and *Loretta Strong* (1974). These plays were published in English by John Calder/Riverrun Press in 1976. Copi also published short stories, eight cartoon albums, and six novels— *L'Uruguayen* (1973), *Le Bal des folles* (1977), *Une Langouste pour deux* (1978), *La Cité des rats* (1979), *La Vie est un tango* (1979), and *La Guerre des pédés* (1982). *A Tower Near Paris (La Tour de la Défense)* was published in 1978 and premiered in Paris in 1981. The production was directed by Claude Confortès with a cast that included Bernadette Lafont and Pierre Clémenti. *Grand Finale (Une Visite inopportune)* is Copi's last play, written shortly before his death of AIDS in December 1988. The Paris production was directed by Jorge Lavelli and starred Michel Duchaussoy of the Comédie Française. It played to packed houses at the Théâtre National de la Colline in February 1988, and it received the award for best production of the year by the French Critics Guild. The play was given a second run in October 1988, and it subsequently toured France and Spoleto, Italy.

MARK O'DONNELL graduated from Harvard, where he won the Academy of American Poets Prize and the BMI Varsity Show Award. His plays include *Fables for Friends, The Nice and the Nasty, That's It, Folks!* and *Strangers on Earth.* O'Donnell's humor has appeared in *The New Yorker, The Atlantic, Spy, The New*

York Times, and many other publications. A collection of his comic pieces, *Elementary Education*, has been published by Knopf and Faber and Faber. He has received a Guggenheim Fellowship and the Lecomte de Nuoy Prize.

CHARACTERS

LUC, *a callous young man*
JEAN, *an unhappy young man*
DAPHNEE, *a young woman on acid*
MICHELINE, *an expansive transvestite*
AHMED, *an Arab youth*
JOHN, *an American*

The action takes place in an apartment in La Defense, a district just outside Paris. There is a living room with bay windows, a kitchen, and doors to the bathroom, the bedroom, and the corridor. It is New Year's Eve, 1976.

TRANSLATOR'S NOTE
I have preserved Copi's convention of referring to Micheline as "she" in the stage directions, though the part is to be played by a man. When the characters are speaking in English, their speech is italicized and slightly stilted; most of this dialogue is over the telephone. I would like to thank Jean-Marie Besset and Hal Walker for their advice and assistance in preparing this translation.

JEAN: *(after a thoughtful silence)* I should have killed myself when I was seventeen. Now it's too late.

LUC: *(after a pause, annoyed)* Oh, all right. Why when you were seventeen?

JEAN: Because when I was seventeen I had a revolver my father gave me.

LUC: There are plenty of other ways to kill yourself. You could always try an overdose.

JEAN: No. For me, suicide is a gun or nothing.

LUC: Why a gun?

JEAN: Because I had one when I was seventeen. And I'm not seventeen anymore.

LUC: Well, who cares?

JEAN: No one. I'm just talking to talk.

LUC: So shut up.

JEAN: Why? Why should I?

LUC: All right, then, talk to yourself.

JEAN: Well, since *you're* here . . . .

LUC: My ears are closed—as far as you're concerned.

JEAN: You mean your *ass* is closed, don't you?

LUC: Will you stop? Talking about sex, you think you're at a cocktail party?

JEAN: And when did you become a righteous landlady?

LUC: I'm going to the Tuileries.

JEAN: Don't you want to go eat at Club Seven?

LUC: No.

JEAN: I wouldn't go to the Tuileries. It's freezing, for one thing.

LUC: I don't recall asking you to come with me.

JEAN: If you don't come back tonight, call and tell me where you are.

LUC: Maybe you'll kill yourself first. Where's my leather jacket?

JEAN: At the cleaners.

LUC: I'll take your raincoat.

JEAN: Then you have to come back tonight. I'll need it tomorrow, I'm having lunch at my mother's.

LUC: Never mind, I'll go like this.

JEAN: You'll get another cold.

LUC: And you'll nurse me through it.

JEAN: That's stupid. Really stupid.

LUC: What's with you tonight? You beg me to stay home

with you when there's a very promising party over at Lucky's—and then you don't stop insulting me all night.

JEAN: We haven't made love in nine months.

LUC: Oh, stop. What do you want me to do?

JEAN: Today makes nine months since we made love.

LUC: Don't be ridiculous. What's the significance? The birth of the baby we would have had if we'd been a straight couple?

(The doorbell rings.)

LUC: Who could that be? Oh, Daphnee!

DAPHNEE: *(entering)* Am I disturbing you? Don't look at me like that, you scare me! I took some acid. I'm cold. I lost the address of my New Year's Eve party.

LUC: Good! For tonight, then, I'll borrow *your* overcoat.

JEAN: Wait, Luc. I'm sorry, I was foolish.

LUC: Let's not talk about it anymore.

(The telephone rings. Jean rolls a joint.)

DAPHNEE: It's for me. Hello, is that you, honey?... Are you coming? *(to Jean and Luc)* It's a divine Arab boy I met at the flea market! *(into the phone)* There's plenty to drink here! Carrefour de la Defense, thirteenth floor. You have to take the elevator to the fourteenth floor, the thirteenth is broken. There are two doors, ring either one. Take a taxi, someone will pay you back. Hurry to my side!

LUC: If you've invited him over, you'd better go home.

DAPHNEE: Oh, fuck you!

(She leaves.)

LUC: Just because she lives on the same floor is no excuse for her to go on boring us with her amorous adventures day and night. Don't let her in here anymore.

JEAN: Oh, stop! She and you, you're the same. As if you didn't fuck every Arab boy you meet.

LUC: This one I leave to you. Give me fifty francs; I'll go to the Tuileries.

JEAN: The Tuileries are free.

LUC: I might need to rent a room at the Crystal.

JEAN: Bring him back here.

LUC: No, thanks—for Daphnee to try and steal?

JEAN: My wallet must be in my coat. Wait til I finish rolling this joint.

LUC: Here, I took two hundred.

JEAN: Take more if you want. I went to the bank yesterday.

LUC: No, two hundred's enough. What if I got robbed?

JEAN: Got a match? This Pakistani herb is better than the Colombian.

LUC: Roll me a joint to take to the Tuileries.

(Daphnee reenters.)

DAPHNEE: Why did you chase me out like that? Are you hysterical or what? Don't you love me?

LUC: Oh, stop, Daphnee!

DAPHNEE: *(going to the divan)* Get out, you woman hater!

LUC: Fine, I'm going.

JEAN: Wait, I'll go with you. You can drop me off at rue Saint Anne.

DAPHNEE: And you're leaving me alone with an Arab?

LUC: Yes—but at your place.

DAPHNEE: Can't I stay here?

JEAN: *(to Luc)* Oh, let her stay. There's nothing to steal.

LUC: Are you crazy?

DAPHNEE: I don't want to see this Arab anymore! Let me stay here. I'll spend my acid trip alone.

JEAN: *(to Luc)* We can't leave her alone.

LUC: Well, I don't want to go to the Tuileries with her! You take her to Club Seven!

JEAN: Oh, no, she made a scene last time, they won't let her in again.

LUC: Then let her stay in her own place!

(The doorbell rings.)

Oh, shit, that's all we need!

(Micheline, a transvestite carrying a Felix Potin shopping bag, enters.)

MICHELINE: Darlings, what a story, wait til I tell you! Smack, smack! I've invited a sublime young Arab here as a New Year's present for you! Ahmed, come on!

(Ahmed enters.)

DAPHNEE: But—that's *my* Arab! Ahmed, dear, did you have trouble finding the place?

AHMED: *(to Micheline)* I found this lady in the elevator.

DAPHNEE: He's mine, you thief!

JEAN: Calm down, Daphnee. *(to Ahmed)* She took acid.

DAPHNEE: They don't want me here. Come on, Ahmed, we'll go to my place.

MICHELINE: Oh, poor boy!

AHMED: But why can't we stay here?

DAPHNEE: Do you like being surrounded by idiots?

AHMED: It's nice here.

DAPHNEE: Oh, go on, you fag! *(She sits on the arm of the divan.)*

MICHELINE: I brought a leg of mutton! Do you have any parsley?

JEAN: Did you bring wine?

MICHELINE: Don't *you* have anything to drink?

JEAN: Some whiskey.

MICHELINE: Ahmed, would you like a Scotch?

AHMED: *(in the armchair)* I'd like one, yes! A little baby one.

LUC: I'm going to the Tuileries.

MICHELINE: You're not going to the Tuileries! It's New Year's Eve!

LUC: Don't you find yourself just a bit ridiculous, you old cunt impersonator?

MICHELINE: *(to Jean)* What's wrong with *him*?

JEAN: Nothing. Let it drop.

MICHELINE: *(to Luc)* Not everyone can carry off that butch style, you have to be built. Even if no one ever sees your little dick!

LUC: I think you'll all be going. As soon as possible.

DAPHNEE: Come on, Ahmed, we'll go to my place while they calm down.

LUC: Take your Felix Potin shopping bag and all of you go to Daphnee's!

DAPHNEE: Oh, no, that'll mean dirty dishes, I'm terrified of them! Why doesn't she go to her apartment? She has ten fucking rooms. Why is she always foraging over here? She only comes to drool on my hard-won tricks!

JEAN: Calm down, Daphnee.

MICHELINE: You are contemptible. I'm going. *(She gathers her things.)*

LUC: Don't forget your onions.

JEAN: *(to Micheline)* Oh, stop, please! We *do* have to eat, stay for dinner!

MICHELINE: No, I'm going.

JEAN: Oh, Micheline, don't have a crisis.

MICHELINE: Don't touch me, you piece of shit, you, you—*fashion designer!*

LUC: All right, if you aren't done gathering your groceries, I'll help you.

MICHELINE: *(to Jean)* What is with him?

LUC: Put it all in your Felix Potin shopping bag and go party with the homeless!

JEAN: Luc, stop it, please stop!

LUC: It's nothing, I'm just insane. See you! *(He puts on Jean's overcoat.)*

JEAN: Can't you wait two minutes?

(Luc leaves and slams the door.)

DAPHNEE: Wait, I'll go with you! Luc, wait! My darling Luc!

(She leaves.)

JEAN: *(to Micheline)* Don't take it wrong, dear, this has been going on all day. Here, peel me two heads of garlic.

MICHELINE: I'll go home and finish my novel.

JEAN: Well, how many pages do you have to go?

MICHELINE: Oh, an eternity. I don't even know how it ends yet!

JEAN: Have her kill herself in the last chapter.

MICHELINE: Oh, no, she's more the housewife type. I think she'll return to her husband. Here's the garlic. Ahmed, do you have any matches?

AHMED: *(sitting)* Yes, here.

MICHELINE: Don't listen to these fools, dear, they're hysterics! Look how well-hung you are, come sit by me!

AHMED: Not right now.

JEAN: *(to Micheline)* So, where's the garlic?

MICHELINE: *(opening Ahmed's fly)* Uh, on the shelf.

JEAN: Where?

MICHELINE: I put it on the shelf.

JEAN: But you only cut one head.

(Daphnee enters.)

DAPHNEE: Luc is hurt!

JEAN: *(dropping a plate)* Where is he?

DAPHNEE: *(leaning against the wall)* On the landing.

JEAN: Luc!

(Jean and Micheline rush out. Daphnee throws herself on Ahmed.)

DAPHNEE: Hold me! I just need to be held!

(Jean and Micheline enter, supporting Luc, whose forehead is bleeding.)

DAPHNEE: He hit his head against the elevator door!

LUC: It's nothing! Let go of me! Give me some peace!

JEAN: But what happened?

DAPHNEE: He wanted to jump down the elevator shaft! He's out of his mind!

LUC: I'm going to take a shower.

(He goes into the bathroom.)

JEAN: Luc!

(He goes into the bathroom)

LUC: *(off)* Leave me alone.

(He chases Jean out and shuts the door.)

DAPHNEE: Oh, God, and me on acid!

(Luc comes out of the bathroom in his underwear.)

LUC: Any clean towels, Jean?

JEAN: *(tossing him a towel)* Here!

LUC: Thanks.

(Luc goes back into the bathroom, leaving the door open. He showers. We see the steam as he sings or whistles. Jean and Micheline go to the kitchen.)

DAPHNEE: They're all insane! I don't want to stay here anymore! Ahmed, let's go to another party.

AHMED: Where?

DAPHNEE: At Les Halles.

MICHELINE: Whose party?

DAPHNEE: What do you care? You weren't invited! Come on, Ahmed.

MICHELINE: *(to Jean)* Did you put the mutton in the oven?

JEAN: Yes, but it's a shitty oven, you can't control the heat.

DAPHNEE: Come on, Ahmed!

AHMED: Let's wait til we eat.

MICHELINE: *(to Jean)* Don't you have a can opener that works? We've got to cook the beans.

JEAN: Of course, here.

LUC: *(off)* Don't we have any dry towels? This one's soaked.

JEAN: Yes, wait a second!

LUC: *(off)* And another one for my hair.

(Jean goes into the bathroom.)

JEAN: *(off)* Luc! What's gotten into you? That was stupid!

   (Jean reenters.)

MICHELINE: *(to Jean)* Your can opener is for shit!

DAPHNEE: *(sitting with Ahmed)* Your religion doesn't forbid you to eat mutton, does it?

JEAN: *(to Micheline)* Give it here! *(He takes the can opener.)*

MICHELINE: Oh, I forgot I left the ice cream in my refrigerator.

JEAN: That was smart!

MICHELINE: Ahmed, would you like to take a taxi over to my place to search for the ice cream in my refrigerator?

AHMED: Where is it?

MICHELINE: Boulevard Saint-Germain.

AHMED: Isn't there some cheese here?

MICHELINE: Cheese? Ice cream is better!

AHMED: Cheese is fine.

JEAN: *(to Micheline)* He's right. It would take hours to cross town, it's New Year's Eve, remember!

MICHELINE: Do you have anything like dessert at your place, Daphnee?

DAPHNEE: Nothing.

MICHELINE: Not even fruit or yogurt?

DAPHNEE: Nothing but olives and some potato chips.

JEAN: Oh, shit, I cut myself!

MICHELINE: You sure did!

(Jean goes into the bathroom.)

JEAN: Luc, I cut myself!

LUC: *(off)* Leave me alone! Can't I have two minutes by myself in the shower?

(Luc chases Jean out, snaps him with a wet towel, and slams the door.)

JEAN: He's beserk!

MICHELINE: Here, sweetheart, run your finger under the faucet!

DAPHNEE: Ahmed, come over to my place. All right? Come over to my place. Come over to my place. Come over to my place. Ahmed, . . . are you listening?

AHMED: A little later.

MICHELINE: The beans are covered in blood, it's gross!

JEAN: That's nothing, we'll blend it into the sauce.

(Luc enters, wet, wrapped in a towel, a bandage on his forehead.)

LUC: I wasn't trying to kill myself. I opened the elevator door by mistake between floors. I'm sorry, Daphnee, I was a little drunk. *(to Jean)* Here's your bandage.

JEAN: Thanks.

LUC: What's that cooking?

JEAN: A leg of mutton.

LUC: You're crazy, you don't have to put it on high!

JEAN: But, look, I couldn't adjust it.

LUC: You don't know how to do anything. Did you put in some garlic?

JEAN: Yes, two heads.

LUC: Two heads? Take it out of the oven, we've got to remove the garlic.

MICHELINE: Oh, you're crazy! Garlic is good for you!

LUC: What barbarians! Isn't there any more whiskey?

DAPHNEE: I have some. Come on, Ahmed, let's go look for it.

LUC: Ah, but here's some good wine!

MICHELINE: I pinched it from my mother's wine cellar!

LUC: Daphnee and Ahmed, set the table.

DAPHNEE: I didn't come here to work. I'm on acid, I can't do anything.

AHMED: *(to Luc)* I can set the table.

LUC: Fine, there's the cloth, there's the plates, there's the glasses. Open a couple bottles of wine while I'm dressing.

MICHELINE: Why is it you don't have any parsley?

LUC: *(off, to Jean)* Where's the djellaba you bought me in Agadir?

JEAN: In the linen closet. *(to Micheline)* I don't have any parsley, I don't have any parsley, what do you want me to do?

MICHELINE: What if we put in some bay leaves? Bay leaves are good.

JEAN: Yes, wonderful, put in some bay leaves! Here, give me that knife, Ahmed.

(Luc enters, nude, holding a revolver in his hand.)

LUC: *(to Jean)* What's this?

JEAN: It's a revolver. I forgot to tell you I hid it in the linen closet.

LUC: A revolver! You don't hide a revolver under a pile of clean sheets!

JEAN: Where would you like me to hide it? We can't just leave it lying around!

LUC: Is it loaded?

JEAN: Of course it's not loaded! It's a gun my father gave me for my seventeenth birthday, I found it when I was at my mother's on Christmas.

LUC: Throw it in the incinerator!

JEAN: I can't throw a gun down the incinerator chute!

LUC: Get rid of it however you like, but do it now!

AHMED: But, no, it's good, this gun! You mustn't get rid of it! Don't you see? It's a Colt, that's a good gun!

(Jean takes the revolver and puts it in a dresser drawer.)

JEAN: I'll take care of it. I don't want to get rid of it. I'll take it back to my mother's tomorrow. There.

(When he closes the dresser drawer, we hear a gunshot. Everyone cries out except Ahmed.)

Shit!

LUC: That could have killed someone.

(Daphnee faints. Everyone hurries to her, except Ahmed.)

Is she hurt?

AHMED: No, the bullet passed through the other side of the dresser. There's the hole.

DAPHNEE: *(reviving)* You're all in a plot to frighten me!

LUC: It's you who's scaring yourself.

DAPHNEE: You know I'm on acid! I want my little girl. Where's my little girl?

MICHELINE: *(to Luc)* Has her husband taken Katia?

LUC: He took her away a week ago. She's on acid, she doesn't remember anything before yesterday.

DAPHNEE: I thought she'd be safe here! I couldn't reach my lawyer, he was skiing.

JEAN: *(to Micheline)* Her husband went back to his family in New York, with Katia. You get the picture.

DAPHNEE: I thought he was at his mother's in Fontaine-bleau, but it looks like he went back to New York. If I was sure, I'd go to New York right away, but I want to talk to my lawyer first.

LUC: But what could happen to Katia? They're not going to let her die of hunger or cold, you'll get her back one of these days. Here, cut the sausage, Ahmed.

AHMED: Where should I put it?

LUC: On a plate. Where do you want to put it?

DAPHNEE: *(to Luc)* Fucking bastard! It's your fault I've become what I am.

LUC: And what have you become? It's moronic! Just because everyone takes acid doesn't give one the right to insult everyone around her! Fuck off! Go home!

JEAN: Luc, please, leave her alone. She has to calm down.

MICHELINE: *(to Daphnee)* Calm down, darling.

(Ahmed dices up the sausage.)

AHMED: *(to Luc)* Like this? I could cut it in big thick slices.

LUC: That's good. Here, Ahmed, help me take the mutton out of the oven. Hold the door open, don't burn yourself! The mutton looks scorched!

JEAN: Oh, shit, I completely forgot.

(Daphnee faints.)

MICHELINE: *(who holds Daphnee)* She's passed out! Quick, a damp towel!

LUC: You take care of her! *(dropping the mutton)* Shit, I burned my fingers!

JEAN: That's lovely! You dropped the mutton on the floor!

LUC: We can save some of the sauce with a spoon. Where are the spoons?

JEAN: Ahmed, go get a spoon from the table.

MICHELINE: A damp towel!

LUC: What is happening?

MICHELINE: Quick, a damp towel!

JEAN: Here!

MICHELINE: She took too much acid. Let's put her on the couch.

LUC: What a circus!

MICHELINE: Do you have any milk? She should drink milk. It's the best antidote for acid.

JEAN: She must have milk over at her place. Ahmed, go see if there's some milk across the hall, it's open.

(Ahmed leaves.)

MICHELINE: Fuck! She is sick!

LUC: But what does she have?

DAPHNEE: *(recovering)* You all look like horrible monsters to me!

LUC: Well, fine, she can talk. Shit, the mutton! *(He goes to pick up the mutton off the floor.)* Quick! A fork! Where's the big fork!

JEAN: Here!

LUC: We'll have to wash it, it's covered with dirt!

JEAN: It's disgusting!

MICHELINE: Quick, a basin! She's going to vomit!

LUC: Oh, no!

(He hurries over with a bowl. Daphnee vomits in the bowl, then faints.)

MICHELINE: Some eau de cologne! Hurry!

LUC: It's nauseating! Drag her back to her place!

MICHELINE: Oh, let her be!

LUC: Did she vomit on you?

MICHELINE: She just missed me! Where's the eau de cologne? Rinse this out in the john!

JEAN: It's sickening!

(He goes into the bathroom, followed by Micheline.)

MICHELINE: *(off)* All you have is Chanel? Don't you have anything better?

LUC: *(from the kitchen)* Christ! The mutton!

JEAN: *(off)* What do you want? All I have is Chanel!

(Jean reenters.)

It smells like vomit in here! *(He opens the window.)*

DAPHNEE: *(recovering)* I'll be going. You'll see, I'm going. I'm sorry. I won't bother you anymore. Where's my purse?

JEAN: If you want to go, you certainly may! Your purse is at your place! . . . The beans are burning! Micheline, you let the beans burn!

(Micheline reappears.)

MICHELINE: I can't do everything!

(Ahmed enters, with a baby bottle and a jar of olives.)

AHMED: This is all I could find like milk. And a jar of olives.

DAPHNEE: It's Katia's bottle! Give me that, Ahmed! Don't touch it, it's sacred! Bunch of clods!

(Daphnee goes into the hall.)

AHMED: *(eating the olives)* The mutton smells good! It's really dirty over there. There's vomit in the refrigerator.

MICHELINE: *(to Jean)* Cut this for me, dear.

(Daphnee reenters.)

DAPHNEE: May I use your telephone? I have to call my husband.

MICHELINE: Ahmed, if you would, open this bottle. *(to Jean)* You let everything burn!

JEAN: No, you did!

LUC: And nobody made vinaigrette for the salad?

JEAN: Shit again, I forgot! Peel me a head of garlic, Ahmed.

LUC: We have to put the mutton back in the oven. It's ice cold.

JEAN: But it's burned!

MICHELINE: Never mind. Let's eat the sausage first.

DAPHNEE: *(on the phone, deliberately trying her English)* Fuck, it's an English operator. *"Hallo, operator. It is my wish to call over the seas, New York. It is from person to person! I am Miss Daphnee O'Donnell. I want to call my husband from person to person, in Manhattan, New York! Mr. O'Donnell. I will give you the number soon."* ... Where's that number? Ahmed, go find my address book. It's on top of my refrigerator.

AHMED: I didn't see it.

DAPHNEE: It must have fallen behind; the top of the refrigerator is warped. Everything slides off.
(Ahmed leaves.)

LUC: Who's going to pay for this call?

DAPHNEE: Some day I'll give you a check .... *"Just one moment please, I did lose the number."* ... She doesn't understand a thing, the idiot! ... *"Just exactly one moment, please!"*

(Ahmed comes back with the address book and gives it to Daphnee.)

Here..... *"Just one second. Plaza eight forty nineteen. P-L-eight-four-zero-one-nine.... Yes, nineteen. Very quick, please, I must be hurried!"*... Ahmed, get me a glass of red wine.

(Micheline and Jean set the table.)

LUC: Dinner time! Ahmed, Daphnee, dinner is fucking served!

(Ahmed sits at the table.)

DAPHNEE: I'm calling my husband.

LUC: *(to Micheline)* This sausage is disgusting! Where did you buy it?

MICHELINE: I stole it from the servants.

LUC: Ugh, it's spoiled!

MICHELINE: Sausage doesn't spoil, stupid!

JEAN: It's creole sausage, it should have been boiled!

MICHELINE: That's why it's so horrible!

LUC: Don't you know how to do anything? It's frustrating! Give me that, I'll boil it!

AHMED: You know those little Algerian sausages?

JEAN: Oh, yes, they're excellent.

DAPHNEE: *(on the phone)* *"Hello, John? Where is Katia?...She is there? I want her back.... What did you say?"*...He doesn't want to give her to me!... *"I would want to speak to Katia. Please, John."*... Allo, Katia! Darling, it's your Mommy! It's me, Daphnee! Are you all right, my love?... You aren't cold? You're not sick?...Yes? You have what?...What? A bear? A stuffed teddy bear, darling?...You have to tell Daddy that you want to come back to me. Do you understand?... *"Hello, John? Please, I want Katia back!...Please, John, please!"*...He hung up.

JEAN: Calm down, Daphnee. Calm yourself, dear.

DAPHNEE: I'm going to kill myself.

LUC: Enough suicides for tonight. I'm going. *(He pulls on his trousers and removes his djellaba.)* I'll be dining elsewhere.

MICHELINE: You're not going to leave all alone at eleven-thirty at night in Paris on New Year's Eve! It's depressing!

AHMED: Look, fireworks!

(They all go to the window, Daphnee first, and they look at the fireworks.)

LUC: Where are they firing them from? La Concorde?

AHMED: The Tuileries!

LUC: That isn't likely. They're all over the sky! Well, I can't cruise the Tuileries if there's fireworks going on!

AHMED: Look, look, that star, there!

(Daphnee tries to throw herself out the window. They restrain her with great difficulty.)

LUC: You fucking whore! You stupid slut!

JEAN: Hold her! There! There!

MICHELINE: Oh, dear God!

AHMED: Look, she hit her head! We must lie her down!

(They put her on the divan.)

MICHELINE: I'm going to pass out! Ahmed, a glass of wine, darling, if you would.

AHMED: Another centimeter and we'd have lost her! Fuck, I cut my wrist! Is there any alcohol?

(Jean goes to the bathroom.)

JEAN: Here, come on.

AHMED: Oww! Wait, I need a bandage!

LUC: Daphnee! Daphnee! She has a hell of a bump on her head!

AHMED: She hit it against the windowsill. Put some ice on the bump!

LUC: Get her out of here! *(to Daphnee)* Stand up! Now shove off!

AHMED: She can't walk. If you want, I'll carry her over to her place.

JEAN: Leave her here. She'll sleep.

(They lie her on the bed.)

LUC: My God, she's boring!

DAPHNEE: I'm falling, I'm falling . . . . *(She sleeps.)*

MICHELINE: I want a glass of wine, or something alcoholic!

I entreat you!

AHMED: Hold on, Micheline!

LUC: To the table, everyone! The blood sausage is boiled. Here, Micheline, while it's hot!

MICHELINE: I feel sick!

(She goes to the bathroom. Ahmed, Jean, and Luc stay and eat.)

AHMED: This blood sausage is good!

MICHELINE: *(off)* AAAIIIEEE! A snake!

(She runs back into the room. Jean goes to the bathroom door.)

JEAN: Luc, there's a huge snake in the toilet bowl!

(Luc and Ahmed rush to the bathroom door.)

LUC: A snake, how? Shit, a snake! And it's looking at us!

(Jean closes the door.)

AHMED: It's a boa constrictor. Those are the animals that can travel through drainpipes!

JEAN: I'll go call the firemen!

AHMED: They are not evil creatures. It's the people who buy them when they're little for their children, and then when they get big, they flush them down the toilet—the snakes, I mean. Then they travel throughout these enormous buildings. They look for warmth in the heating pipes and sometimes they come out of the drains, because in the big apartment houses, all the pipes connect. But they're not evil.

LUC: What should we do?

MICHELINE: Call the building manager.

JEAN: Sure, on New Year's Eve?

MICHELINE: Lock the bathroom door!

JEAN: There's no key, we'll have to block it with some furniture!

LUC: Don't touch the dresser, it has the gun in it! Dammit!

JEAN: Oh, shit!

LUC: Let's use the divan.

JEAN: The door opens inward!

AHMED: But they aren't evil beasts. He must have smelled the vomit. They like that.

MICHELINE: We'll have to nail the door shut and call the fire department!

AHMED: The firemen won't come, they don't bother about snakes anymore. They'll just give you instructions on how to kill them. I know, because my brother-in-law is a fireman. I can kill it if you want.

MICHELINE: Oh, no. Not here!

LUC: We'd better kill it.

AHMED: All right, where's the kitchen knife? You have to drive the knife in between the head and the spine.

JEAN: No, that's dangerous, have you seen the size of that thing? What if we killed it with the gun?

AHMED: Oh, no, with a gun, you have to aim for the brain or else you'll make it suffer needlessly. A knife is better. Hold the door half open in case it wants to escape.

(Ahmed enters the bathroom and cries out.)

LUC: The snake has climbed up on the door!

MICHELINE: Oh, God. What horror!

DAPHNEE: *(waking up)* What's going on?

JEAN: I'll go help him.

(He goes into the bathroom.)

LUC: Jean! Careful! Oh!

(Ahmed enters, holding the headless body of the snake. He's covered with blood, as is Jean. Daphnee screams. Jean throws himself on the divan, drained. Luc caresses his head.)

AHMED: Here, look, it came off quickly, his head! *(He throws the serpent in the sink.)* And it's still moving, look!

DAPHNEE: Now what have you invented to frighten me?

AHMED: I killed a snake, look!

DAPHNEE: You are all monsters!

MICHELINE: Daphnee, my dear! It's true, he killed a real snake that climbed up through the pipes! Calm yourself, honey!

LUC: Jean, do you feel all right?

JEAN: Yes, all right. Come here.

LUC: No, you're covered with blood. Go take a shower! What's wrong with her again?

DAPHNEE: Oh, Luc, I know you're plotting against me, but please, don't kill me!

LUC: It's you who wants to kill yourself, babe!

DAPHNEE: But it's because you frighten me!

LUC: Then go home! Kill yourself by yourself! Enough already!

DAPHNEE: But I'm on acid!

(Ahmed returns from the bathroom again.)

AHMED: Here, Micheline, the snake's head. You dry the teeth til they become white, and you can make a necklace with them, you thread them using a red-hot needle.

MICHELINE: Thanks, I'll put it in a plastic bag and keep it in my purse.

DAPHNEE: Luc, please!

LUC: Daphnee, stop, come on! Here, Jean. Come stand under the shower. Get undressed.

(Luc helps Jean undress.)

JEAN: Shit, that gave me a shock. I'm groggy!

LUC: Whew, the bathroom's full of blood! Where are the rags?

JEAN: No problem, the blood will wash away under the shower. It isn't dried yet.

LUC: But it's all over the walls. Here, I'll wash you at the same time.

(They both go into the bathroom.)

You've got a lot of blood in your hair!

MICHELINE: *(to Ahmed)* Want a whiskey?

AHMED: Oh, yes, to settle my nerves.

JEAN: *(off)* Oh, it's too hot!

LUC: *(off)* Wait til I get my pants off, you're spraying me!

(He throws his trousers out of the bathroom. They land on Ahmed, who stands at the door and watches the scene.)

AHMED: Say, Luc, can I wear your djellaba? The djellaba you were wearing before? My shirt is soaked with blood. Look!

LUC: *(off)* Come under the shower.

AHMED: Thanks, but I showered at my sister's.

MICHELINE: Here's the djellaba, darling.

JEAN: *(off)* Ow, you're scalding me!

AHMED: *(undressing)* Look, these are the briefs my sister gave me for Christmas.

MICHELINE: You want to come home and sleep with me? I

have a house with ten rooms, with servants and everything. I live alone with my mother.

AHMED: *(putting on the djellaba)* Maybe later.

LUC: *(off)* Oh, no, you're not going to take advantage of
this by trying to fuck me! Here, wash your own ass!

JEAN: *(off)* You're crazy! What are you doing?

MICHELINE: Let's tactfully close the bathroom door, there
are ladies fucking in there. Come on, Ahmed, enough fun.
We've got to think about dinner.

AHMED: Would you like me to roast the snake?

MICHELINE: Let's eat the mutton, it's already cooked.

AHMED: Have you ever had snake?

MICHELINE: No, how is it?

AHMED: Have you ever had cod?

MICHELINE: Yes, but not snake.

AHMED: Snake is better. Here, let's do it. You dice up the
mutton. We'll stuff the snake with it. First, we gut the
snake. Shit, it's still moving! It's like a spring!

JEAN: *(off)* Luc, stop!

LUC: *(off)* I'm going to drown you!

DAPHNEE: I'm going! There's a party in Le Marais, they're
waiting for me. Bye.

(She leaves. Ahmed opens the bathroom door.)

AHMED: Those two haven't stopped kissing yet! *(to Jean and Luc)* Hey, do you two want to dine on snake?

LUC: *(off)* Yes, yes. Let's have snake!

JEAN: *(off* Yes, yes. Some snake!

(Daphnee reenters.)

DAPHNEE: I forgot my Hermes bag!

AHMED: The skin you have to cook in vinegar to soften the scales.

MICHELINE: Well, look at you! You must be quite the cook!

AHMED: I love to cook!

DAPHNEE: I lost my address book. *(She opens the bathroom door.)* Jean, can you loan me a hundred francs? I'm out of cash.

JEAN: To go where?

LUC: Let her leave already!

(Daphnee is sprayed with water. Jean and Luc laugh uproariously.)

JEAN: Stop, you'll make me slip!

LUC: Oh, no! I've got water up my nose!

DAPHNEE: *(to Micheline)* He drenched me! That asshole! Have you got a hundred francs?

MICHELINE: Well, where is Daphnee going?

DAPHNEE: To find a man in the Tuileries.

MICHELINE: Did you hear that, girls? Daphnee's going to cruise the Tuileries!

LUC: *(off)* You'll need a false mustache, Daphnee.

JEAN: *(off)* Try a hat and trenchcoat.

LUC: *(off)* Put aftershave on your pussy!

(They laugh.)

DAPHNEE: You are assholes! You're all jealous of me! You wish you *had* my pussy! *(She sits on the divan.)*

MICHELINE: Now look who's talking about pussy! *(to Ahmed)* Look, sweetheart, I've cut it into little pieces.

AHMED: Now soak it in warm water with some sugar, and then we'll stuff the snake with it. The snake should be nice and crispy. Any green pepper here?

MICHELINE: No. Here's a box of truffles.

AHMED: Oh, no. They're too expensive. Here, take out the organs and drain the blood into this salad bowl.

MICHELINE: No, that's repugnant! I couldn't possibly touch it.

AHMED: But you'll eat it, won't you? This is a fine snake, really meaty. He ate lots of rats in parking lots.

MICHELINE: Isn't that dangerous? Rats cause illness!

AHMED: That's a myth. Rats are good, you know why? They nibble on wood, that makes their flesh fragrant, like rabbit. But it doesn't matter what snakes eat, because they only eat living things. Here, look, I told you. He just ate a rat! *(He removes a rat from inside the snake.)* It's not even digested yet. Let's put it in the stuffing. Is there a meat grinder here?

MICHELINE: Over there.

AHMED: Oh, it's electric. How does it work?

MICHELINE: Who knows? I'm horrified of gadgets like that.

LUC: *(off)* Stop, you're a madman! You're ripping my anus!

(Luc enters, nude and wet.)

Christ, there's no more hot water! I'm freezing!

(He wraps a towel around himself. Jean enters, nude.)

JEAN: The water is turning to ice!

LUC: Here.

(He passes Jean a towel. Luc puts on his pants.)

Nuts, I lost my T-shirt!

JEAN: I'll get a djellaba! Have you seen the red one we bought in Marrakesh?

LUC: I haven't see that one for at least a year!

JEAN: It was hanging up just before!

MICHELINE: I gave it to Ahmed.

JEAN: Oh, never mind.

AHMED: Is this yours? Would you like it?

JEAN: No, don't be silly. I have another one.

LUC: Go put on that 'thirties robe you never wear. For once, we're screwing.

MICHELINE: Did you come?

LUC: You said it! She came right away.

JEAN: That's normal! He takes hours to get hard! Oh, Luc, you took my shirt!

LUC: Put on your bathrobe, you housewife!

JEAN: No, I'll put on pants. Here, I'll wear these poncho pants!

AHMED: Here, Luc, look! Isn't this a good-looking snake? Have you ever eaten snake? Here, touch it! Put your hand inside it. Don't be scared.

(Luc goes to the kitchen. Jean and Micheline stay in the living room.)

MICHELINE: You're acting like two insane little girls! How long has it been since she fucked you?

JEAN: Nine months.

MICHELINE: No wonder you came so fast. You should have worn white tonight. It becomes you.

JEAN: Do I look radiant? It isn't because he fucked me, I'm eternally eighteen.

MICHELINE: Getting fucked has raised your spirits! Your skin looks so supple and fresh.

LUC: *(to Ahmed)* I can put my hand in up to my elbow! Brrr, it's cold!

AHMED: That's normal, it's a snake! Snakes are cold-blooded. That's why the meat is always good. Here, look at the rat he had in his belly. Ever had a rat?

LUC: It had swallowed a rat?

AHMED: Touch it.

LUC: Shit, it's all gristle!

AHMED: We'll have to put it through the meat grinder to make stuffing!

JEAN: A real rat?

LUC: A big gray one. Look!

JEAN: Oh, you're scaring me!

LUC: All right, now you have to eat it! Tonight's menu is snake stuffed with rat! *(to Daphnee)* Well, my dear one, haven't you left for the Tuileries? You never went to the Tuileries?

DAPHNEE: You've never been with a real woman in your life, have you? A real woman, the kind that get you hot and bothered and keep you awake nights.

LUC: Daphnee, the woman in my life! And do you think my mother would accept a divorced woman in the family?

DAPHNEE: She's already accepted me on the same floor as you.

LUC: *(impressed)* What's this? Is she becoming intelligent?

MICHELINE: She's acting like a drag queen. How futile!

DAPHNEE: I'm going to get you, Luc. You can be sure of that!
I'm going to get you! I'm going to kill myself and they'll
accuse you of the crime!

LUC: Kill yourself first and we'll discuss it later!

DAPHNEE: You don't think so, huh? Do you know how I
drove my first husband to death? I gave him a heart attack,
and I inherited all this. Look, look! *(She takes some jewels from
her purse.)*

LUC: Oh, look, she's got a lot of rubies!

AHMED: Luc, would you show me how to work this? And
then, would you grate the nutmeg?

LUC: All this?

AHMED: Oh, yes, you have to have a lot to cover the taste of
rotten rat.

MICHELINE: *(to Jean)* She was married before the
American?

JEAN: I don't know anything about it. But anyway, these are
real rubies. And pretty valuable! She only takes them when
she's going to the Tuileries.

MICHELINE: But she is completely fucked up! She'll get
them stolen !

JEAN: Haven't you ever seen her walk the night in the Tuileries, nude, with her jewels? She leaves her dress in the car.

MICHELINE: But she's out of her mind!

JEAN: She sure is! And she's passive, she gets fucked up the ass, and by the worst kind of men!

MICHELINE: Where did you find her?

JEAN: She lives across the hall.

MICHELINE: But was she already crazy?

JEAN: Not at all. She was a middle-class girl married to a big American asshole, a professor of philosophy at Cambridge. He's from Boston. That's where they met. She was studying American law.

MICHELINE: That's incredible! We've got to throw her out of here!

JEAN: But how? You've seen her technique.

DAPHNEE: *(to Luc)* Luc, would you like my rubies? I leave them to you, darling. They're for you. All for you. Here, you, too, Ahmed, here, here, a topaz. It's a New Year's present for you all. I'm taking the first plane to New York. I'm going to pack my suitcase.

(She leaves.)

AHMED: She's not all there, that one!

MICHELINE: Completely cracked!

JEAN: Here, let's put the rubies in a drawer, so they don't get lost.

LUC: But you're crazy, let's keep them.

JEAN: We can't keep them, they're worth a fortune!

LUC: All the more reason. We can sell them!

MICHELINE: You wish! She'll be back for them instantaneously!

(Daphnee enters, nude under her overcoat, carrying a big crocodile suitcase.)

DAPHNEE: Give me my rubies, I have to put them in my beauty case. If John dumps me, they're all I have to live on! Call me a taxi, Jean.

JEAN: And you're going to get on the plane nude?

DAPHNEE: Oh, Christ! I forgot to get dressed! I'll look for a dress in my suitcase. It's cold in New York. All I have are summer dresses.

JEAN: That's all you have? What happened to all your things?

DAPHNEE: I threw all my winter dresses down the incinerator. I thought it was summer. I'm still on acid. Don't call a taxi yet. I'm going to take a shower. I'm completely gone.

(She goes into the bathroom.)

Oh, shit, I've got a lump on my head. Isn't there any hot water?

JEAN: You'll have to wait fifteen minutes.

MICHELINE: Take a cold shower, it'll do you good!

DAPHNEE: *(off)* Oh, it's freezing!

MICHELINE: *(to Jean)* Do you think she's actually going to go?

JEAN: Of course not! She's always about to leave and never does!

MICHELINE: But now she has a reason! Her husband's taken Katia!

LUC: The snake's on fire! The oven's too hot! Oh, fuck, an explosion! Turn off the gas, Jean!

JEAN: What is happening?

LUC: Who knows?

AHMED: The snake is too cold for an oven that's already hot. But never mind, it's almost done. We can eat it this way.

(Daphnee enters, nude and soaking.)

DAPHNEE: Oh, that's cold! Aren't there any dry towels?

JEAN: No!

DAPHNEE: Never mind, I'll put on a dress to dry mself. *(She puts on a light linen dress, which becomes quicky soaked.)* I'm better now, don't worry! Call me a taxi, Jean. Please. I've got to get to Orly! *(She puts on her shoes.)* I'm going crazy, good, I'm going crazy. I've bothered you enough! Anyway, I'm going.

LUC: Fine, but go before we sit down to eat.

DAPHNEE: I'll go when you tell me you don't want me anymore. Because I'm hopelessly in love with you, Luc.

LUC: Put on your coat, fat girl! Go on, go! Here's your suitcase and your clothes!

(Luc forces her into the corridor with her suitcase.)

DAPHNEE: Let go of me! Let me in!

(Luc locks the door.)

LUC: That's enough. Let's eat!

JEAN: I think you're being a little hard.

LUC: Would you like to go with her? Or do you want some snake? Come on, Ahmed, serve it! Micheline, Jean, sit down at the table, all right?

MICHELINE: *(to Luc)* I've already invited him to my house tonight, but if you want you can come have him at teatime tomorrow. I'll be tired of him by that time, then you can have him. Have you noticed how well-hung he is?

DAPHNEE: *(off, knocking)* Open up! Luc, I'm on acid! Please!

JEAN: Luc, you'll have to open the door! Otherwise, she'll knock all night.

MICHELINE: When she's had enough, she'll go sleep at her place. Believe me, Luc's right, she's insufferable!

DAPHNEE: Luc, please, Luc!

AHMED: Here, I put it in a bucket, so it can soak in its juices! Here, Micheline, serve the stuffing!

MICHELINE: Oh, my God! It's the rat!

AHMED: Now cut it up like you cut quail.

DAPHNEE: *(off)* Luc, do you hear me? Do you hear me? I love you!

JEAN: Listen, it's too much! I'm going to open the door!

(He lets her in.)

DAPHNEE: I can't handle taking that elevator, Jean! Let me stay here a minute.

JEAN: Can't you stay at your place? Don't you realize after a certain point you become a real pain in the neck? Go to New York, do what you want, but not here, please! Daphnee, be considerate!

DAPHNEE: Okay, I'll go. Wait, all my things are on the floor. Excuse me, dear, I promise you this is the last time I'm bothering you. I'm going to rest a bit and tomorrow I'm going to New York. *(She faints.)*

JEAN: Oh, shit, she's fainted again!

AHMED: Oh, come on! Here, let's put her on the bed.

(They lay her on the divan.)

It's a good thing she's not heavy, because this is never going to stop! Plop!

JEAN: Thanks, Ahmed!

(He brings Daphnee's suitcase and things in from the hall and closes the door. Jean puts the coat over Daphnee. Luc and Micheline remain at the table.)

AHMED: You know what's going on, Luc? She's in love with you. Once she's satisfied, she'll go. This I promise you, if you don't fuck her, she won't go!

LUC: Fuck her yourself! You like girls!

AHMED: That wouldn't help. She could be fucked by all of mankind. She only wants you. She's like a child, like my little niece—when she wants a toy, and you buy it for her, she throws it in the garbage! But if you don't buy it, she goes crazy!

LUC: Thanks, I got the point! But I hardly want her to throw me in the garbage! I'd rather throw her in the garbage!

AHMED: You're very sly! But you better be careful. Look at her sleeping there! What do you think she's dreaming of? It's you she's dreaming of! She's dreaming of some way to have you! Here, Luc, have a piece of snake. Micheline, here. Jean, here, taste this.

MICHELINE: Oh, but it's delicious!

AHMED: Isn't it good?

MICHELINE: And the stuffing is sublime!

JEAN: Oh, I've got the rat's leg! Can I trade it for some white meat?

LUC: This is great! Have you tasted this? It's a treat!

JEAN: Mmmm, it's good!

AHMED: Here, try this, Jean, it's the snake's balls. They're inside the animal. Here, try a ball.

MICHELINE: What about me? Can't I have one of the balls?

JEAN: Here, have half of mine. It's exquisite!

MICHELINE: Very fragrant!

AHMED: Try this, try this, Micheline!

MICHELINE: What is it?

AHMED: It's the snake's heart.

MICHELINE: Sublime again!

AHMED: The heart is the caviar of the snake!

JEAN: It's better than caviar! It's divine!

LUC: The rat tastes like pig's feet! It's very spicy!

MICHELINE: It's better than Indian food!

AHMED: Try this, try this, it's the anus of the snake! See how round it is? Snakes have only one hole besides the mouth. They use this to fuck and to lay eggs. See how elastic it is? Here, Luc, this asshole's for you!

LUC: It looks like a foreskin.

MICHELINE: *(to Ahmed)* Oh, what an obsession! Do you like assholes that much?

AHMED: I don't like anything else! Me, I don't like girls, I like boys!

MICHELINE: *(admiringly)* What a fool! Where are you from, anyway?

AHMED: I'm from Lyon. And I was born under the sign of Leo the lion!

MICHELINE: So was I!

JEAN: Me too!

LUC: Well, everyone's a lion! That's rich! Who'd like another slice?

MICHELINE: You're eating too fast!

AHMED: To the sign of the lion!

ALL: To the lion! *(They drink.)*

MICHELINE: Oh, it's snowing!

AHMED: Snowing? *(He goes to the window.)* This is the first time I've seen snow.

MICHELINE: Isn't there snow in Lyon?

AHMED: Can I touch it?

LUC: Go on, it won't burn you!

AHMED: Oh, it's cold, but it's sweet! It's melting, it's turning into water! It's like a fine summer rain, only cold!

LUC: They're crystals of water! Here, look, it's in the encyclopedia. Snow. Snow seen under the microscope. That's what melts in the heat of your hand, these microscopic crystals. And they're all different, look! No two are alike!

AHMED: It's the loveliest thing I've ever seen. Can I stick my head out the window? Oh, I like this! I like this!

(The bells of Paris start to ring.)

Oh, the bells! They sound so near!

LUC: The snow is muffling the sound, but you can hear them from far away.

AHMED: Happy New Year, Luc!

(They embrace. Jean embraces Micheline.)

JEAN: Happy New Year, kiddo!

MICHELINE: Happy New Year, you mad boy!

AHMED: Happy New Year, Jean!

JEAN: Happy New Year, Ahmed!

AHMED: Happy New Year, Micheline!

MICHELINE: Happy New Year, my prince!

LUC: *(to Jean)* Happy New Year.

JEAN: Happy New Year, my love.

LUC: Happy New Year, Micheline!

MICHELINE: Happy New Year, dear!

(Daphnee sleeps through all this on the divan.)

(End of Act One)

Act Two

(The situation is the same)

AHMED: Look! A bird!

LUC: A seagull lost in the snow!

JEAN: But where's she from?

LUC: She's lost. Sometimes they fly up the Seine!

MICHELINE: She's turning in circles!

LUC: She thinks the tower is a lighthouse! The foghorn! Where's your grandfather's foghorn, Jean?

JEAN: Haven't you seen it lately?

LUC: Yes, here it is! *(He blows on it out the window.)*

MICHELINE: Look!

AHMED: It heard you!

JEAN: Oh, shit! The snow is getting thicker! Can you see her?

AHMED: Here, give it to me! I can blow it louder than you! *(Ahmed blows on the horn.)*

JEAN: Look there! She's afraid of the sound. Get away from the window!

(They do. The gull enters the window and bumps into the furniture. Ahmed catches it. The gull flounders and cries.)

AHMED: It's hurt!

LUC: She's afraid!

AHMED: We'd better put it in the bathroom.

(He takes the gull into the bathroom, followed by Jean and Luc.)

(off) Do you have any frozen fish?

JEAN: No.

MICHELINE: Give her the rest of the rat. They eat rats in harbors!

(They follow into the bathroom with a plateful of food. Daphnee wakes up; she goes to the window and shuts it. She takes a biscuit. The snow thins out, almost disappearing. Meanwhile, the seagull's cries are heard as well as running water and other noises.)

AHMED: *(off)* Don't turn the faucet up so high, it's afraid!

LUC: *(off)* She must think the faucet is a sewer pipe!

JEAN: *(off)* God knows what's going through her brain!

MICHELINE: *(off)* Careful! She's trying to get away!

AHMED: *(off)* Oh, calm yourself, bird!

JEAN: *(off)* She's terrified! Poor girl! Careful! Catch her!

MICHELINE: *(off)* Oh, it's frightening me! Or she is, whatever!

AHMED: *(off)* You're strangling her! Here, hold her like this! Look how scared she is! She wants to peck me! I think she's having a heart attack!

MICHELINE: *(off)* She's pecking because she's hungry.

LUC: *(off)* Let's give her some caviar. She'll love that! Isn't there some caviar in the refrigerator?

JEAN: *(off)* Sure, two jars!

LUC: *(off)* Let's give her some caviar on a sponge.

(He reenters.)

(to Daphnee) Oh! You're awake!

DAPHNEE: Yes, for now. I'm totally high, you realize. A week's worth of acid!

LUC: Fine, fine....

DAPHNEE: What are you doing?

LUC: Getting some caviar from the refrigerator.

DAPHNEE: For the gull!

LUC: Well, you can bet it's not for you. We ate the snake. There's not one vertebra left. You shouldn't have fainted.

DAPHNEE: Never mind, I'm not hungry. I ate a biscuit I found over there, on the floor.

LUC: Nuts, this jar is empty!

AHMED: *(off)* Careful! Careful! She wants to fly!

JEAN: *(off)* Shit, she's strong!

MICHELINE: *(off)* You're strangling it! Or, her!

LUC: What are you doing?

AHMED: *(off)* There! She's calmed down now!

JEAN: *(off)* She's exhausted, poor thing!

MICHELINE: *(off)* Look how she floats! Like a rubber duck!

DAPHNEE: Luc, can I talk to you for a minute?

LUC: I'm fetching some caviar for a seagull in distress.

DAPHNEE: Can I help?

LUC: Well, you've calmed down. What's going on?

DAPHNEE: I came down all of a sudden. The shower did me good. I'm insane to take drugs all the time!

LUC: I've been telling you that for months!

DAPHNEE: I know. But it was necessary. I had to.

MICHELINE: *(off, overlapping)* Oh, she's flapping her wings!

AHMED: *(off)* Hold her!

(The gull cries.)

JEAN: *(off)* You're going to drown her!

AHMED: Shit!

LUC: Don't start breaking my back with your high drama, Daphnee!

DAPHNEE: Please don't blame me for anything. I'm going to New York to see John.

LUC: What did I blame you for?

DAPHNEE: Nothing, I know. I'll go and you'll forget me, fine. I never meant anything to you.

LUC: Daphnee, don't you realize after a certain point this kind of talk is ridiculous? Did I ever ask anything of you?

DAPHNEE: But I love you.

JEAN: *(off)* Look out! She's plunging her head under the water!

MICHELINE: *(off)* She's crazy!

LUC: Really, Daphnee, if this is love, we're doomed.

(Luc returns to the bathroom.)

(off) Here's the caviar!

(During the following, Daphnee goes to the dresser, takes the re-volver, and puts it in her purse.)

MICHELINE: *(off)* Oh, it's Iranian caviar! You have to feed it to her with a tiny spoon!

JEAN: *(off)* It's the soap she wants to eat.

(They all laugh.)

MICHELINE: She's addicted to detergent!

JEAN: *(off)* She's swallowed the soap!

LUC: *(off)* You're kidding! She swallowed the soap?

MICHELINE: *(off)* She thought it was a fish! She's trying to vomit!

LUC: *(off)* She's having convulsions!

MICHELINE: *(off)* She's going beserk!

JEAN: *(off)* Careful! Careful!

AHMED: *(off)* Catch her! Catch her!

JEAN: *(off)* She's dead.

LUC: *(off)* She's dead?

AHMED: *(off)* Yes, see, her heart isn't beating anymore.

MICHELINE: *(off)* She choked on the soap.

AHMED: *(off)* She must have died of exhaustion. Who knows how long she'd been lost in Paris? Poor animal!

JEAN: *(off)* Let's not leave this dead seagull in the bathroom.

LUC: *(off)* Most of all, let's get that soap out, it was a bar of Chanel! We'll have to open her up!

MICHELINE: *(off)* Oh, no, don't be disgusting!

AHMED: *(off)* No, she must be buried. That's what you do with gulls.

(He reenters, carrying the dead gull, followed by the others.)

Oh, look, Daphnee, the gull, it's dead.

DAPHNEE: We should bury it in the sand on the beach. If we don't, its soul will wander forever around the towers in this neighborhood.

AHMED: I think they're supposed to be magical, there's a lot of them in Algeria.

DAPHNEE: I spent my childhood by the sea, in Maine. When I was little, I used to bury seagulls who died on the beach. Give her to me. I'll take her to New York with me and bury her in Maine. I'll ask them to put her in the refrigerator unit on the 747.

AHMED: You would do that?

DAPHNEE: Yes. Wrap it in newspaper. I'll bury it next Sunday with my little girl on the beach in Maine. We'll take the bus.

MICHELINE: You seem to be doing better, Daphnee.

DAPHNEE: Yes, much better. Thanks!

JEAN: You're all wet in your dress. Aren't you cold?

DAPHNEE: Yes, I am.

JEAN: Here, change out of that.

DAPHNEE: *(undressing)* All I have are summer dresses. Can you give me a sweater?

JEAN: *(handing her a sweater)* How's this?

DAPHNEE: Good, thanks. Oh, no, here. I'll wear this. Look what I found in my suitcase, I don't know how it got there. It's a dress of my grandmother's. She was named Daphnee too. She went to Maine because she fell in love with a whaler there. Look, it's the dress of a fisherman's wife in New England.

MICHELINE: *(dubiously)* It's a poem!

DAPHNEE: Would you like it?

MICHELINE: Thanks, but I only wear my mother's dresses.

DAPHNEE: And she was my size! *(She puts on the dress.)* Too bad it's coming unstitched, here.

LUC: It's very appropriate for burying a seagull in Maine. Until then, you can wear it on your head, like a hat.

MICHELINE: She found that dress at the flea market! I saw that dress last week at the Malik market!

JEAN: That's nonsense! Do you think she sees herself as a drag queen?

MICHELINE: Absolutely! But not of this era.

AHMED: *(to Daphnee)* I wrapped the bird in a wet towel. When you bury it, think of me, promise? Here.

DAPHNEE: Thanks, Ahmed. *(Daphne puts the gull in her suitcase.)*

AHMED: Won't that get your clothes wet?

DAPHNEE: That doesn't matter. Oh, look what I found! Pink champagne from California!

LUC: Ugh! But is it cold, at least?

DAPHNEE: Almost. Here, Ahmed, you open the champagne, you're a man.

AHMED: Where's the corkscrew?

JEAN: Here, you can open it with your fingers!

DAPHNEE: Look, I found this, too, some dope!

LUC: All right! It's a holiday! Give it here and I'll roll a joint.

DAPHNEE: I have more in my kitchen and some bourbon, too! Go get them, Ahmed.

AHMED: It's open?

DAPHNEE: Oh, no, maybe not. Here's the key.

JEAN: They're tough, these American corks, like wood.

LUC: *(to Ahmed)* See what else she has. Bring all of it.

AHMED: And the refrigerator? Are you leaving that?

MICHELINE: Leave it in the hall! I'll have the chauffeur pick it up tomorrow.

AHMED: Thank you, Daphnee.

(He leaves. Jean opens the champagne and serves it.)

LUC: *(to Daphnee)* You should also leave your rubies while you're away.

DAPHNEE: I would, but I can't. They're all I have in the world.

MICHELINE: A present from your grandmother?

DAPHNEE: No, from John, when Katia was born. They belonged to his mother.

MICHELINE: There you are. When you die you can leave them to Katia, they'll be back in style.

DAPHNEE: Yes, of course, if I keep them. In the state I'm in, God knows if I'll even make it to New York.

MICHELINE: Come on, dear, we'll go with you to the Airport.

DAPHNEE: Good, thanks, but I'd better call John so he'll come get me at Kennedy airport. That place terrifies me.

JEAN: Do you have your American passport, at least?

DAPHNEE: Yes, here it is! Oh, shit, it's wet! It's unusable! Oh, God, what am I going to do?

JEAN: All your things are soaked. Oh, the gull threw up in your suitcase. It's disgusting! *(He empties the suitcase into the sink.)* Oh, it stinks of rotten fish!

(There is the sound of a creaking refrigerator in the hallway.)

DAPHNEE: What's that?

LUC: It's your refrigerator being moved out! Micheline, have you got a match?

MICHELINE: You've made an enormous joint!

(Ahmed enters, carrying a case full of bottles.)

AHMED: Not too many bottles here! Enough for a store!

(He exits again.)

MICHELINE: Oh, that's strong stuff!

LUC: Pass it here.

MICHELINE: *(coughing)* There must be speed in it!

LUC: Not speed, ammonia! The Colombians piss on it so it seems heavier when they sell it! Here, look! See these little mushrooms in the flower? These mushrooms are in the urine of the Indians. That's what makes this herb a little hallucinogenic!

MICHELINE: Oh, this isn't Colombian! It's thyme! It's a sprig of thyme, you asshole!

LUC: Are you crazy? Haven't you ever seen Colombian?

JEAN: Oh, this bird is disgusting! She's thrown up all over everything!

(Ahmed enters with two suitcases, one large and one small.)

AHMED: Here, Daphnee, you forgot this suitcase!

DAPHNEE: Thanks. Oh, I didn't forget that one! Leave it in the hall or throw it out!

AHMED: What's in it? It's heavy! It's locked.

DAPHNEE: A statue. A Greek statue that belongs to my husband.

MICHELINE: I know. Take it to him, that'll soften him up!

DAPHNEE: No, it's too heavy. Leave it here.

MICHELINE: They can store it in the airplane, dear. *(to Ahmed)* Is that all she has?

AHMED: There's also a mattress on the floor and a large crib. But the mattress smells terrible. Can I take the crib for my little niece?

MICHELINE: Why not?

JEAN: Oh, shit! The gull is still alive!

(Luc and Ahmed go to the sink; Micheline goes halfway.)

LUC: What?!

JEAN: Her wings are moving.

LUC: You're crazy!

AHMED: She's alive!

JEAN: Oh, it's atrocious! She's vomiting the soap! It's making bubbles like Ajax!

AHMED: Don't touch her!

LUC: Let me see!

AHMED: Look, she's calm for now! Don't touch her! Leave her alone. She'd better rest.

JEAN: These animals have seven lives!

AHMED: I'll take her to my sister. We'll make a nest for her on the mantel.

MICHELINE: No, let's take her to my place. I have an enormous terrace.

AHMED: You do?

MICHELINE: Of course! We have a coop full of doves, too. They can play together.

AHMED: Thank you, Micheline.

MICHELINE: You have kinky hair, you do!

AHMED: Yes, like my mother. But my father has straight hair, like yours.

MICHELINE: But this is a wig, darling!

LUC: *(to Jean)* Here's the joint. But first, wipe your hands! You smell like a fishwife!

JEAN: Wait til I wash my hands. Her things are ruined! *(taking the joint)* Thanks!

LUC: She can't go to New York dressed like that! They'll stop her at Orly!

JEAN: That's for sure! And she'll make a scene with the cops!

MICHELINE: Will you come live with me, Ahmed?

AHMED: Oh, all right, why not?

JEAN: Is this her hash?

LUC: It's old, like everything else! It doesn't have any taste!

JEAN: She's probably had it in her suitcase for three years. It's not so bad. Here, Ahmed.

AHMED: No, thanks. I don't smoke.

JEAN: *(to Micheline)* Here you go. But where's the bottle of pink champagne from California?

MICHELINE: Is it all drunk already?

JEAN: Already? Let's open another bottle. It's all warm, let's put it in the refrigerator.

LUC: Whoa, this hash is strong shit! *(He opens the window and looks out.)*

MICHELINE: *(to Ahmed)* The only inconvenience is we have to have lunch with my mother every day. The rest of the time you won't have to see her. She stays in her own room.

AHMED: I don't care. I like mothers.

MICHELINE: You do?

LUC: Look! It's stopped snowing! There's a full moon! What's going on in the Tuileries? Some kind of party?

MICHELINE: Oh, shit! Shit! Shit! I forgot to call my mother to wish her Happy New Year. *(She dials the phone.)*

JEAN: Look what I found in the refrigerator! Some chocolate mousse!

AHMED: Are you sad about leaving, Daphnee?

DAPHNEE: Yes.

AHMED: Is it cold in New York?

DAPHNEE: It's very cold. And I'll be alone. I can see myself now, knocking on John's door, which he won't open. I don't know what's to become of me.

AHMED: You're sick, you know. My mother had a nervous depression, but they took care of it. Now she's fine.

DAPHNEE: But I don't want to take care of myself, you get me? I'd rather be like this.

AHMED: You're a crazy woman! I've never seen a girl like you.

DAPHNEE: Me neither. That's what scares me.

AHMED: You always seem to be scared.

DAPHNEE: No, not always. Only since I came here, to this tower. I didn't know he'd be here too. Luc.

AHMED: You're in love with him, right?

DAPHNEE: Maybe. But when I speak of love, I'm talking about something else.

AHMED: Everyone goes a little crazy when they fall in love.

DAPHNEE: Oh, shut up! I don't want to talk about it!

AHMED: Don't get angry with me. I do like you.

DAPHNEE: Yes, I know. But shut up.

MICHELINE: *(on the phone)* Hello, Mama? Are you sleeping? ...What's going on?...No, I'm not coming home right now. Did you dine alone?...Oh, and your Brazilian consul friend.

JEAN: Here, Daphnee, want some mousse?

DAPHNEE: Mmm. Thanks! This is the first solid thing I've had since taking the acid.

JEAN: Want any, Ahmed?

AHMED: Oh, yes!

MICHELINE: *(on the phone)* But where are the servants? How could they leave you alone this way?...But I *can't* come back right now. Besides, I won't be coming back alone. Go to bed and get some sleep. Take a sleeping pill. It's almost one a.m., and tomorrow you're having lunch with your cousin from Madrid.... Mother, don't start crying, please!

JEAN: Want some mousse?

MICHELINE: No, thanks.... *(on the phone)* Mother, go to bed. Mother, I'm not coming home to undress you. Go to bed as you are. I'll undress you when I get back.

DAPHNEE: Shit, my hands are trembling! I can't eat any mousse. I'm cracking up!

AHMED: Here, open your mouth! I'll feed you with this spoon, Daphnee.

DAPHNEE: Oh, thanks! This is good chocolate! Why hasn't anyone cleared the table? It's revolting, the remains of that snake!

AHMED: You're right. Help me clear the table.

DAPHNEE: I can't, I have trembling hands.

MICHELINE: *(on the phone)* You can go to sleep by yourself, do you hear me?... You're afraid of *what*?

AHMED: All right, I'll clear it. Here, finish the mousse. Can you eat it by yourself?

DAPHNEE: Thank you.

JEAN: Luc?

LUC: What?

JEAN: Do you want any chocolate mousse?

LUC: No, thanks. Leave me alone, I'm watching the stars!

JEAN: What?

LUC: Bzzzzzz! A sound from science fiction!

JEAN: I don't hear anything.

LUC: You're deaf. Listen, can't you hear it?

JEAN: Oh, that.

LUC: Look! A flying saucer!

JEAN: Where?

LUC: *(pointing)* There!

JEAN: Christ, there's a light approaching! What, it's fading!
No, it's exploding! Shit! What is that?

AHMED: Isn't it a flying saucer?

LUC: Isn't it a flying saucer?

JEAN: Are you demented? It's a helicopter! It's crashed into
the tower over there! Look! It's caught fire!

LUC: There aren't any helicopters in Paris!

JEAN: Well, look!

(The lights go out.)

Jesus, a blackout! Where's your grandmother's candelabra,
Luc? . . . Oh, here it is!

LUC: Look, it's started a fire in the tower!

JEAN: Oh, shit! It crashed into some apartment!

AHMED: It could have crashed into us!

MICHELINE: *(on the phone)* Mother, you're a pain! Go to sleep! I'll come back when I please! *(She hangs up.)* What's up? *(She goes to the window.)* Christ! The building next door is on fire!

LUC: Which way is the wind coming from?

JEAN: The flames could never reach over here. Forget that. It's at least fifty meters!

MICHELINE: Why isn't there any electricity? Don't they have their own generators in these towers?

(The lights come back on. Daphnee is gone.)

LUC: Why aren't the firemen already there?

AHMED: It is New Year's Eve.

MICHELINE: Good point, the whole town is dead drunk! That's why those guys crashed! They were having some fine wine in that helicopter!

LUC: I doubt that! Whose helicopter was it?

MICHELINE: It's a city helicopter. I think they were launching fireworks from that helicopter.

LUC: Oh, don't be ignorant! Why did they crash here? There, there's the firemen!

MICHELINE: But where's Daphnee?

JEAN: She must have gone back to her place.

MICHELINE: In the state she's in, she could fall down the elevator shaft!

LUC: The one shaft doesn't have a car!

(Micheline and Ahmed go into the hall.)

MICHELINE: *(off)* Daphnee! Daphnee!...Her place is locked!

AHMED: *(off)* I left it open.

MICHELINE: *(off)* Daphnee, sweetheart, open up!

(Sounds of knocking.)

JEAN: *(with sudden significance)* Luc, I'm leaving you. I'm going to use my vacation in India to begin to forget you.

LUC: All right, I wish you well. When you devote yourself to a task like that, it can take a lifetime.

AHMED: *(off)* We'll have to break down the door.

MICHELINE: *(off)* Do you think you could do it?

(Sounds of bodies hurled against a door.)

JEAN: You're very hard, Luc.

LUC: That's the second time you've said that to me tonight. I am hard. I think you're thinking of my cock, really. The hard cock you have in your head. Go on, forget me! In time, even my cock will soften in your memory.

MICHELINE: *(off)* Careful, you'll hurt yourself!

AHMED: *(off)* Here, wait! I'll try to open it with my sister's key.

LUC: I'm carved in marble! Isn't that right? You think you can spend your time pummeling me and it's only your fists that get hurt. I'm like that tower out there, look! The helicopter crashes into it. The pilot dies. But the tower isn't shaken. My cock is unbreakable.

JEAN: Luc, it's you who put yourself in a tower.

LUC: And what does that make you? A passerby? Go on, forget me! Don't touch me, asshole!

(Sounds of hammering on the door.)

MICHELINE: *(off)* I smell gas! Daphnee!

JEAN: You know I can never leave you. Why do we have to live in this hysterical fashion?

LUC: Speak for yourself! My head is elsewhere! Your talk has never interested me! Go buy fabrics in India!

JEAN: The firemen have taken care of the fire! It's out! Look!

(Micheline enters.)

MICHELINE: She turned on the gas! Is there any more ice? She passed out!

(The telephone rings.)

JEAN: Yes .... Oh, hello, John. Pardon my English. *(deliberately)* "Here is Jean, a Happy New Year.... Thanks. How are you? ...Daphnee's not here. Just one minute." *(to Micheline)* It's her husband.

MICHELINE: She's in no state to come to the phone. Are you crazy? She's really sick!

JEAN: What happened?

MICHELINE: Well, she's practically asphyxiated! She put her head in the oven! Ahmed's giving her artificial respiration.

JEAN: Fuck! *(into the phone)* *"Hello, John? Daphnee is not here. She does sleep. It's late in Paris, you know? I can't get her up . . . . What do you mean, where is Katia? She's not with you? . . . Well, she's not here! Just one minute again, John."* The child isn't with him. *"But where are you, John? . . . Fontainebleau? What do you mean? You are not in New York?"*

MICHELINE: How is this possible? Didn't she just talk to him?

(Ahmed enters.)

AHMED: She's breathing. Give me some ice, Micheline. I'll give her some ice cubes.

(Micheline hands Ahmed some ice. He leaves.)

JEAN: This is incredible! He didn't take Katia. *"Give me your telephone number, John! I'll say her to call you back . . . . Well, I don't know where is Katia. I can't wake up Daphnee, she is sleeping! . . . Well, just one more minute, John."*

MICHELINE: The child must have wandered off somewhere.

JEAN: But where?

MICHELINE: In a big department store, like everyone else!

JEAN: Very funny, but what do I tell her husband? He insists on talking to her.

MICHELINE: Well, at least she didn't kill her. *(Awkward long pause.)*

JEAN: What would she do with the body?

LUC: In the suitcase!

MICHELINE: Oh, lord! Go look!

JEAN: It isn't possible.

LUC: It's locked.

MICHELINE: Pick the lock. Here, a knife!

LUC: *(opening the suitcase)* Oh, shit, it's true! This is horrible!

MICHELINE: Close it, close it!

JEAN: Oh, God!

(Ahmed enters.)

AHMED: She's doing better!

LUC: Ahmed, listen to me. We have something very serious to tell you. Daphnee has killed her little girl. She's in this suitcase. Look!

MICHELINE: He's about to faint, slap him!

LUC: Ahmed, be strong! Drink this!

JEAN: Her husband is still on the phone.

LUC: Give it to me! *(deliberately)* "Hello, John. I am Luc. You are in Fontainebleau? Something horrible is happened. I want you to be strong before you listen to me. Good? . . . Katia is dead, John. I think the best to do for you is to come to Paris as soon as possible. Daphnee's going very bad. She will need you . . . . Daphnee did kill Katia, John, or it may be she only let her die . . . . I don't know. We did just find the*

body in a suitcase. . . . I didn't see Katia for the last week. When did
you leave Paris, John?. . . A week ago? On Christmas day?. . . I
didn't see Katia after that. Well, John, she's dead. Understand that,
please? Excuse my poor English. Know it's Daphnee who is in
danger."

(Daphnee enters.)

"Be careful on the highway, John. Many people is drunk tonight.
Don't lose your self-control, John, promise?. . . John, you are ill,
right? I will not call the police before you are here. It means about half
an hour. . . . She's here in my apartment, she just came in. I don't
know if she can take you at the phone, John! Just a moment."
Daphnee, it's John. Do you want to talk to him? "She has no
understanding, John, I'll take care of her. Be strong, John, we are
waiting for you. Bye-bye, John, I kiss you."

(He hangs up the phone.)

MICHELINE: We should call the police. That's what they
usually do.

LUC: You're crazy. So she should spend twenty years in
prison? Or who knows, get the death penalty? It's a psychiatrist we should call!

MICHELINE: No, the psychiatrist comes after. If we don't do
this right, we're accomplices! First the cops, then a lawyer.
They'll pick a psychiatrist. Call them, Jean.

JEAN: It doesn't matter, there's no dial tone.

MICHELINE: It must still be connected to international long
distance. Wait a minute.

LUC: Daphnee, do you hear me?

DAPHNEE: Yes, I hear everything.

LUC: We must give you to the police, dear. We'll find you the best lawyer. You must refuse to talk except in the presence of your lawyers. You have to pass for crazy, do you get me?

DAPHNEE: Yes, I got you. I'm not an idiot. But it's not me who killed her.

LUC: What happened?

DAPHNEE: She must have climbed into the refrigerator and closed the door behind her. I found her frozen, but I was on acid. So I thought I could get her heart started again. I tried to warm her in the oven, but she was dead all right. I want to bury her in Maine, that's where she was born. There must be a way to get her through Customs. And then I'll kill myself. See, I took the revolver from the drawer!

(Luc takes it and puts it in his pocket.)

Please take that suitcase out of here! I can't bear looking at it!

MICHELINE: Don't touch it, Luc! It's evidence!

LUC: You phony mock-up of a cunt! What kind of prissy drag queen are you?

JEAN: Luc, don't act like this now. It's atrocious!

LUC: Stupid bitch! Call the cops, then. Go call the cops!

JEAN: Luc, you know very well I'm not going to call them.

MICHELINE: You're all mad, I'm getting out of here!

LUC: You're staying here, Micheline. I've got the gun.

MICHELINE: What's this, Luc? Have you finally snapped?

LUC: You'll wait with the others!

MICHELINE: Wait? For what, then?

LUC: The end of the story. Then you can tell the police whatever you want. Daphnee, do you hear me?

DAPHNEE: Yes.

LUC: John will be here soon. Then we're going to take you to the police. Do you understand?

DAPHNEE: Yes, I understand everything.

LUC: Good. I'm going to wash Katia in the bathtub. And put her in her crib. She'll look more presentable for John.

DAPHNEE: That's for me to do.

LUC: Are you sure you're capable?

DAPHNEE: Yes.

LUC: You really want to do it?

DAPHNEE: Yes.

LUC: Here, Daphnee.

(He puts the body in Daphnee's arms. Micheline looks ill; she goes to the window and opens it.)

DAPHNEE: Oh, she's heavy!

LUC: Yes, she's very heavy! Don't you have a proper dress for her?

DAPHNEE: The little Indian robe I bought for her last Christmas that she never wore. It's folded in the suitcase.

LUC: Here, is this it? Very pretty.

DAPHNEE: Will they let me bury her myself?

LUC: Yes, Daphnee, she's your daughter. And for now, we'll wash her little body with cold water and rub it with eau de cologne. I'll help you.

DAPHNEE: Thank you.

(They go into the bathroom. The sound of running water is heard. Luc reenters.)

LUC: Ahmed, do you feel better?

AHMED: Uh-huh. I had a shock there. Shit!

LUC: Just hold on! We're going to be interrogated all day tomorrow, and who knows, maybe the day after that. They may give you more of a hassle because you're an Arab. Do you have a clean police record?

AHMED: I do, but I have a cousin in prison.

LUC: That means absolutely nothing. We'll get very good lawyers, trust me! Have a shot of bourbon, that'll help. Jean, is the telephone still dead?

JEAN: Yes.

AHMED: This bourbon is strong!

LUC: *(to Jean)* When it starts working, tell me. How's our panicky queen?

MICHELINE: Honestly, Luc, I feel sick.

LUC: Go undress your mother, it *is* late for you!

MICHELINE: Please, Luc, don't!

LUC: Ahmed, go find the crib!

AHMED: Okay, Luc.

(He goes.)

DAPHNEE: *(off)* Luc, come look at her. I've washed her pretty well.

(Luc goes into the bathroom.)

MICHELINE: This is awful! It is awful!

JEAN: *(listening on the phone)* Control yourself! What are you going to do when your mother dies?

MICHELINE: Well, whatever happens, it won't be a sordid spectacle like this.

JEAN: You're the sordid spectacle! You're the only sordid spectacle here!

MICHELINE: Jean, please, it's not worth the trouble to say terrible things to me!

JEAN: Everyone says terrible things to you. You're a selfish freak!

(Ahmed reenters with the crib.)

AHMED: Luc! Where shall I put it?

LUC: *(off)* In the center of the room! Move the furniture to make room for it!

AHMED: *(to Jean)* Are you going to have any weepers? You know, hired mourners?

JEAN: That's the last thing we need! Well, what shall we do?

AHMED: Shall I put the chairs over there?

JEAN: I don't think that's necessary.

MICHELINE: Why don't we do all this over at her place? Why here?

JEAN: *This* is her home, idiot! Just shut up! *(He goes to the window.)*

LUC: *(off)* Is she all dry? Here, put some cologne on her, she already smells a little bad.

DAPHNEE: *(off)* Thank you, Luc.

JEAN: Look, Ahmed, over there, the tower is still burning!

AHMED: The fire must be in the interior of the building, in the heart of it. What shit, these towers! It's no fun for the firemen!

JEAN: That's why they cut the telephone. They need all the lines! Brr, it's cold!

(He closes the window. Luc and Daphnee enter. The body of Katia is dressed in the djellaba.)

LUC: Come on, Daphnee.

DAPHNEE: *(putting the corpse in the crib)* Thank you. I forgot to do her hair.

LUC: Go get a brush, Daphnee.

DAPHNEE: You have to use a comb on her. She has very fine hair.

LUC: Would you give me your comb, please, Micheline? I thank you. Here, Daphnee.

MICHELINE: Is her place open? I'd rather wait for the police over there.

DAPHNEE: Oh! She's monstrous, this she-creature, and look how she's dressed! You're just an ape, you poor old thing! You can tell at a hundred meters that she's just a drag queen!

MICHELINE: Can I have her key, Ahmed? I'll wait for the police over there.

DAPHNEE: Wait in the hall, honey! You're not waiting in my place!

LUC: Go wait in the parking lot! Maybe you'll get raped!

AHMED: *(laughing)* Go on, calm yourself, Micheline!

MICHELINE: Give me her key, you dirty Arab!

AHMED: *(slapping her)* How's this, then? Who are you talking to?

LUC: Calm down, Ahmed!

JEAN: Have a bourbon, Micheline!

(Micheline collapses in Jean's arms, and Jean helps her to the sofa.)

MICHELINE: Oh, God!... That's better, thanks.

DAPHNEE: I need some air!

(She and Luc go to the window.)

Don't worry, I'm not going to jump. I only want to breathe.

JEAN: Ahmed, can I ask you for something? Please take of Micheline.

AHMED: She insulted me!

JEAN: She's not in her normal state, Ahmed, she's frightened, that's all! Go on, don't complicate things.

AHMED: My apologies, Micheline. I saw red, that's all.

MICHELINE: I'm the one who should apologize! My God, how could I have said that?

AHMED: I forgive you, Micheline. Don't cry anymore. You'll make me cry myself.

MICHELINE: Well, I don't want to make you cry. Here, roll me another joint, dear, I have the stuff in my purse, over there! Here, it's good Afghan dope.

AHMED: But I don't smoke.

MICHELINE: But I *do* smoke. I need it, dear. Roll me a joint, please! Here, here's the paper! Oh, Ahmed, Ahmed! I'm afraid of cops.

AHMED: Wait til I roll the joint. That will calm you. Don't be afraid of the cops, they can't do anything to you.

DAPHNEE: Luc, you see over there, far off, is that really Sacre Coeur?

LUC: Yes, dear, and beneath that, over there behind the Tuileries, you see, there, that's lit up, that's Notre Dame! And to the right, the Eiffel Tower, if you lean a little. Is this the first time you've looked out a window since you came here?

DAPHNEE: I never really looked out! At my place the windows are covered with yellow paint. It looks very nice. What year is it?

LUC: 1977.

DAPHNEE: Already? Do you realize how old I'll be when I get out of the slammer?

LUC: You won't go to the slammer, as you put it. You'll go to a psychiatric clinic for a few months and you'll come out like a shiny new penny. Your brave American husband will take care of all that, trust me! You can spend your time reading the classics and they'll give you Valium instead of acid and you'll sleep a lot and you'll leave and start a new life like everyone else's!

DAPHNEE: Yes, like everyone else's! I believe that! You've done me a lot of good, Luc. I'll become like anyone else.

JEAN: Private chat? Here's your horrible California champagne, baby! It's just barely cool. Here, Luc.

MICHELINE: Olé! Here, Ahmed.

AHMED: I don't have a hand free. I'm rolling your joint.

MICHELINE: I'll hold your cup.

(Daphnee heaves a long despairing sigh and goes to the crib.)

LUC: Daphnee!

DAPHNEE: Oh, I forgot she was dead.

LUC: Daphnee, my dear, calm down. She's very much dead. Sit down, dear.

DAPHNEE: Oh, my God! It's so hard to come down after acid. My brains are like marmalade.

LUC: All right, come down easy now, not too suddenly. First of all, you should change, you can't meet the cops dressed like that. You're the mother of a family, mad but decent. What do you have like a dress in your baggage?

DAPHNEE: I don't know, look!

(She takes off her clothes.)

MICHELINE: Don't look, Ahmed!

LUC: Look, a nice tailored suit!

DAPHNEE: Oh, that's my little tailored suit. It's perfect for seducing the judges! Here, should I take my rubies?

LUC: Positively not!

DAPHNEE: There, I'm ready. All we have to do is wait for John. Well, are you keeping that joint for yourselves? *(She takes the joint.)* Here, Luc!

LUC: Thanks.

DAPHNEE: Somehow I don't think I'm truly presentable for these police!

LUC: None of us are. But you're fine as you are!

DAPHNEE: Fine, okay, if you say so. I've heard all the instructions, I won't screw up any. I washed Katia. I put some perfume on her, I'm presentable for the cops and the headshrinkers, ta daah! I won't have anything more to do with your life. I'll leave with the body for New York like you wanted me to do. You won't have anything more to do with this mess. You think you're doing me good by telling me to play the repentant mother. Fine, but I'm not repentant, because I'm not guilty! She climbed into that refrigerator by herself.

JEAN: Daphnee, no one said you were guilty.

MICHELINE: *(tartly)* No one *said* it.

DAPHNEE: That's even worse! You treat me as an innocent, then? Don't you think that's worse? Katia's already dead, she's already dead. I'm going to bury her in Maine. That's it. I think that's normal enough. Why shouldn't I be able to take her with me? I've already smuggled ten kilos of hash. Why not Katia? At airports, they don't look for anything but guns, their machines only detect metal. So, . . . I'm an American citizen. They don't mess with American suitcases, especially if I'm in first class.

LUC: Wait for John, Daphnee.

DAPHNEE: He's going to turn me in, that's guaranteed! I have to disappear before he arrives! I'm getting out now. Call a taxi for me, Jean! I've got to get Katia back in the suitcase.

MICHELINE: No, no, that's horrifying!

DAPHNEE: Where's the suitcase? Help me, Luc!

LUC: It's too late to go anywhere with Katia, Daphnee. She's practically decomposed. But she will be buried in Maine, you'll see, I promise you. Only she's not going to travel in a suitcase, she'll go in a hermetically sealed coffin with certificates from the American consulate, all perfectly legal. Believe me, your husband can take care of this better than you.

DAPHNEE: Dirty bourgeois.

(Ahmed laughs.)

MICHELINE: What are you laughing at, Ahmed?

AHMED: Nothing, I don't know, but I can't stop! *(He has a fit of mad laughter.)* What's wrong with me?

MICHELINE: Control yourself or you'll choke! *(She slaps him on the back.)*

AHMED: Oh, I'm going to put my head under cold water!

(He goes into the bathroom, still laughing.)

(off) Oh, the water's freezing! Oh, my head's under freezing water!

JEAN: Did he smoke too much hash?

MICHELINE: Not at all, not even a puff. It must be his nature. I hope my mother will die of a heart attack when I bring him back to the house. In any case, he'll be a good reason to move out on her!

JEAN: Oh, you're dreaming!

AHMED: Micheline, a towel!

MICHELINE: I'm coming, my prince! *(to Jean)* You see, it's not a dream. It's a reality.

(She goes into the bathroom.)

(off) Here, sweetheart, there are no towels, but come here and I'll dry you with my handkerchief. Stop it, what are you doing? Don't be crazy.

AHMED: *(off)* Come into the tub with me.

MICHELINE: Wait til we get to my house, dear, I don't want to give up my maidenhead in a tub!

(Sounds of laughter and running water are heard.)

JEAN: What trash! *(He closes the bathroom door and goes to the window.)* Oh! The tower across the way! Look!

LUC: What's wrong? It's burning! That's impossible! Still? What are those firemen doing?

JEAN: You think it's easy? A helicopter crashes into a tower, it's complicated! Why aren't they evacuating the building? Oh, it's nothing but offices, no one lives there.

LUC: Look! Isn't that John's car? The firemen won't let him through! There! Look!

JEAN: He must be having trouble finding a place to park. There, he's left the car in the middle of the street! He'll be here in a minute.

LUC: *(to Ahmed and Micheline)* Get dressed! Come on! John's here! Go! Go! Go!

MICHELINE: *(off)* But I am dressed! *I* am, anyway! Oh, this is all madness!

(Micheline reappears, dressing herself.)

LUC: *(shouting into the bathroom)* Ahmed! Your pants!

(Ahmed reenters.)

AHMED: There! That's better! But I'm all wet!

LUC: You make some coffee, Ahmed, and don't open your mouth without my permission. The guy who's coming here is in a state of shock, got it?

AHMED: Yes, Luc.

MICHELINE: Make mine nice and strong, dear! I'll help you.

LUC: Daphnee? John is here. He's coming up. Don't you want to say anything?

DAPHNEE: John is here. I got it. I know John.

LUC: Jean, are you all right?

JEAN: Yes. Fine. Asshole.

LUC: And Micheline, no crises, please!

MICHELINE: I've never been so calm!

AHMED: Don't worry, I'll take care of Micheline.

MICHELINE: Don't slap my behind, I'll drop the cups!

LUC: *(at the phone)* Still no dial tone.

JEAN: I think we'd better cover her face. It's so bloated. It's monstrous.

LUC: Leave it as it is.

(Luc opens the door and John enters.)

LUC: *(deliberately)* *"Hello, John. Come in."*

JOHN: Hello, Luc? Hello, Jean? Hello, Micheline?

JEAN: Hello, John.

MICHELINE: Hello, John. This is Ahmed.

AHMED: Good evening.

JOHN: Hello, Ahmed. *(John goes to the crib and looks in.)* What happened, Luc?

LUC: Maybe you should ask Daphnee, John.

JOHN: Daphnee, do you hear me?

DAPHNEE: I listened to everything and everybody, John. I'm absolutely all right.

JOHN: What's happened?

DAPHNEE: She crawled into the refrigerator. She crawled into the refrigerator, that's all. It happens to children. In the United States, there are constantly children being suffocated in refrigerators! Everyone knows refrigerators were built for adults to use, dammit.

JOHN: Oh, my God! *(He breaks down.)*

DAPHNEE: Ahmed, please, a cup of coffee for my husband, please. Put a lot of bourbon in it.

(Daphnee goes into the kitchen. Jean holds John while he cries.)

JEAN: John, please!

JOHN: I don't understand. She was alive and beautiful and perfectly healthy on Christmas day. She was playing with her toys. How could it happen?

DAPHNEE: She crawled into the refrigerator. She crawled into the refrigerator. She crawled into the refrigerator. She crawled into the refrigerator.

MICHELINE: Why didn't you tell anyone about it, Daphnee?

DAPHNEE: What would that have changed? She was already dead! Where's the bourbon coffee? Don't just stand there with your mouth open like an asshole. Take this, John, it's strong like you like it! Quickly, John, we're going to the police. Hurry! Come on! Where's my coat? Let's go to the police! Why hang around here, now? Why didn't I tell anyone right away? Because she was my daughter, not yours! I can do what I want. And I waited here as long as possible, because I knew it would be the last time Luc and I would spend together. There's no danger with a gay man. He has his dream—and I have mine. You didn't understand that, did you, Mister Yankee? My dream was of *you*, Luc! Yes, it happens to everyone, but for me it was stronger, I don't know why, it blinded me. Please, John, let's go! I'm very tired!

JOHN: Of course, Daphnee.

DAPHNEE: Take Katia's body, please! We're going back home.

JOHN: Yes, of course. But we must go to the police station, first.

DAPHNEE: Let's not leave her body here. Jean and Luc have had enough trouble as it is. Let's keep her at my place til the police arrive, and you and I can go to the station ourselves.

JOHN: Okay, Daphnee. *(He breaks down again.)*

JEAN: I'll do it, John. Ahmed, would you help me?

LUC: John, remember, it's just an accident.

JOHN: But who will believe it?

LUC: You will believe it! You! If you don't believe it, nobody will! Do you understand?

JOHN: Yes, I do, Luc. Thank you. Oh, God!

AHMED: This is a bullet hole.

JEAN: Oh, Christ, Luc! Come here! She has a bullet hole in the back of her neck!

AHMED: Micheline, the child was killed by a bullet!

MICHELINE: Yes, I understand. Be quiet!

JOHN: I'm not following. What's happened?

LUC: Katia was killed by a gun.

JOHN: Oh, Katia!

DAPHNEE: *(to Jean)* I killed her with your revolver. I took it because I saw it in the linen closet, under the sheets.

JOHN: Bitch! Oh, you bitch!

(He tries to strike Daphnee. Jean, Luc, and Ahmed separate them. Micheline gives John a glass of bourbon, while Jean sits Daphnee in the armchair and holds her hand.)

JEAN: *(to Daphnee)* Did he hurt you?

DAPHNEE: No, I'm all right.

JOHN: I'll kill you, bitch! I'll kill you!

(He breaks away and tries to strangle Daphnee. Luc and Ahmed separate them.)

LUC: Under the shower! Put him under the shower!

(Luc and Ahmed carry John into the bathroom. Sounds of a struggle and running water are heard.)

JOHN: *(off)* My baby, my little baby.

LUC: *(off)* Put his head under the shower.

DAPHNEE: A bourbon, please, Micheline. Thank you.

(Micheline gives her the bottle.)

JOHN: *(off)* Let me go, you bastard!

(Luc and Ahmed enter, holding John. All three are soaked.)

I'll be quiet, I promise. I promise. I only want to ask Daphnee a question.

DAPHNEE: It's pronounced DAPHNAY, not DAFFNEE. Daffnee is the name for a dog . All right, your question?

JOHN: Why did you kill our baby?

DAPHNEE: Because she was just like me, helpless! She didn't want to be separated from me for a second, and my head was elsewhere. It was Luc who took up all my thoughts! I wasn't a mother anymore. I was in love.

LUC: Not this routine, Daphnee!

DAPHNEE: I'm talking to John! Do you understand me, John? No, you don't! You're an American, you don't understand anything!

JOHN: I'll kill you. I will kill you!

(He throws himself on her. Ahmed and Luc restrain him.)

LUC: John, please!

JOHN: Oh, God! Oh, God!

(He breaks down. Jean protects Daphnee.)

LUC: *(at the phone)* There! There's the dial tone.

MICHELINE: Good, call the police! The number's on the dial! John? Come on, Jean, you have to take care of John, I don't speak any English. He's in some sort of cataleptic state.

JEAN: You're used to servicing men, aren't you?

MICHELINE: Here comes his crisis. He wants one, too! Here, sit down, John. Ahmed, help me sit him down.

AHMED: The poor man, he's in shock!

JOHN: I would like some coffee, please!

MICHELINE: Is there any coffee?

AHMED: It's cold.

MICHELINE: That doesn't matter. *"Don't you want a drink, John?"* How's my English? *"Whiskey?"*

JOHN: No, thanks. I feel better.

AHMED: *(bringing a cup of coffee)* Here's some coffee, John.

LUC: *(at the phone)* The cops aren't answering.

MICHELINE: It's New Year's Eve. The line is flooded!

LUC: Hello? Hello? Shit, I got cut off! *(He redials.)*

DAPHNEE: Jean, you don't have to cling to me. I might want to move!

(She goes to the window and opens it. Ahmed follows.)

Oh, the fire's finished. The firemen are leaving. You left the Cadillac in the middle of the street, John.

LUC: Shit! There's no answer!

DAPHNEE: Never mind. Let's all go to the station. We can put Katia in the trunk. She's getting used to it. We can drive really fast along the Seine. That'll sober us up. And you can drop me off at the emergency room with Katia. I'll say she crawled into the refrigerator while I was drunk. They won't give it too much attention, they must have plenty of emergencies tonight. I'll play my role to the hilt, but John, I need your help.

JOHN: I won't say anything but the truth, Daphnee.

DAPHNEE: Ah, no, I see. I'm in for twenty years in prison. The truth. The truth. All right, what's taking the cops? They're chatting away. No answer yet?

LUC: *(hanging up the phone)* Daphnee?

DAPHNEE: Are you talking to me?

LUC: Yes, to you, and you're going to answer me. Why did

you kill Katia, Daphnee? Tell me.

DAPHNEE: She made me sick. That's all I know. Do you have any normal cigarettes? Look at all that neon out there, doesn't it ever let up?

LUC: It's New Year's Day.

DAPHNEE: Oh, that's right. 1977! Those are fireworks!

LUC: Yes, the end of the celebration.

DAPHNEE: You're so intelligent. That must be what attracted me most to you. That and the smell of your hair. Your whole aroma, it drove me crazy as long as I can remember. The odor of your armpits and your feet. That's what I lived for. I used to steal your dirty clothes and sleep with my nose buried in them, you didn't know that. I was obsessed, I went mad. But, for now, I'm cured. See? No need to say anything else.

LUC: All the better, Daphnee. Do you want me to come with you to the station?

DAPHNEE: No, I want you to let me leave with Katia. I want to bury her in Maine, myself!

LUC: You know that's impossible.

DAPHNEE: Not if you help me. I killed her, I should bury her. It's a matter between her and me. Drive me to the Orly Airport.

JOHN: You are sick, baby! You are very sick! It may be my fault, but you are very sick! I will find the best doctors for you and everything you need. Trust me, Daphnee.

DAPHNEE: I've been waiting for hours. Let's go to this police station, already. Let's go, I'll call the elevator!

LUC: *(restraining her)* Daphnee!

DAPHNEE: Let go of me, pederast!

JOHN: Daphnee, it's better to wait here.

DAPHNEE: I don't want to stay here. I want to take a walk. I haven't been out of this tower in an eternity. I'll walk to my arrest on foot. All I have to do is follow the banks of the Seine. Who wants to come? Nobody? You prefer the air-conditioned Cadillac? Have it your way! You'd rather see me die than see me suffer. You'd be relieved if I burst. That's why I killed her. She was like me. It relieved me to kill her.

LUC: We'll all go with you, Daphnee.

DAPHNEE: Thank you, Luc.

(Luc holds her and calms her.)

JEAN: John, put on your overcoat, please.

JOHN: Thank you. It was raining in the country.

JEAN: It did snow here in Paris, just at midnight. Do you have the keys to your car?

JOHN: Yes, thank you.

JEAN: Give them to me, I will drive. Luc, is there any point in having Ahmed and Micheline come?

LUC: No. Anyway, someone should stay here with Katia. But you can stay if you want.

JEAN: Don't be mean. I'm coming with you. Get your coat.

LUC: My coat! You took it to the cleaners.

JEAN: Right, I'm such a jerk. Put on your other one. I'll get mine.

LUC: Thanks.

JEAN: Micheline, they'll be calling you soon about what's happened here. Maybe you should take Katia next door. You might have to wait here for hours.

AHMED: We'll keep here here with us, Jean. It's bad to leave dead children all alone. Are you afraid, Micheline?

MICHELINE: Absolutely not! But in my opinion, John should phone the American embassy before going anywhere.

JOHN: Before I came I did call my father in Boston, he's very influential. He'll do what he can.

JEAN: That's perfect, John. Your coat, Daphnee.

DAPHNEE: Thank you. Oh what's this in my pocket? Not the revolver? *(She backs toward the door, menacing them with the gun.)* Don't come near me, I'm leaving.

   (She exits.)

JEAN: Luc, you put that in her pocket! You're insane!

   (A gunshot is heard. Everyone but Luc rushes outside. They bring in Daphnee. She has a scratch on her throat. They lie her on the couch.)

LUC: *(distracted by another development)* What's that? The seagull! The gull was trying to fly in the bathroom! It's alive again!

AHMED: She's not dead. The bullet only scratched her throat, here!

LUC: She wants to fly, look!

(Gull cries are heard. Luc takes the gull and carries it to the window.)

Fly! Fly! She's flying!

DAPHNEE: Luc! Luc! Luc! Luc! Luc!

MICHELINE: I'll call an ambulance! *(She dials.)*

JOHN: Oh, my God!

JEAN: John, be strong! I'll look for some alcohol.

MICHELINE: Carrefour de la Defense, an ambulance, please! ... Isn't this police emergency?... This is urgent. There's an injured woman and a dead baby! No, the fire's in the building next door.... But that's insane! *(She hangs up.)* He told me to look for an ambulance down on the street. He says lots of people have been hurt in the fire. All the ambulances are there.

AHMED: But they haven't put out the fire. Look how it's burning, that tower! Shit, what a job for the firemen!

JEAN: What, again? It's a catastrophe!

AHMED: Oh, the gull! Over there! She's flying over the fire! Hey, gull! Fuck! She's going to get burned! Like a moth into the fire!

MICHELINE: Where's the fog horn? Here! Come back, stupid! That gull is out of its mind! Go on! Louder, Ahmed! I think she heard! Oh, no, the idiot! She's turned back toward the fire. Louder, Ahmed!

LUC: I'm here, Daphnee.

DAPHNEE: I missed. God, what a jerk! I missed!

LUC: Here, I'll take care of it.

JEAN: Here's some alcohol. Like an idiot, I'm standing here with it.

LUC: It's nothing, just a superficial wound.

DAPHNEE: Thank you.

AHMED: She must have smelled the sea. See, she's headed that way.

MICHELINE: Back down the Seine!

LUC: Daphnee?

DAPHNEE: Yes?

LUC: I like you very much.

DAPHNEE: Thank you.

LUC: Can you walk? Come on, we'll go down, you and me, and walk to the police station.

DAPHNEE: Okay, help me up.

LUC: All right?

DAPHNEE: All right.

LUC: John, Jean, are you ready?

JEAN: Let's go, John.

JOHN: I'll take the body with me in the car.

JEAN: It's better to leave it here, John.

JOHN: I said I'll take it with me!

LUC: Whatever you want. Let him do it!

JEAN: Then put it in a blanket, John.

JOHN: Thanks.

DAPHNEE: Good-bye, Micheline.

MICHELINE: See you soon, Daphnee.

DAPHNEE: Good-bye, Ahmed.

AHMED: Be well, Daphnee.

JEAN: Stay here, Micheline. I'll call you. Be brave, dear.

DAPHNEE: *(to Ahmed)* Will you send me oranges?

AHMED: All the oranges in Tunisia!

DAPHNEE: Where's my beauty case? I want my rubies! I'll take them to prison with me.

LUC: Here.

(Daphnee, Luc, Jean, and John leave, John carrying Katia.)

AHMED: Oh, let's hide this crib somewhere!

MICHELINE: Let's put it in the bathroom!

AHMED: Shall I make some coffee, Micheline?

MICHELINE: You'll be an angel one day, Ahmed. I have to admit something to you, I am not rich. I'm a compulsive liar. In fact, I live in a maid's room on the rue Monsieur le Prince. I only dress up as a woman when I go out at night.

AHMED: What, you too? You live on rue Monsieur le Prince?

MICHELINE: Why, do you?

AHMED: Yes. I moved in yesterday. My brother-in-law found me the room.

MICHELINE: At what number?

AHMED: Thirty-one.

MICHELINE: You're the Arab who moved in yesterday?

AHMED: You're the boy with the glasses who helped me carry in the mattress?

MICHELINE: That's me!

AHMED: Didn't you recognize me?

MICHELINE: I am completely myopic!

AHMED: It's destiny, then!

MICHELINE: Do you prefer me as a man or as a woman?

AHMED: With glasses, as a man. With the wig, as a woman.

MICHELINE: Oh, sweetheart, I love you!

(Explosions are heard outside. They hurry to the window.)

AHMED: Shit! The tower's exploding!

MICHELINE: Do you think we should stay here?

AHMED: Yes, there's no danger to us. Look! There's the Cadillac! They've put little Katia on the luggage rack! They've all gotten in the car and Jean is driving.

MICHELINE: Good, good! He's the only one with a cool head.

AHMED: Well, that's all past, Micheline. Oh, shit! The coffee's burning!

MICHELINE: Ahmed, look! Look! He's driving the car full speed into the fire!

AHMED: Merciful God! They're on fire! They're burning! They've exploded! They must be dead! They've been killed!

MICHELINE: Oh, my God, Ahmed, hold me!

(Ahmed does.)

AHMED: I'm here, Micheline! Don't be afraid!

MICHELINE: Sometimes God arrives so suddenly.

∽

Copi

GRAND FINALE

Translated from the French by Michael Feingold

COPI, whose real name was Raul Damonte, was born in Buenos Aires in 1939. He moved to Paris in 1963 and was already well-known as a designer and cartoonist when he started to write for the stage. His plays were very successful and he rapidly became one of the most talked-about playwrights in Paris. Copi himself acted in some of the productions of his plays, which were often directed by French-Argentine directors such as Jorge Lavelli, Alfredo Arias, and Jérôme Savary. He wrote a total of fifteen plays; among his best known ones are *Eva Peron* (1969), *The Homosexual or the Difficulty of Sexpressing Oneself* (1971), *The Four Twins* (1973), and *Loretta Strong* (1974). These plays were published in English by John Calder/Riverrun Press in 1976. Copi also published short stories, eight cartoon albums, and six novels— *L'Uruguayen* (1973), *Le Bal des folles* (1977), *Une Langouste pour deux* (1978), *La Cité des rats* (1979), *La Vie est un tango* (1979), and *La Guerre des pédés* (1982). *A Tower Near Paris (La Tour de la Défense)* was published in 1978 and premiered in Paris in 1981. The production was directed by Claude Confortès with a cast that included Bernadette Lafont and Pierre Clémenti. *Grand Finale (Une Visite inopportune)* is Copi's last play, written shortly before his death of AIDS in December 1988. The Paris production was directed by Jorge Lavelli and starred Michel Duchaussoy of the Comédie Française. It played to packed houses at the Théâtre National de la Colline in February 1988, and it received the award for best production of the year by the French Critics Guild. The play was given a second run in October 1988, and it subsequently toured France and Spoleto, Italy.

MICHAEL FEINGOLD, a graduate of Columbia University and the Yale School of Drama, is lead drama critic for *The Village Voice*, New York's weekly newspaper. His many translations from the French include works by Molière, Marivaux, Diderot, Musset, and Anouilh, as well as four Offenbach operettas. He is best known, however, for his English versions of the music theater works of Brecht and Weill, *Happy End, Seven Deadly Sins, The Little Mahagonny, Rise and Fall of the City of Ma-*

hagonny, and *The Berlin Requiem,* which are the standard versions in use all over the English-speaking world. His new translation of *The Threepenny Opera* will be premiered on Broadway in the fall of 1989. Experienced in the theater as a director and dramaturg as well as a translator, Mr. Feingold has served as Literary Manager of the Yale Repertory Theatre, the Guthrie Theater in Minneapolis, and the American Repertory Theater in Cambridge, Massachusetts. He has frequently worked as an advisor to young playwrights at the National Playwrights Conference of the Eugene O'Neill Theater Center and teaches classic drama in the Dramatic Writing Program at New York University.

This year, Feingold's English version of Joshua Sobol's *Soul of a Jew* will be produced at River Arts Repertory in Woodstock, New York, while the Classic Stage Company in New York City will produce *The Tower of Evil,* his adaptation of Dumas père's *La Tour de Nesle.* A translator of poetry and songs as well as plays, Mr. Feingold has been the recipient of a Guggenheim Fellowship, a National Endowment for the Arts Fellowship in Translation, and the Walter Lowenfels Prize in Criticism.

CHARACTERS

CYRIL
NURSE
HUBERT
REPORTER
REGINA MORTI
DR. BACKSLEIDER

SCENE

A room in a Paris hospital. One door leads to the hallway and another to the bathroom.

>   *(Cyril is in bed. Nurse enters.)*

NURSE: Your new dressing gown's here.

CYRIL: I didn't order that horror.

NURSE: It's a present from your sister-in-law.

CYRIL: My sister-in-law would do anything to ruin my birthday.

NURSE: You're in an impossible mood this morning. You didn't even eat your croissant. And did you take your pills?

CYRIL: Yes.

NURSE: All of them? But I see you've retouched your hair. Is that what kept you in the bathroom for an hour?

CYRIL: Is that your business?

NURSE: Are you expecting that little blond thing who brought you roses at Christmastime?

CYRIL: I forbid you to interfere with my private life!

NURSE: I just said that to please you. Hold still while I put that needle in.

CYRIL: Another i.v.?

NURSE: It's the day for your suramin.

CYRIL: You're hurting me!

NURSE: Your veins are a mess.

CYRIL: What do you expect when you keep sticking needles in me? Ow!

NURSE: That's it. Make sure you don't shake the needle out, you're overexcited today. I'll add a pinch of valium to your medication.

CYRIL: No chemical tranquilizers! I'd rather smoke my opium.

NURSE: You really must let me try that one day.

CYRIL: Not a chance! You'd never hold a hypodermic straight again.

NURSE: Come on, give me a little bit. I'll try it this weekend with my husband.

CYRIL: Here! But be careful, don't put more in your pipe the first time than you can put on the head of a pin, otherwise you'll get palpitations.

NURSE: Is it good for sex?

CYRIL: Oh, no; it's guaranteed to ruin it.

NURSE: In that case I won't give it to my husband, I'll smoke it all myself. Did you take your temperature?

CYRIL: Yes. Light the water pipe for me.

NURSE: It'll make your fever go up.

CYRIL: I adore having a little fever.

NURSE: I hope you'll have your cleaning woman come today. I'm sick of throwing out the leftovers from your chic picnics every day. This hospital's never seen such goings-on. You're the Sarah Bernhardt of the charity ward.

CYRIL: You talk like a gay man.

NURSE: I often ask myself if I wouldn't have done better to be born gay. You seem to have led quite a life.

CYRIL: I adore you! When I get out of here I'm going to take you around to all the great fashion houses. You're my ideal woman.

NURSE: You're not the first who's promised me the moon when he gets out of the hospital. You'd do better to leave me something in your will.

CYRIL: All I'd have to leave you is debts.

NURSE: After all, it's mainly thanks to me you're still alive today. You should be giving *me* a birthday present.

CYRIL: I've already given you my pearls!

NURSE: That dressing gown your sister-in-law sent you, if you really hate it—

CYRIL: Don't tell me you'd dream of wearing such a thing!

NURSE: I'd love to stay home and loll around in my dressing gown, but somehow I never have the time. No, it would be a present for my husband, who does stay home all day, cooking up gourmet treats for me.

CYRIL: Sounds like your husband has weird tastes. You must introduce me.

NURSE: No, I'll keep him for myself, thank you very much. But your friend's here, early for a change.

CYRIL: What friend? Hubert? Tell him I'm dying, let him come back some other day.

NURSE: If I tell him that, he'll insist on staying here till you're dead.

CYRIL: Well, tell him I've died already! I'm on my way to the morgue!

(Enter Hubert.)

Too late! Hubert, what are you doing here at this hour of the morning?

HUBERT: I want to be the first to wish you a happy birthday. I took the liberty of bringing you this present.

CYRIL: *(opening it)* A dressing gown! Mary Jo, take a look at this embroidery! Your husband will be in hog heaven!

NURSE: Oh, this one's much too nice for him, I'll keep this for myself! *(Exit.)*

CYRIL: Well, Hubert darling, what's the world been doing since I left it?

HUBERT: Turning, as always, dear genius.

CYRIL: Too bad! I'd love to make it stop. And what do you do with your evenings now that I'm not there to amuse you?

HUBERT: Nothing, dear genius. Paris isn't the great city it used to be. Since they closed the baths, there's no place to hang out after the show. Of course, there's no more shows either. And even if there were, these days they're hardly a meeting place for people like us, of ambiguous sex and indeterminate age. There's always the park, but I'm afraid of getting mugged. You're so lucky having AIDS; here you don't run any risks.

CYRIL: Ah, Hubert, you always know the right thing to say.

HUBERT: It's true, I'm jealous of you. Now that I no longer know how to spend my days, I'm terrified I'll live to be a hundred.

CYRIL: So go live in the third world! With all your money, you could be king of a court of little boys, waving banana leaves over you to brush away the flies.

HUBERT: I've had fantasies about that. But I'd be afraid of getting cut off from all my friends.

CYRIL: All your friends are dead.

HUBERT: You're still alive, dear genius.

CYRIL: Well, not for long. And when I'm dead like all the others, how'll you spend your time?

HUBERT: I'll go to Père Lachaise.

CYRIL: Who told you I'd be buried there?

HUBERT: Everyone else is.

CYRIL: Exactly!

HUBERT: But then where will you be?

CYRIL: I won't tell you. I have no intention of leaving anyone my forwarding address.

HUBERT: But what about your tomb?

CYRIL: What tomb?

HUBERT: Well, I hadn't meant to tell you, but you are already the proud owner of a tomb in Père Lachaise. Dear genius, I took the liberty of presenting you this posthumous gift.

CYRIL: Hubert, I despise you.

HUBERT: I bought a plot right across from Oscar Wilde, and almost next door to André Gide. The excavation's already started. I've been dying to show you these aerial photographs.

CYRIL: And that, what's that supposed to be?

HUBERT: Your monument, dear genius.

CYRIL: That atrocity? You will tear it down at once, to the last pebble!

HUBERT: Maybe you would have preferred the Montparnasse cemetery; it's a little cozier.

CYRIL: I don't want to be buried anywhere! I've been turning you down since we were at school, don't think you're going to possess me once I'm dead. You are an elderly necrophile!

(Enter Nurse.)

NURSE: You're in good form today. They can hear you shouting all the way down to the kitchens. There's a reporter who wants to see you.

CYRIL: He doesn't have any cameras, does he?

NURSE: Don't worry, I frisked him.

CYRIL: Hubert, my makeup mirror. I will permit you to stay for the interview as long as you promise not to say a word about my age. Especially make sure you don't tell him I was well-known before the War!

HUBERT: But you weren't well-known before the War.

CYRIL: All the more reason! You knew me as a baby in my mother's arms, you fought side by side with my father in the Résistance. *(to Nurse)* Show him in!

NURSE: *(ushering Reporter in)* Mr. Hubert, will you play hostess? It's time for my rounds and I'm already behind schedule. You'll find the drinks in the ice chest under the terrace. *(Exit.)*

CYRIL: Approach without fear, young man, you may kiss my hand without risk, nothing I have is contagious, except my vices, of course. Hubert, a chair. What's your name, young man?

REPORTER: Jean-Marc, sir.

CYRIL: Has anyone ever told you that you resemble a Botticelli? It's true; a Botticelli that's in Verona, a young shepherd wearing a sheepskin, third row from the Virgin, on the left. Don't you think so, Hubert?

HUBERT: It's the image of him. A Botticelli, absolutely.

CYRIL: Of course, you'll have a taste of this little vino bianco from Verona? Botticelli wouldn't have sneered at it. Hubert, hurry up with the drinks! First of all, tell me what this interview is supposed to be about. Because I warn you, there are topics I won't discuss, my mother doesn't know I'm gay.

HUBERT: Oh, she does too!

CYRIL: Hubert, I'm giving this interview!

HUBERT: Would you like a slice of candied orange peel in your white wine, young Botticelli?

REPORTER: Yes indeed, thank you.

HUBERT: You realize, dear genius, the whole world knows you're gay.

CYRIL: But not my mother!

HUBERT: She's known since you were a little baby. Mothers have no illusions.

(Nurse enters.)

NURSE: Well, what a nice party! If you keep on jumping around like a carnival barker, your medication will go into the system too fast. You know how weak your heart is. Every time you look at a young man, you're risking a cardiac arrest. And there's a lady outside to see you.

CYRIL: A lady, here? That has to be my sister-in-law. Tell her I despised the dressing gown and I haven't the least intention of seeing her.

NURSE: It's not your sister-in-law.

CYRIL: Then why does she want to see me? First of all, who is she? Does this woman have a name by any chance? What's that, her card? Regina Morti? Sounds Italian. Is she?

NURSE: I wouldn't know.

HUBERT: Isn't that the opera singer you used to run around Verona with before the War?

CYRIL: Regina Morti? It means "Queen of the Dead"! What a morbid name!

HUBERT: But it's the perfect stage name for an opera singer.

CYRIL: Does she look like an opera singer?

NURSE: I don't know what opera singers look like.

HUBERT: Does she have an imposing look?

NURSE: Well, apparently she isn't afraid to wear her diamonds in the subway.

HUBERT: Then she must be an opera singer.

CYRIL: I despise opera singers. It's impossible to make them shut up, and even worse, if she sees a reporter she'll try to steal the interview from me . Oh, well, show her in; I know how to defend myself.

(Nurse goes out.)

My dear Jean-Marc, . . . but that sounds so ordinary, Jean-Marc . . . . What about letting me call you Gianmarco?

REPORTER: Of course, sir.

CYRIL: Gianmarco Botticelli, I'm truly happy to see you here at my side. You have the serene beauty of an Italian Renaissance masterpiece. Promise me that you won't say naughty things about me in your magazine. People have spread such insane stories about my so-called bad character! They say I like to slap my co-stars. It's true that, now and then, you feel the need to work off some nervous tension in the wings. But I have never treated any colleague badly on the stage itself.

(Enter Regina Morti.)

Madame Regina Morti—why, it's Regina! Darling Regina, how sweet of you to come and see me! That's right, I read somewhere that you were at the Paris Opera for a few days with your Carmen—or was that last season? Let me introduce Gianmarco, who is really French, but nonetheless adorable, and Hubert, who was in the army with my father.

HUBERT: *(presenting himself formally)* Hubert Dubonnet.

CYRIL: Hubert, would you take Regina's coat? My dear Gianmarco, you see before you the creature with the most miraculous organ in the world. One last encore, Regina, let me hear the last notes of "Libiamo."

(Regina Morti sings the closing bars of the Drinking Song from La Traviata.*)*

NURSE: *(running in)* What's going on here? You'll wake up the whole ward!

CYRIL: *Brava! Bravissima! Sei una divinità! Un Negroni per Regina!* Listen, Mary Jo, I didn't ring for you. Go take care of your sick people!

NURSE: They'll move you into Intensive Care if you go on working yourself up like this. You were in a coma only last week! What about your tension? You could explode!

REGINA MORTI: I don't usually make my listeners explode, miss.

NURSE: Shut your face! I'm in charge here! And I don't feel

like practicing resuscitation at lunchtime! I'm going, but watch out: If this heathen uproar continues, I'll have all your visitors barred! Got that?

(Exit Nurse.)

CYRIL: You see, Regina darling, how they treat me here? And to think that heartless woman will be the one to overhear my farewell sigh.

REGINA MORTI: Count on me, my little wolf cub. I'll protect you from that wicked nurse. The minute I knew you were on the verge of death, I made up my mind to abandon everything and stay at your side through the grand finale. I've cancelled all my contracts! I still treasure that little note you sent me the morning after my Tosca at La Scala, look, here it is: "*Regina, ti amo! Regina, ti amo!*" This is the first time I've seen you since then, but I always knew we would find each other again one day. The Bishop of Genoa, who's my cousin, is just waiting for the phone call to fly here and join us.

CYRIL: Darling Regina, I can't marry you. I have AIDS.

REGINA MORTI: What a sublime disease! What apotheosis could be greater than to be brought crashing down under the weight of so many scandalous adventures! What a magnificent end for a true artist! And what an opportunity for a widow! I'll have someone compose me a cantata to sing at your funeral! Mr. Dubonnet, would you by chance have any leftovers there in your ice chest? I need to calm my diaphragm. A chicken? But I don't want to eat a whole chicken! A half will suit me fine.

CYRIL: Hubert, that chicken is for me! You eat the salmon.

REGINA MORTI: Salmon? Pink salmon? There's nothing better for keeping the diaphragm fresh. But I see that you have roast beef too. I didn't realize people were so well treated on welfare. If I'd known, I never would have spent such fortunes at the Ritz every time I descend on Paris. I shall take a suite in your ward.

CYRIL: The hospital's full.

REGINA MORTI: Now, don't be a naughty little wolf cub. Is that the way you greet me after such a long absence? With a family quarrel?

CYRIL: I never sent you that ridiculous note! As soon as you've finished dining I shall thank you for your visit and bid you farewell.

REGINA MORTI: And you don't even want to know how large a dowry I bring?

CYRIL: What do you take me for, you old sow? A gigolo?

REGINA MORTI: You aren't the gigolo, the boys who ruined you are! All your old sets and costumes sold off for nothing!

CYRIL: But what do you think I could do with your money in my condition?

REGINA MORTI: I will build you *il più bel panteon* in the world, in the *cimetario* at Genoa, overlooking the Mediterranean.

CYRIL: Thanks, I already have one at Père Lachaise.

REGINA MORTI: You're not going to compare Père Lachaise to the *cimetario* at Genoa!

CYRIL: Excuse me, Regina dear, but I'm handling this matter, and my answer is "no." My tomb at Père Lachaise is already habitable, all it needs are a few finishing touches.

REGINA MORTI: But he could spend his summers in Italy. *Un panteon sulla baia di Genova, il più bel tramonto al'mondo!*

CYRIL: I hate the bay at Genoa!

HUBERT: As you can see, my dear friend, your proposal doesn't have the least chance of being considered. And I must warn you that it is strictly forbidden to take the dead on vacation trips, even within the boundaries of the Common Market; if for no other reason, think of the vivid fright it would give schoolchildren on holiday.

CYRIL: Hubert, stop this discussion and give her her coat.

REGINA MORTI: Oh, my love! What deep distress your contempt throws me into! I who planned to share peace and happiness with you at the end of a hectic life, I who wished to wear mourning for you like a proud banner of theatrical genius, what a deep abyss I have landed in! Your indifference has hurled me into a hell of shadows!

CYRIL: It's just a case of widow's nerves, madame. Take your coat and run to your psychiatrist.

REGINA MORTI: Sooner than leave you, I choose to put an end to my days here in your presence. Where is the carving knife? Oh, sunlight of my life, look me in the eye one last time! If it is your will that I should cease to exist, then I shall obey you!

(Enter Nurse.)

NURSE: Where do you think you are, madame, on Broadway? Give me that knife, that's dangerous!

CYRIL: You're just in time, Mary Jo. Madame Morti has concluded her visit, you can show her out.

NURSE: All right, out, before I get angry.

REGINA MORTI: *(fainting, in the Reporter's arms) Addio, mondo crudel'!*

CYRIL: Not on my bed!

NURSE: What is wrong with her! You'd think she was choking, she's turning blue! She must have swallowed something! Quick, somebody with long fingers, try and get it out of her throat! What is it?

REPORTER: It's a chicken leg.

CYRIL: She swallowed a whole chicken leg?

HUBERT: Like a python!

CYRIL: Send her to emergency. Quick, before she comes to!

REGINA MORTI: *O profonda notte dell'infortunio!*

(Enter Dr. Backsleider.)

CYRIL: Dear doctor!

DR. BACKSLEIDER: Dear genius, I took the liberty of bringing you these sugared almonds. As of today I've had you under treatment for exactly two years.

CYRIL: What a charming idea to remember the birthday of my AIDS. How thoughtful of you, dear doctor! And how am I getting along?

DR. BACKSLEIDER: How do you feel?

CYRIL: I'm in agony. I'm terrified at the thought that I'll die without ever having played Richard the Third.

DR. BACKSLEIDER: Don't let that bother you, you can put on plays in the hospital, like the Marquis de Sade. I can loan you some mental cases from St. Anne's to help out. And I need hardly add how grateful I would be, dear genius, if I were allowed to play a very small part, even a spear carrier.

CYRIL: I'll think it over, dear doctor. Meanwhile, let me ask you a question: When am I going to get out of here?

DR. BACKSLEIDER: You wouldn't think of leaving us! Medical science, like the show, must go on! You ought to be proud to be the hero of all the successes we've had in post-posing death, here in this shrine of science. Is the real death hovering over you any less meaningful than the black-draped death at the end of the play?

CYRIL: Dear doctor, I'm very grateful that you have such affection for the theater; but, in that case, when am I going to die?

DR. BACKSLEIDER: What is that you're taking?

CYRIL: A liter of suramin, as I do once a week, and a million units of interferon once a month, in addition to my daily dose.

DR. BACKSLEIDER: Good, very good. Mrs. Bongo, give me the patient's chart. No crises these last few days?

CYRIL: Two heart attacks and a coma.

DR. BACKSLEIDER: Good, very good.

NURSE: What a day, doctor! This woman keeled over and she isn't even hospitalized, I haven't got a bed for her.

DR. BACKSLEIDER: Well, you'll work it out, Mrs. Bongo. Hmm. Good, very good. Very good. Very very good. Almost too good.

CYRIL: What do you mean, too good?

DR. BACKSLEIDER: In reality, you ought to be dead.

CYRIL: I ought to be dead?

DR. BACKSLEIDER: You've outlived yourself by at least six months.

CYRIL: Are you sure?

DR. BACKSLEIDER: Mrs. Bongo, get a blood sample from the patient's other arm. We must find the explanation for this excess of health. Otherwise we'll be forced to believe in a miracle.

CYRIL: A miracle! I hope I won't be forced to convert. I haven't the least desire to take a dip in the pool at Lourdes.

DR. BACKSLEIDER: Oh, don't worry, it will only be a miracle of science.

CYRIL: Then would I be cured?

DR. BACKSLEIDER: Not at all, not at all. Didn't I just tell you you ought to be dead?

CYRIL: That's reassuring. But to go back to my first question: In reality, when am I going to die?

DR. BACKSLEIDER: You will never die, dear genius. Your fame will outlive us all.

CYRIL: I'm not talking about my fame, I'm talking about me!

DR. BACKSLEIDER: You will live as long as your AIDS does. It's already two years old, we can discuss the matter again on its next birthday. I'll come by to see you again tomorrow morning, as always.

HUBERT: Wouldn't you like to share our lunch, dear doctor? We always wonder how you can stand the food in the cafeteria.

DR. BACKSLEIDER: Thank you, thank you, it would be a pleasure, but I really don't have the time. I've got a lobotomy in fifteen minutes.

HUBERT: Lobotomy is a treatment for AIDS?

DR. BACKSLEIDER: Oh, no, lobotomy is my hobby. I only do it on Sundays. But what's that I see there? A chicken leg?

HUBERT: Oh, not that one, doctor. This one is a little fresher.

DR. BACKSLEIDER: And a roast beef. I don't believe my eyes! Is that real *foie gras*?

HUBERT: Let me fill up a plate so you can picnic before your operation.

DR. BACKSLEIDER: Well, I don't want to strip your cupboard bare.

HUBERT: No problem, we'll get more of the same from Fauchon. Isn't that right, dear genius?

CYRIL: Absolutely! Take it all, doctor.

DR. BACKSLEIDER: How can I think you?

HUBERT: Nothing is too good for you, dear doctor.

DR. BACKSLEIDER: Mrs. Bongo, help me carry these delicacies. You know where I hide things in the operating room, I'll have a snack when we break.

NURSE: I'm not your maid!

DR. BACKSLEIDER: You know, Mrs. Bongo, since you got married you've become impossible. Now get moving!

NURSE: And what should I do with the opera singer?

DR. BACKSLEIDER: Oh, you'll figure something out.

(Exit the Nurse and Dr. Backsleider.)

CYRIL: Hubert, you know Fauchon's isn't open on Sunday!

HUBERT: We still have the doctor's sugared almonds.

CYRIL: I can't live on sugared almonds alone!

(Nurse comes back in.)

NURSE: It's noon! Would you like your welfare patient's lunch?

CYRIL: What is it?

NURSE: Grated carrots and boiled hamburger with noodles. And today you can have two desserts because it's Sunday: strawberry yogurt and a little cube of cheese.

CYRIL: That's revolting.

HUBERT: It must be very healthy, it doesn't have any odor at all.

CYRIL: In that case, you eat it and I'll take the sugared almonds.

NURSE: You two deal with it!

(Nurse hurries out again.)

REPORTER: I could go get you something to eat from outside the hospital, sir.

CYRIL: Oh, are you still here? Don't you ever say anything?

REPORTER: I haven't had a chance, sir.

CYRIL: And that's all you have to say? I warn you, if you publish one word of what you've seen and heard here today, I'll come back from the grave and haunt you.

REPORTER: I'll be careful, sir.

CYRIL: Can't you call me "dear genius" like everyone else?

REPORTER: I'm sorry, dear genius, I'm just not used to it.

CYRIL: What's wrong? Do I intimidate you? Haven't you ever met a sublimely mad queen in your dreary life?

HUBERT: Dear genius, you really should break this bad habit of abusing journalists. Not a moment ago you were comparing him to a Botticelli.

CYRIL: Me, compare this monster to a Botticelli? No! My poor young friend, you belong to a generation of men without charm. Hubert, show him the photo of me at his age.

HUBERT: Which one?

CYRIL: Show him the one of me playing Hamlet.

HUBERT: You've played Hamlet at every age.

CYRIL: Then it doesn't matter which.

HUBERT: I can't find any of Hamlet. Here's one where you're dressed as a butler. You must have been understudying Pierre Fresnay, you're with Yvonne Printemps.

CYRIL: Well, cut out Printemps and just give him the photo of me. No, don't lean down to look at the photo, but hold it a little higher, so it's right by your face. Hubert, my makeup mirror, give it to him. No, take it in the other hand, raise your eyebrows...a little more...a little more...now thrust your chin out, the way mine is in the photo.... That's it; now you have a stage star's profile. You would make an interesting actor if I had the time to give you a few lessons.

REPORTER: But I might not have the talent, dear genius.

CYRIL: I only said that to please you anyway, in reality you have the profile of a sack of potatoes. You're a spineless peeping Tom like all journalists. There, in three phrases I've turned you into a joke. You can remove yourself now, this interview is over.

(Nurse comes in.)

NURSE: Another present from your sister-in-law!

HUBERT: An ice-cream cake from Bertillon's!

NURSE: I've never seen one this big! Your sister-in-law has real class. Since it's your birthday, the doctor told me to take you off this earlier. *(She unhooks the i.v.)* There! Now you'll be able to move around and come closer to your ice-cream cake.

CYRIL: Did the doctor see this come in?

NURSE: The cake? He even dipped his finger in it.

CYRIL: Hubert, we've got to find a way to smuggle supplies in secretly.

DR. BACKSLEIDER: *(entering)* There you are, dear genius, free of your ball and chain.

CYRIL: Dear doctor, how can I thank you?

DR. BACKSLEIDER: How can I thank you for that splendid roast beef? So tender—like butter. But I see that you're about to have dessert, too bad I won't have time to join you. My operation should have been in full swing by now, but my patient's disappeared into thin air. I can't imagine where she's gone.

CYRIL: Hubert, bring the dessert spoons.

DR. BACKSLEIDER: A soup spoon will do fine for me, thanks. Mmmm! Strawberry sherbet! It brings back the aroma of my childhood at Deauville. My first tricycle, ... the boards on the promenade going creak, creak ... and the little girl next door, what was her name? ... She was so pretty with her little pigtails on her little tricycle. ... Lili, her name was Lili. ... Mmmmm .... What a great artist Bertillon is!

NURSE: You know what Sundays are like at the incoming desk, doctor. They probably shipped your patient over to maternity.

DR. BACKSLEIDER: That would amaze me, since I saw her in the hallway, already anesthetized, at least an hour ago.

NURSE: Are you sure? They came by this morning to pick up the dead for the week, they might have taken her along by mistake.

DR. BACKSLEIDER: You deal with it, Mrs. Bongo. Wherever my patient is, I want her on the operating table immediately! That's an order.

NURSE: But the morgue's closed on Sunday afternoons.

DR. BACKSLEIDER: That's your problem, Mrs. Bongo. Go find the key to the morgue.

CYRIL: You've lost your patient, doctor, and meantime I've found one. What am I going to do with this hysterical woman who insists on fainting on my bed? I don't propose to keep her here indefinitely.

DR. BACKSLEIDER: A hysteric? But this is my patient! How did she end up here? Dear genius, it was unkind of you to lure my patient into your bed.

CYRIL: Lure her into my bed? I've been trying to get rid of her for over an hour!

DR. BACKSLEIDER: Mrs. Bongo, did you hear this?

NURSE: The orderlies are on their lunch break.

DR. BACKSLEIDER: So much the worse. We'll carry her like this. Give me a hand, young man.

REGINA MORTI: *(reviving slightly)* I feel transported to Nirvana.... O my noble love, wait for me,...after my lobotomy I will love you all the better....

CYRIL: Make sure you clean out the skull thoroughly, dear doctor!

(Nurse, Dr. Backsleider, and Reporter go out, carrying the prostrate Regina Morti.)

Well, Hubert, have I done it?

HUBERT: Botticelli? Dear genius, he's at your feet.

CYRIL: My old technique still works. A little seduction, a little slap. All I have to do now is drive him till he's insane with love. Tonight I'll play to break the bank! Do I still have my deerskin vest with the fringe? And my Indian silk tie from Cerruti?

HUBERT: All your street clothes are at home.

CYRIL: What? You mean I have nothing to wear when I get out of here?

HUBERT: Nothing, dear genius.

CYRIL: Hubert, I don't think I ever noticed before that you're almost my height and build.

HUBERT: That would amaze me.

CYRIL: Your outfit is very unfashionable, but it'll have to do.

HUBERT: You want my clothes? And what about me?

CYRIL: You can spend the night in my bed. One of us has to stay here or the night nurse will think something's wrong.

HUBERT: And if they try to give me an i.v.?

CYRIL: Then they'll give you an i.v. Don't tell me you're afraid of a little needle.

HUBERT: The mere idea of it gives me chills.

CYRIL: I thought you were a loyal friend, Hubert.

HUBERT: Dear genius, you know I'd do anything for you, but . . . .

CYRIL: All right, off with your pants! Put on these pajama bottoms.

HUBERT: But you'll see my legs!

CYRIL: I may as well see your legs at least once in my life.

HUBERT: I'm dying of shame!

CYRIL: Don't worry, they're exactly what I imagined they'd look like.

(Nurse and Reporter come back.)

NURSE: Mr. Hubert, put your clothes back on! You know that you're absolutely forbidden to do that! You could give us all a heart attack! This time I'll pretend I didn't see anything, but make sure there isn't a next time.

HUBERT: Thank you, dear Mary Jo! You've rescued me from torture.

NURSE: My poor Mr. Hubert, at your age.

REPORTER: I managed to save the *foie gras*, dear genius. It only has a few bite marks on it.

CYRIL: You are a true bloodhound, my boy. Hubert, what time did you plan to lay the table?

NURSE: This'll be the first time I've ever tasted *foie gras*, although I was born in the town of Foix, and my mother was originally from the town of Grasse. Isn't that incredible?

CYRIL: I don't recall anyone's inviting you. Go eat in the cafeteria as you do every afternoon.

NURSE: But today's your birthday.

CYRIL: Well, just one slice. You can't stretch *foie gras*.

NURSE: *(tasting it)* Ugh! It's not fit for dogs. Oh, is that disgusting!

HUBERT: Botticelli, a slice? Mary Jo, a glass of white wine?

NURSE: Thanks, to wash down that garbage. You're not going to believe me, but—that opium? I smoked it. And it hasn't had the least effect on me. *(to Reporter)* You're not bad, you know. You look like my husband, only in white.

CYRIL: Mary Jo, you're stoned! I specifically told you not to smoke that till you were at home!

DR. BACKSLEIDER: *(off)* Mrs. Bongo, anesthesia!

REGINA MORTI: *(off) O, amore! Dal profondo abisso dell'incoscienza penso a te!*

NURSE: Say, when you smoke opium are you supposed to see green people?

CYRIL: You see green people because you have no more imagination than a caterpillar! If that's all you get, it's not worth the trouble of smoking opium!

DR. BACKSLEIDER: *(off)* Mrs. Bongo, scalpel! Mrs. Bongo, corkscrew!

NURSE: So much the better if I'm a caterpillar. I love seeing the world in green. *(She runs out.)*

CYRIL: Alone at last! Hubert, put on a little light music and close the blinds.

HUBERT: Would a little Viennese waltz suit you?

CYRIL: Put on the Beatles. I'm a fan of the 'sixties.

HUBERT: I thought you despised them.

CYRIL: Dear friend, if you want to visit your cousin in Versailles today, it's really time for you to get going.

HUBERT: My cousin in Versailles? She's dead.

CYRIL: Well, aside from me, there must be one person still living among your acquaintances.

HUBERT: No one, dear genius.

CYRIL: Well, then go to Père Lachaise and inspect the work on my tomb. You don't have to spend the whole day glued to my side.

HUBERT: I'm going to take a nap in your bathtub. Wake me in time for the football game. *(He goes out.)*

CYRIL: Don't be afraid, I don't want to rape you, just ask you a few questions. Let me do the interviewing for a change, and you give the answers. How old are you?

REPORTER: Thirty, dear genius.

CYRIL: You can drop the "dear genius." Your sex? You seem to hesitate. Which one did they put on your birth certificate?

REPORTER: Masculine.

CYRIL: You see how easy it is? Married?

REPORTER: No, dear genius.

CYRIL: Are you a Don Juan?

REPORTER: No. Not at all.

CYRIL: You are truly a boring specimen. Haven't you ever had a dream of glory? Not necessarily on the stage, but in life, in the pages of your newspaper, or even in your own living room? Didn't you ever, as a child, help blind people across the street so your followers would admire you?

REPORTER: I don't think anything like that ever happened to me. It seems I was also a boring child, sir.

CYRIL: But as a teenager, you must have had dreams of being a great writer before you went into journalism. Have you ever written anything else? Not even a poem?

REPORTER: I'm afraid not.

CYRIL: Didn't anything interesting ever happen to you, at least once in your life? Even a coincidence. You didn't ever win any kind of prize or award? Do you play any sport?

REPORTER: Yes, tennis.

CYRIL: It's enough to make you tear your hair. This interview is cancelled, you don't deserve a column in my paper.

REPORTER: I'm terribly sorry to have misled you, sir.

CYRIL: You're not the first. Would you care for a puff of my water pipe? It belonged to Cocteau, he gave it to me when he stopped smoking. And I'm still alive! I'm not afraid to die, but to live on always wedged in among my memories! If that's what eternity is, I've been looking for the exit a long time. Isn't my water pipe sublime?

REPORTER: Sublime, sir.

CYRIL: I'll leave it to you in my will, that way you can remember me on those lonely nights.

REPORTER: Thank you very much, sir.

CYRIL: I fooled myself into thinking I could rediscover my own youth in you, but nothing about you tempts me. Maybe thirty years ago I would have found you attractive, but then again I'm not really sure of that, and besides thirty years ago you would have been just a babe in arms. Read back to me what I just said. What, don't you take notes?

REPORTER: Oh, no, sir. I trust my memory.

CYRIL: If your memory is as stupid as you are, you won't write anything but stupidities. Look, take this notebook from the welfare office and my Mark Cross pen. How many pages do you propose to darken? I want to measure out my effects.

REPORTER: How many pages would you like?

CYRIL: The number of pages isn't important, as long as I get my picture on the cover. Hubert, what happened to that photo of me as Hamlet?

HUBERT: *(off)* Help! Help!

(Reporter goes out.)

CYRIL: Poor Hubert! Nightmares even in his afternoon nap!

(Reporter returns, helping in Hubert.)

HUBERT: Aiee! There was a bee in the bathtub!

CYRIL: We'd better get the stinger out fast, don't forget you're diabetic.

HUBERT: I sat on it.

CYRIL: Mary Jo! She's never here when you need her.

REPORTER: Let me help you, sir.

HUBERT: Aiee!

REPORTER: It's all right, the stinger didn't go into the flesh. Here it is.

HUBERT: Thank you, my dear friend. You've saved my life.

NURSE: *(entering)* Mr. Hubert! Not again! I would never have thought it of you! Shame on you!

REPORTER: There are bees in the room.

NURSE: Bees? Aiee!

CYRIL: They must have been attracted by the ice cream. It's crawling with them! Mary Jo, get that thing out of here!

NURSE: Where should I put it?

CYRIL: Throw it near their hive.

NURSE: I'm scared!

CYRIL: Don't yell, you'll frighten them....Walk slowly towards the door....They're drunk on wild strawberries....

. *(The Nurse goes out with the ice-cream cake.)*

REGINA MORTI: *(off) Mi sento ritornare alla vita, amore mio!*

(Regina Morti comes in, escorted by the Doctor.)

DR. BACKSLEIDER: Dear genius, permit me to dedicate to you a worldwide scientific first. I have just grafted in my own invention—an artificial brain!

REGINA MORTI: Oh, my love! My silicon-cell brain thinks only of your happiness. As proof of my loyalty I give you this, my former brain, in which I have left all my memories of my former lovers. In this wad of gray matter I offer you my entire past!

CYRIL: Give your past to the cat! And stay back, you're frightening me! *(He hides behind the Reporter.)* Doctor, do something!

DR. BACKSLEIDER: Her behavior is perfectly normal. She's only trying to demonstrate her affection for you.

REGINA MORTI: *Questo cervello col quale sono nata é per te, amore mio! Devi mangiarlo per provare la tua passione! Tieni, mangialo tutto! Quando tu sarai morto io mangerò il tuo cuore!*

(She throws the brain at Cyril, in the process landing it on the Reporter, who is protecting him. Reporter goes out, wiping himself off.)

DR. BACKSLEIDER: More inspired than ever! A true theatrical genius!

NURSE: *(running in, in a panic, with the ice cream)* Help! Help! Bees!

(She falls, ice cream and all, on top of the Doctor.)

CYRIL: Bravo, Mary Jo!

HUBERT: A real theatrical *coup*!

NURSE: Oh, doctor! Forgive me! What have I done!

DR. BACKSLEIDER: Try and save some of it with a spoon, Mrs. Bongo!

REGINA MORTI: *E adesso, amore mio, che cosa devo fare? Sono la tua schiava!*

CYRIL: Talk to the doctor! It's his brain you're wearing! Let him tell you what to do!

REGINA MORTI: *Mio caro professore, che cosa devo fare?*

DR. BACKSLEIDER: I've already explained to you that your brain works all by itself, it doesn't need to be told what to do. You are an independent woman!

REGINA MORTI: *Oh nobile vestare, che cosa devo fare?*

NURSE: When you sing, I don't understand what you're saying. If you want something, ask like everybody else.

REGINA MORTI: *Caro signor Dubonet!* Good, handsome Signor Dubonnet! Fate, after hurling me from master to master, has designated me to be your slave! *Voglio un' ordine! Che cosa devo fare?*

HUBERT: My dear Regina, I order you to shut up.

DR. BACKSLEIDER: Oh, no, you mustn't tell her that! She has to keep singing all the time, or her brain will have a breakdown. *Cara diva,* sing us something sweet on the ear, like a lullaby. Well, you see, now she no longer wants to open her mouth. But don't worry, it's just a little post-op shock.

CYRIL: We can do very well without her voice. Her presence takes up enough stage space. Hubert, put her in a corner.

HUBERT: And I, dear doctor, when will I be able to sit down again?

DR. BACKSLEIDER: We'll know in a week.

NURSE: And me? Who's going to take care of me? You take care of everyone in the world except for me! Even though you know I've been smoking opium and I need you!

DR. BACKSLEIDER: Mrs. Bongo, please, no public scenes!

NURSE: Let the whole world know who you are, you cheat! Ever since I got married, you've stopped inviting me up to your flat. You don't want me anymore because I married a black man. Racist!

DR. BACKSLEIDER: Mrs. Bongo!

CYRIL: Bravo, Mary Jo!

HUBERT: What dramatic temperament!

NURSE: I'm going to send your wife an anonymous letter! I'm going to tell her how you made love with me on your tricycle!

CYRIL: A real acrobatic feat!

DR. BACKSLEIDER: However, I did tell you, Mary Jo, that I had no desire to share you with another man! I have my masculine pride to think of! But I swear to you, no other woman has been on that tricycle since.

NURSE: Liar! I saw you go in there with the maid!

DR. BACKSLEIDER: I didn't have her on the tricycle, but on a broomstick.

CYRIL: On a broomstick? How divine!

HUBERT: Like the witches in Shakespeare!

NURSE: On a broomstick? You scum! I never would have dreamed you were capable of it!

CYRIL: More anger! Show your temperament!

DR. BACKSLEIDER: Are you going to stop it, bitch? *(He slaps Nurse.)*

HUBERT: A slap! What realism!

DR. BACKSLEIDER: Jo-jo, are you crying? Did I hurt you?

NURSE: I love you, Jean-Pierre! I forgive you everything!

CYRIL: A happy end, what a letdown!

DR. BACKSLEIDER: Want to ride my tricycle?

NURSE: Don't be crazy, we're on duty. . . .

DR. BACKSLEIDER: Come on, let's go in the operating room.

CYRIL: Out, lewd creatures!

HUBERT: You can never depend on such mediocre actors!

(Dr. Backsleider and Nurse go out.)

CYRIL: What's happened to Botticelli?

HUBERT: He must have gone for a walk in the garden.

CYRIL: And if he doesn't come back?

HUBERT: He'll come back, I'm sure of it.

REGINA MORTI: Send them away from our house! Let the living go with the living! Our kingdom is unaware of them! Oh, my love, when will we consummate our marriage?

CYRIL: Are you insane? We're not married!

REGINA MORTI: We are in the kingdom of the dead.

CYRIL: You may be dead, but I'm not.

REGINA MORTI: *Ti voglio adesso! Andiamo subito consommare il nostro amore sul' letto!*

HUBERT: But Regina, you've just recovered from a very delicate operation!

REGINA MORTI: If you don't want me alive, then I'll kill you so I can have you in death. Our love will only be the more exalting for it. Where is the carving knife?

CYRIL: Not again!

HUBERT: Dearest Regina, you have every right to a consummation, but in my opinion you aren't dressed for the occasion. Your undergarments aren't suited to it. To enchant a man's heart, you really must have more seductive underthings. Do you know what I mean? Later today I'll take you around to all the boutiques in Pigalle, and then tomorrow you can consummate your marriage with no problem at all.

REGINA MORTI: *Andiamo subito a Pigalle, bello e buono signor Dubonnet!*

CYRIL: That's it, take her to Pigalle, you can ditch her there.

HUBERT: Not right now, dear Regina.

REGINA MORTI: *Subito! Voglio andare a Pigalle comprare le mutande sexy!*

HUBERT: I said, later!

CYRIL: Strike while the iron's hot, Hubert, it just means getting rid of her that much sooner!

REGINA MORTI: *Subito, subito!*

HUBERT: You're strangling me!

REGINA MORTI: *Subito, subito, la morte subito!*

(Reporter, coming back in, seizes Regina Morti and drags her off Hubert, who grabs the lamp and hits her over the head with it.)

REGINA MORTI: Do—re—mi—fa—fa....

(The Reporter drags Regina Morti to the bed.)

CYRIL: Botticelli! You've rescued us from strangulation! You've saved our lives! Where've you been, my angel?

REPORTER: Sir, I was putting money in my parking meter.

CYRIL: Hubert, stay near her with your lamp. I don't want to die murdered by a woman. I've spent my whole life running away from women.

HUBERT: I can testify to that, a real nightmare of a life.

CYRIL: Every time I went offstage, they'd be waiting in the wings, whole clusters of them! Sometimes they'd climb onstage through the prompter's box. I'd have to have my dressing room cleared by the emergency squad. How many times have I found them hiding behind the wardrobe rack? Or under my couch?

HUBERT: In Manaos, they had to call out the army to get him out of the theater.

CYRIL: And the campier I was onstage, the more they adored me.

HUBERT: A curse, a real curse!

CYRIL: My dear Hubert, you got me out of so many dangerous situations.

HUBERT: Don't even mention it, we must have at least a dozen suicides on our conscience!

CYRIL: But you aren't saying anything? Look at me. Do I frighten you?

REPORTER: No, sir.

CYRIL: This dreadful hospital atmosphere, where everything reminds you of death! That horrible woman obsessed with death! Me here waiting for it.... Don't you see that Death herself is here, in this room?

REPORTER: No, sir.

CYRIL: She's come looking for me, I can feel her standing right behind me.

HUBERT: No doubt she's there, but who is she looking for? It might not be you at all.

DR. BACKSLEIDER: *(entering)* Dear genius, gentlemen, you are no doubt surprised to see me in this tropical outfit. I am leaving for Africa to continue the struggle against AIDS down there. It's the only thing left for me to do; otherwise I'll go insane.

CYRIL: Leaving for Africa? But what about your patients?

DR. BACKSLEIDER: Doctors can be replaced almost as easily as patients.

CYRIL: But what about me, dear doctor?

DR. BACKSLEIDER: Don't try to sway my feelings, I am inflexible. My situation here, pulled back and forth between my legal wife and Mrs. Bongo, has become insupportable. Do you want me to tell you the truth about the tricycle? I've always been revolted by the thing. In Africa, at least, they've never heard of tricycles.

CYRIL: Give me a minute to think about this, doctor. Don't do anything so drastic on a whim. You're a doctor, consult your colleagues before you make a decision.

DR. BACKSLEIDER: They're the ones urging me to resign my chair on the faculty. My treatments strike them as more and more dubious. My medicine is too humane for the icy world of laboratories. In Africa I'll be able to give my emotional impulses free rein, there'll be no lack of human material there. You can explain all this to Mrs. Bongo, I've sent her to clean up the surgical storeroom, to get rid of her for a few minutes. I'm terrified at the prospect of a farewell scene with her. As for you, if you want my parting advice, think about herbal medicine. You're going to die in any case, and at worst a cup of chicory is more pleasant than an i.v.

CYRIL: A cup of chicory! But I already have my opium!

DR. BACKSLEIDER: Use both. Goodbye, dear genius. Perhaps we will find each other again, somewhere outside this world of sound and fury signifying nothing, perhaps somewhere in another galaxy. You were always my favorite patient.

CYRIL: Dear doctor, I don't know what to say.

DR. BACKSLEIDER: Forgive this momentary distress, I don't usually cry in public.

CYRIL: Hubert, your handkerchief.

DR. BACKSLEIDER: Thank you. It's the sadness after intercourse. The ancient Romans knew all about it.

HUBERT: True, Mrs. Bongo is rather like a Roman matron.

DR. BACKSLEIDER: How can I express my gratitude to you at this melancholy moment?

CYRIL: It will pass. Everyone knows about sadness after intercourse. That's why smoking was invented.

HUBERT: Don't be so cheerful. Sadness after intercourse can last a lifetime. Take me, for example. One night of intercourse and then a half-century of sadness. But I won't tell you who my partner was on that one night, you'd laugh.

CYRIL: I always knew; it was your nanny.

DR. BACKSLEIDER: What, you too?

HUBERT: There's a femme fatale in every man's life, and so often it's your nanny.

(Cyril, who has been smoking his water pipe, offers it to Dr. Backsleider.)

DR. BACKSLEIDER: Is this opium? But what will my wife say if I come home high?

CYRIL: You can tell her it's your birthday.

DR. BACKSLEIDER: All through my childhood, my family spent the holidays in a rented villa at Deauville. My nanny was big and blonde; her name was Yvonne. I begged and pleaded for my parents to buy me a tricycle, but she was against it. She liked keeping me in the stroller where she could tie me down whenever she pleased. And my parents only listened to her, even though I was already six years old. One day, I made up my mind to steal my little neighbor Lili's tricycle, thinking nanny was asleep under a tree. Bad mistake! I found myself on an insane race down the planks of the promenade, with nanny in hot pursuit. And then, suddenly, kaboom! A broken nose, a split lip, my baby teeth scattered across the planking, I was bleeding all over the sand when nanny caught up with me, pulled my pants down and whipped my behind right there, in public! But the worst was that my parents, finding the punishment insufficient for my crime, made me spend the night hung from the clothesline by my ears. Look! Ever since then, my ears have stuck out.

CYRIL: That's monstrous!

DR. BACKSLEIDER: And I never did get a tricycle of my own.

HUBERT: My poor doctor, nannies are the most savage race of beings on earth!

DR. BACKSLEIDER: Fortunately, I believe they're dying out.

HUBERT: At last a true victory for mankind!

DR. BACKSLEIDER: But there will always be parents, my dear Mr. Dubonnet.

HUBERT: Alas, alas!

REGINA MORTI: *(coming to)* Dubo—dubon—Dubonnet!

CYRIL: Quick, doctor, do something! She's already tried to strangle Hubert!

REGINA MORTI: Du bo—du bon—Dubonnet! *Voglio il mio aperitivo preferito!*

DR. BACKSLEIDER: But what are you saying? Her behavior is completely normal, it's afternoon and she wants her aperitif. *Cara diva, come ci sentiamo?*

CYRIL: Dear Botticelli, pour Madame Morti a Dubonnet, would you? And look, just slip this pill in her glass.

REGINA MORTI: Where am I performing tonight? Is this my dressing room? And who are all of you?

DR. BACKSLEIDER: We're your friends, *cara diva.*

HUBERT: The most passionate admirers of your talent.

REPORTER: Your aperitif, *cara diva.*

DR. BACKSLEIDER: You have morally slapped me, dear genius. If that's the way you feel, we are headed for Africa for good.

REGINA MORTI: Africa? How much is my fee?

NURSE: *(Enters pointing a revolver.)* Hands up! I knew you were planning to run off to Africa with that opera singer! Bastard! I saw you rape her on the operating table!

DR. BACKSLEIDER: Mrs. Bongo, you are making a severe error of judgment. This lady is my work, my creation. I can't leave her in the hands of whoever comes along. The real reasons for my departure for Africa are entirely humanitarian.

NURSE: So, you're giving me the heave-ho, you scum?

DR. BACKSLEIDER: I might reconsider my position, but only in a humanitarian context. I offer you the post of surgical orderly in Africa, on condition that you occupy yourself exclusively with the care of our *cara diva*. You will be to some extent my right hand, Mrs. Bongo, but our personal relations will cease to exist at the border. It's a formal requirement, and you will have to sign a paper to that effect.

NURSE: And you think that a modern woman like me, who dared to marry a black man, would let herself be turned into a slave to an old crackpot like her? And in Africa at that?

REGINA MORTI: *Chi è questa? Una cantatrice rivale? Signorina, un po' di rispetto! Cui la diva sono io!*

NURSE: You see how she treats me?

DR. BACKSLEIDER: She treats you as a rival opera singer. That's already pretty good for an ordinary nurse.

NURSE: An ordinary nurse? Is that what you thought I was when you made me get on your tricycle? That I was just an ordinary nurse?

DR. BACKSLEIDER: Mrs. Bongo, I am sick of your jealous tantrums. You are fired! Leave your smock in the cloak-room and go home!

NURSE: And you think it's going to be that easy? Here's what I think of your opera singer!

(She fires several shots, one of which hits Regina Morti. Reporter disarms her.)

DR. BACKSLEIDER: *Cara diva!*

REGINA MORTI: *Ancora una volta mi ritrovo dell'altra parte del si-
pario della morte!* Goodbye, world of illusions that we call life!
Addio, notevole signori, ci rivediammo presto!

DR. BACKSLEIDER: You've destroyed my masterpiece!

NURSE: That's right! Now go and graft an artificial heart
onto your mechanical doll and take her to Africa! You can
sell her by the pound!

HUBERT: Calm down, dear friend, have a Dubonnet. It's the
preferred drink of murderesses everywhere.

REPORTER: *(to Cyril)* Sir, are you all right? Sir! He's
wounded!

DR. BACKSLEIDER: Dear genius! A bullet grazed his neck!
Can you hear me?

CYRIL: This little scratch is a message from Fate. Could I
have a kKeenex, please? Thank you. Mary Jo, let this be
the last time you ever smoke opium. Hubert, I am preparing to die at 5 P.M. In the hatbox under my bed you will
find the wig I wore as Hamlet. The costume is in the closet.
You will make sure that my collar is starched and my shoes
polished.

DR. BACKSLEIDER: Not tonight, dear genius! I couldn't bear
to lose both of my finest creations on the same day!

CYRIL: Human material is easily replaced, dear doctor.
Dream of Africa!

DR. BACKSLEIDER: But I will never find another actor of your
greatness. Dear genius, deign to allow me one sole day of
your life! Don't die tonight! Wait till tomorrow at least!

CYRIL: One day is an eternity and you aren't worth that

much time. Invariably, when I get to the last scene, I can't wait for the show to end. I want to get rid of my character as fast as possible. When the curtain comes down, there's a moment, before you get back to your dressing room, when you aren't anyone. It's an unbelievable pleasure. I'm going to try and slip into the hereafter through one of those black holes. Hubert! My makeup mirror and a tube of white base.

HUBERT: Clown white or dead white?

CYRIL: Dead white! You don't want me to look like a clown in your tomb, do you?

HUBERT: Eye shadow?

CYRIL: Lilac, always lilac.

HUBERT: A stroke of eyeliner?

CYRIL: You can take care of these details later. And you'll do my nails every morning, after my bath. By the way, is there a bathtub in your tomb?

HUBERT: Even better, dear genius, a sauna!

CYRIL: Hubert, I've never complimented you enough on your good taste.

HUBERT: You flatter me. But you haven't seen the best part yet: the TV room; it's encircled by lapis lazuli columns, and the chairs are covered in giraffe skin.

CYRIL: I don't think I'll have much occasion to watch.

HUBERT: It's for my breaks. I find I love television more and more.

CYRIL: You're planning to forget me.

HUBERT: What do you want, I'm getting old.

CYRIL: Take this Kleenex. I've scribbled a few last words on it. My dear Hubert, you are the only person in the world to whom I owe an apology.

HUBERT: An apology? To me?

CYRIL: One night in spring, the year has escaped my memory, I dishonored your family in the person of your sister Adeline. Our friendship has blossomed on the ruins of that scandal, but I know how much it cost you to maintain that friendship.

HUBERT: What trivia! In any case, you had dishonored me long before you dishonored my family. As for my sister Adeline, don't be upset, but I dishonored her long before you did.

CYRIL: Hubert, you're diabolical.

HUBERT: I may have been when I was fifteen. But my demon has left me.

NURSE: Let them send me off right now! I want to be judged and condemned to death! And I'll write my memoirs! Because I know, believe me, I know what death is. I've seen hundreds drop off before my eyes, and I've given one or two a helpful push into the grave! I unhooked them or I shot them up with morphine so I could be like her, like Death! Death and I are sisters!

(Dr. Backsleider slaps Nurse.)

DR. BACKSLEIDER: Mrs. Bongo, who do you think you are? A Jean Genet heroine? The welfare system asks you to do your dirty job, not tell your life story. They're ringing in every room! Get to your station! I want temperatures for the whole ward immediately!

REPORTER: Here.

NURSE: What's that?

REPORTER: The revolver. I unloaded it.

NURSE: Thanks. I have to return it to my sister-in-law.

DR. BACKSLEIDER: And look what you've done to us with our *cara diva*. I can see I'll be forced to reopen the skull to get back the prosthetic brain! And it'll be a double blessing if it doesn't have one of your bullets in it!

REGINA MORTI: *Grazie, notevole signori. E bebbiamo al' trionfo de stassera!* By the way, what time do I go on? Have I already signed my contract? How much is my fee? Who's singing opposite me? But I know you! You're the dresser from La Fenice! Are you the one who's dressed me up in these bandages? Is my character supposed to have a head wound? This must be a modern opera! Who is the composer? And are you the conductor? And you, who are you? Ah, it's you! It's you! I knew that sooner or later our paths would cross again, my dear actor! You seduced me and abandoned me long ago when I was a little street singer. Your contempt has blighted my whole career. I swore I would murder you if I ever found you again! I've waited for decades, but the moment for my dark revenge has at last arrived! Where is the carving knife?

CYRIL: What an obsession!

DR. BACKSLEIDER: My dear diva, you can't kill this gentleman before you go onstage, don't forget you're singing tonight.

REGINA MORTI: Who are you to tell me what to do!

DR. BACKSLEIDER: Your conductor, *cara diva*.

REGINA MORTI: Oh, *caro maestro*, you are right. I have all eternity to savor my revenge. Tie him up and keep him for me in my dressing room. I will cut him into little bits and dine on him after the performance.

CYRIL: Kindly stop playing this awful melodrama in my presence!

DR. BACKSLEIDER: It's you, dear genius, you theatricalize everything you touch. We are all inspired by your theatricality!

CYRIL: That revolts me! Get this woman off my back before she commits a crime! And you go with her! Weren't you about to catch a plane for Africa? Well, take her with you. Make her sing Wagner to the crowds of African AIDS patients.

NURSE: Goodbye, dear genius! I'm leaving welfare hospital work and going home, to take care of my husband and make a lot of babies. I can see my career isn't going anywhere in this dump. Better to drop the whole thing. I will always be an ordinary person, but I promise you that I'm going to make all my kids grow up to be actors like you, so they can all be celebrities.

CYRIL: If you really want celebrities, make them all doctors.

NURSE: That's beyond my income level. Goodbye, Mr. Hubert. I'll come visit you at your tomb on Sundays, with my kids.

HUBERT: You'll all be welcome, dear Mary Jo.

NURSE: Goodbye, Mr. Reporter. Give him a nice article in your magazine; he deserves it. Believe me, he was an exceptional man, even if he was awfully demanding. It took me a year to figure out the difference between all his bottles of cologne. And he had slippers in every color, one pair for each day of the week. And if I got the wrong color by mistake, it was a major scandal, I can tell you. But he was a good and generous man, he left me all his jewelry and his dressing gowns.

CYRIL: Do us one last service, Mary Jo. Take my water pipe. Soak the opium pellet in the liquid from this little vial, and then relight it.

NURSE: What is it?

CYRIL: An Aztec poison.

NURSE: You just can't do anything the normal way, can you, not even this!

REPORTER: Should I stay, sir?

CYRIL: Of course, you must stay. I'm absolutely counting on you. You are the only newcomer in the cast of this comedy of death, and our last audience. Hubert, you will pay a condolence call on my sister-in-law, you know how concerned she is with form, but I particularly do not want her seated in the first row at my funeral. Set up a more theatrical light for me here, lower the curtains and mask that lamp over the dresser. Has that grande dame's heart stopped beating, dear doctor?

DR. BACKSLEIDER: Her heart no longer beats, and my new brain may as well be sold for scrap. But I wouldn't make a definite diagnosis, dear genius. I must tell you, I'm more and more inclined to believe in miracles.

CYRIL: Hubert, you can see what I'm thinking, can't you?

HUBERT: Of course, there's plenty of room for her in the tomb. We have a soundproofed vault which we can use as her suite.

CYRIL: I owed it to women to make some gesture to them before I died. She is certainly the last female companion I would have chosen, but she is the one Fate picked out for me.

HUBERT: I agree. It's never too late to make amends honorably, and it always makes a handsome final gesture.

CYRIL: It only remains for me to thank you, dear doctor, for the gift of this posthumous fiancée. It's the most original birthday present I've ever received.

DR. BACKSLEIDER: Dear genius, you overwhelm me!

NURSE: You truly are amazing, dear genius!

DR. BACKSLEIDER: My two masterpieces on display side by side at Père Lachaise! You will be the Abelard and Heloise of the twentieth century! I will head a foundation named for you! Thanks to you I will get the grants to build my clinic in the African jungle. You are my benefactor!

CYRIL: Use my name any way you like. It's only a stage name anyhow. Botticelli, I want you to promise me something.

REPORTER: Yes, sir?

CYRIL: Get a new line of work! You are the biggest nothing of any journalist I've ever met! You have yet to ask me a single question!

REPORTER: I don't know what to say, sir.

CYRIL: This is your last chance.

REPORTER: I don't have any questions to ask you.

CYRIL: Are you afraid of death?

REPORTER: Yes, sir.

HUBERT: You are a real shit, Cyril. And after the handsome gesture you just made! You know the way the audience last sees a character is what decides how beautiful the show is.

CYRIL: I made a big mistake in life. I should have hired you as my director.

HUBERT: I always have been your director, really.

CYRIL: Is the makeup all right?

HUBERT: Perfect, dear genius.

CYRIL: But what the hell have you done with that picture of me as Hamlet?

HUBERT: You never played Hamlet.

CYRIL: What are you saying?

HUBERT: You're daydreaming, Cyril. Tonight is the night you play Hamlet for the first time. Get ready for your entrance.

CYRIL: My entrance? I'm in the process of making my exit!

HUBERT: That's life in the theater. When you're finished, you just start all over again. Here's your wig, Cyril.

CYRIL: But I haven't played Hamlet for centuries! I don't remember a word of it....

HUBERT: It doesn't matter which role you play; they're all important.

CYRIL: True, there are no small parts. We can play everything except our own life. That's the one thing we can't do.

HUBERT: You can play your own life anytime.

CYRIL: I don't know what scene I'm in, cue me.

HUBERT: Sleep in peace, angel of my youth.

CYRIL: But that's not Shakespeare! *(He dies.)*

HUBERT: The final curtain has fallen.

DR. BACKSLEIDER: Dear genius, what a sublime ending!

NURSE: My God, what an actor! When you see that, you feel like nothing next to it.

HUBERT: Are you all right, young man?

REPORTER: Yes, sir.

DR. BACKSLEIDER: Good, very good. Very good. In a sense, everything has been put back in order.

NURSE: Go home, Mr. Hubert; you need rest. I'll take care of him, and deliver him to you all beautiful tomorrow morning.

DR. BACKSLEIDER: Get my motorcycle out of the garage, Mrs. Bongo. I'll spend the night in Deauville. And cancel all my appointments for tomorrow!

NURSE: Yes, doctor.

DR. BACKSLEIDER: I'll take my leave of you, dear friend. And if you turn out to have any health problems, you know where to find me. Be brave!

NURSE: Go on, Mr. Hubert, we'll see you at Père Lachaise.

DR. BACKSLEIDER: After you, Mrs. Bongo.

NURSE: Oh, please, doctor.

DR. BACKSLEIDER: After you, after you.

NURSE: Oh, no, never, doctor!

DR. BACKSLEIDER: Really, Mrs. Bongo, I insist!

NURSE: You're too kind, doctor....

(Dr. Backsleider and Nurse go out.)

REPORTER: Can I drop you somewhere, sir? I have my car.

HUBERT: Thank you, no; my carriage is waiting.

REPORTER: Fine, then I'll say so long.

HUBERT: Don't forget your water pipe.

REPORTER: Oh, sir, I wouldn't want to deprive you of a souvenir like that.

HUBERT: It's only a prop, a backstage imitation; I've got the real one at home.

REPORTER: In that case, thanks, sir. Before I go, I've got to tell you something: I'm not really a reporter.

HUBERT: Somehow I guessed.

REPORTER: I'm your sister Adeline's son.

HUBERT: I guessed that too. Why the hell didn't you say so?

REPORTER: Every time I got close, something interrupted me. I had the feeling he already knew.

HUBERT: He may have.

REPORTER: I'm really happy to have met you, sir, even under these circumstances. Goodbye, sir. I've found this whole occasion very moving.

HUBERT: That's the second time you've said goodbye.

REPORTER: I'm sorry, sir.

(He goes out with the water pipe.)

HUBERT: Now, Cyril, what is this nonsense about Aztec poison?

CYRIL: Just nose drops, my dear Watson. Your nephew is the most insensitive, mediocre, flabby and tiresome human being I have ever met. He is the image of your sister Adeline.

HUBERT: What do you want, he's a typical young man of our time! Would you have liked him better if he were gay?

CYRIL: Frankly, yes.

HUBERT: Unfortunately, it's not hereditary.

CYRIL: That's enough talk about the gender of angels; let's get down to business. Tonight, I'm going to play for you my very first drag role. Where's Regina Morti's cape?

HUBERT: You, dear genius? But you always swore you'd never. . . .

CYRIL: Today I take back everything I ever swore and its opposite to boot. What do you think of me, Hubert?

HUBERT: Terrifying, dear genius.

CYRIL: You always were my best audience. And don't forget that to the world, from now on, I will be Mrs. Dubonnet.

HUBERT: Dear genius, what an honor! I would never have dreamed it would end this way!

CYRIL: In life anything can happen, Hubert. But I will be unbearable as Mrs. Dubonnet, get ready to submit yourself to a female tyranny that shows no mercy.

HUBERT: I'm used to it, dear genius.

CYRIL: Miss Genius to you. Are there at least monogrammed sheets in your tomb, I hope?

HUBERT: We have everything, dear Miss Genius.

CYRIL: Then let's get going.

HUBERT: When we get there, the cherry orchard will still be in blossom.

CYRIL: A real cherry orchard?

HUBERT: Well, a little one.

CYRIL: Tonight we'll dine by the light of the moon, and I'll recite to you from the poetry of Lorca. Help me, Hubert, I've just got to get to your carriage.

REGINA MORTI: *O miserabile fortuna!* The very day of my marriage, my flaming new husband stole my cape and left me for dead! *Al ladro! Al ladro!*

CYRIL: Quick, Hubert, let's get out of here! Oh, shit! . . . .

HUBERT: Cyril! Your heart?

REGINA MORTI: *Questa umiliazione postuma non posso tolerarla!* My honor will not allow me to sink so low! *La Regina dei Morti si uccide!* Where is the carving knife? *Addio, umiliante realtà! (She stabs herself.) Addio, caro publico!* I wait for you in the hereafter *per il grande finale! (Dies.)*

CYRIL: Hubert, what time is it?

HUBERT: *Las cinco en punto de la tarde, señor.*

CYRIL: It's time. *(He dies.)*

HUBERT: Keep the cape, tonight you'll be cold. *(He goes.)*

NURSE: *(entering with a huge floral wreath)* Another present from your sister in law! Oh, crap! I forgot you were dead!

   (Curtain.)

∿

Hervé Dupuis

THE RETURN OF
THE YOUNG
HIPPOLYTUS

Translated from the French by Jean Vigneault

Fugues pour un cheval et un piano
(Return of the Young Hippolytus)
was given a trial performance
in the writing workshop of the
Centre d'essai des auteurs dramatiques
and
the preproduction workshop of the
Théâtre d'Aujourd'hui.

I would particularly like to thank
Linda Gaboriau
Marie Laberge
Lorraine Hébert
Lorraine Pintal
and
Robert Lalonde
for the interest they have shown in my work.

To them I gratefully dedicate this play.

Fugues pour un cheval et un piano
(Return of the Young Hippolytus)
by **Hervé Dupuis**
was performed in Montreal
on 27 April 1988
at the Théâtre d'Aujourd'hui
in a stage production of
Alain Fournier
assisted by **Claire L'Heureux**, stage manager
with the following cast:
BENJAMIN: **Hubert Gagnon**
MICHAEL: **Éric Brisebois**
Musical director and sound track producer:
Pierre Moreau
Scenery and costumes:
Mario Bouchard
Lighting:
Jocelyn Prouix

HERVÉ DUPUIS was born in Saint-Barthélemy (Quebec) in 1941. In 1970, at the Université d'Aix-Marseille in France, he obtained a doctorate in Latin Classics, besides studying theater at the Micheline Palliard School at Aix-en-Provence; he was also trained in the techniques of group dynamics at the Montreal Institut de Formation par le Groupe. In 1966 Dupuis joined the staff of the Department of Classics at the Université de Sherbrooke, and he subsequently (1972) launched a theater program that provides training for future stage directors. He has three theoretical works to his credit, dealing with the theater and group dynamics: *L'animateur de théâtre et sa formation* (1978), *Les rôles de l'animateur et de l'animatrice de théâtre* (1981), and *L'auto-animation dans une troupe de jeune théâtre* (1985).

Aside from his university teaching, Dupuis has been actively involved in stage production. Between 1973 and 1985 he produced no fewer than 40 plays in Sherbrooke (Quebec). He has also been a rather prolific dramatist. Of the 10 plays he has written, the following have had fairly extensive runs. *Ti-Jean-Déconnecté* (1974), produced by the Théâtre du Sang-Neuf, tells of the alienating forces in the life of a Quebecker; *Dewors les chiens pas d'médailles* (1976), produced by l'Option-théâtre, deals with the theme of Quebec independence; *La Symphonie en oui majeur* (1980) extols the merits of the "oui" option in the Quebec Referendum; *Les Peaux-Roses* (1983), written in association with Jacques Jalbert, documents the emergence into the limelight of the gay community; *J'veux faire mon show* (1984), produced by the Théâtre Entre Chien et Loup, satirizes the backstage shenanigans of a summer troupe; and *Dédales* (1988) dramatizes the rebellion of a neurotic young adult whose life has been much perturbed by videogames. *Fugues pour un cheval et un piano (Return of the Young Hippolytus)* was written in 1986 and produced in Montreal by the Théâtre d'Aujourd'hui in 1988.

JEAN VIGNEAULT has taught at the Université de Sherbrooke since 1963. A graduate of the University of London (Ph.D. 1971), he has specialized in teaching basic English-writing techniques to francophone students. He has also been a prolific translator of expository prose. In association with Hervé Dupuis, Vigneault is translating and anthologizing a number of lesser-known Quebec plays that deserve the notice of an English-reading public.

CHARACTERS

BENJAMIN,[1] *42 years old, a concert pianist*
MICHAEL, *18 years old*

The action takes place in Benjamin's apartment. I picture a kind of loft, the spacious upper story of a once derelict but now renovated factory situated just on the outskirts of Montreal, in the old popular quarter of Outremont.[2] The apartment has an ultramodern look; its furnishings are both tasteful and simple. Right in the middle of it stands a grand piano. On a wall behind hang a painting of a horse and a photograph of Benjamin's father. On the piano there is a pair of crescent-shaped spectacles for a farsighted person. Smoke is rising from a lighted cigarette in an ashtray.

Benjamin is alone. He is seated at the piano and has placed a cup of coffee next to him. It is late May, about eight o'clock one Sunday morning. Sunshine is streaming through the windows. The atmosphere is relaxed and pleasant. Benjamin is repeatedly addressing a difficult passage from a Chopin composition. Unable to give it the finish he wants, he starts up an elaborate virtuoso exercise that will help him master the problem. Stopping, he gets up from the piano and starts pacing up and down the room, performing finger-stretching exercises as he does so. Then he goes back to the piano and addresses the same musical phrase. His manner indicates great concentration, along with considerable annoyance. The doorbell rings. Surprised, Benjamin looks at his watch. He gets up from the piano and reaches for the intercom button.

BENJAMIN: Yes?

MICHAEL: *(speaking on the intercom)* It's Michael. Hi!

(Pause. A look of dismay spreads over Benjamin's face.)

BENJAMIN: Hello.

(Pause)

MICHAEL: Well, ... aren't you going to ask me in?

BENJAMIN: What do you want?

MICHAEL: To say hello; to see you.

BENJAMIN: It's pretty early.

MICHAEL: It's eight o'clock. *(Pause)* Are you going to let me in?

(Pause)

BENJAMIN: O.K. You can come in for five minutes, but not

any longer. I've got work to do.

(Benjamin presses a button that unlocks the door admitting people from the outside. Obviously very disturbed, he waits a moment, then opens the door to his apartment.)

MICHAEL: *(walking in)* Relax. Nobody's seen me come in.

(Michael is wearing cyclist's gear. He is perspiring heavily. A handsome, well-built young man, he is clearly a figure of these times; the way he dresses, and his slightly punk hairstyle, shows it. On entering the apartment he stops close to the door and casts a quick look around.)

Wow! I've never seen a pad like this before! Look at all that space! You've got to be making lots of bread to be able to stay here! *(He walks towards the piano. Benjamin leaves the apartment door open.)* I don't know why I'm surprised, really, considering what you are. *(He sits at the piano and starts wildly mimicking the gestures of a pianist, hammering out impossible chords and trying to drown them out with the sound of his own voice.)* A Steinway! Now that's a damn good make!

BENJAMIN: Stop that. You're going to untune it.

MICHAEL: *(sarcastically)* Oh! Do forgive me! *(Pause. Michael turns his head this way and that.)*

BENJAMIN: Is there anything I can do for you?

MICHAEL: *(pretending to be unconcerned)* Nothing at all. It's like I said: I just came in to say hello.

(Michael walks toward the painting of the horse. Benjamin's embarrassment is steadily mounting.)

BENJAMIN: O.K. Now that you've said hello, I'll say hello too. So that's over and done with. Now I'd appreciate being left alone so I can work.

MICHAEL: Hey, man, cool it! Put on the brakes a little. My five minutes aren't up yet. *(looking toward the horse)* Far out, eh? *(Pause)* Does it bring back memories?

BENJAMIN: Now, listen, if it's not too much to ask, I'd prefer it if you left.

MICHAEL: You're not gonna let me see the other rooms?

BENJAMIN: There aren't any.

MICHAEL: What about your bedroom?

BENJAMIN: The bed's in that back wall over there.

MICHAEL: Everything's so squeaky-clean. I bet it must take a lot of work keeping this place in shape.

BENJAMIN: I get somebody to do it for me.

MICHAEL: Who's that?

BENJAMIN: Listen, it's really nice of you to have dropped in. But I'm much too busy today to have you visit my apartment. I've got this concert to rehearse for.

MICHAEL: It's not as if you've never rehearsed for concerts before...!

BENJAMIN: We're never ready enough.

MICHAEL: When is it?

BENJAMIN: Next Tuesday evening.

MICHAEL: You've still got three whole days.

BENJAMIN: What's to stop us from seeing each other some

other time? You couldn't have come on a worse day. Let's make sure to call before, O.K.? And let's meet in some other place than here.

MICHAEL: Are you scared I'll catch you in bed with somebody you don't want me to see? . . . or who might see me?

BENJAMIN: *(taking him by the arm and pulling him toward the door)* Now that's enough. Get out of here!

MICHAEL: *(defiantly)* I thought you'd put your goddam music aside to give me a little attention . . . today, at least.

BENJAMIN: What's special about today?

MICHAEL: It happens to be my birthday.

(Pause. Benjamin is at a loss for words.)

BENJAMIN: Today!

MICHAEL: Yeah! I'm 18 today.

BENJAMIN: I see . . . . Well, happy birthday.

MICHAEL: You'd forgotten it.

BENJAMIN: Yes.

MICHAEL: Like a lot of other things.

BENJAMIN: O.K. I've said hello; I've said happy birthday. What else do you want?

MICHAEL: Guess.

BENJAMIN: Just a second. *(He reaches into his pocket and pulls out a bill of large denomination. He then hands it to Michael.)*

MICHAEL: Why are you giving me money?

BENJAMIN: *(taken aback)* Well, it's . . . my birthday gift to you.

MICHAEL: That's not what I want for a birthday gift.

BENJAMIN: What is it, then?

MICHAEL: What I want'd take a little time, and of course you gotta practice for that goddam concert of yours.

BENJAMIN: Michael! It seems to me we know where we stand toward each other.

MICHAEL: Well, I don't.

BENJAMIN: I've nothing more to tell you.

MICHAEL: But I've got a few things to tell you.

BENJAMIN: Does your mother know you're here?

MICHAEL: I didn't tell her I was coming. *(Pause)* I'm 18 now.

BENJAMIN: You know I don't want to open that can of worms again.

(Pause. Michael is close to tears, but he is desperately trying to hide it.)

MICHAEL: You don't even have one lousy little hour for me today.

BENJAMIN: We'll get together some other time, O.K.?

MICHAEL: O.K. You're the boss! *(Pause. Michael tries one final ploy.)* Could you at least give me a glass of water before I leave? I'm thirsty.

(Benjamin heaves a long exasperated sigh. He fetches the glass of water without trying to hide his annoyance. Michael stands next to the door, waiting.)

(He dreams. He hears a horse galloping.)

BENJAMIN: *Boy! We've really forged ahead, dear buddy of mine!*

MICHAEL: *We're goin' to become the two best horsemen in the world.*

BENJAMIN: *You're not too tired?*

MICHAEL: *No, but it's hot and I'm thirsty.*

BENJAMIN: *What d'you say we find the spring?*

MICHAEL: *Sure. And we'll take a dip at the same time. Gee!*

(The horses start galloping again. The voices of their riders spurring them on can clearly be heard.)

(Benjamin returns with a glass of water. Michael starts to drink it, but does so in a very leisurely fashion, taking one little sip at a time.)

MICHAEL: So it seems you still get up pretty early.

BENJAMIN: *(making the best of a bad situation)* Yes. Early morning is the only time I can bring myself to practice my scales.

MICHAEL: You even work Sundays now!

BENJAMIN: Seven days out of seven. *(Pause)* But it seems you like getting up early too.

MICHAEL: That's what country living does to you. Besides, it's so much more fun cycling at that time of day. There's barely any traffic, and a lot less pollution too. *(Pause)* How was your tour in Poland?

BENJAMIN: Excellent.

MICHAEL: A first-class success, as always.

BENJAMIN: I've no complaints, really. Everything went well.

MICHAEL: The reporters, at any rate, were certainly very... *(deliberating what word to use)* enthusiastic.

BENJAMIN: *(aping a modesty he does not feel)* Well, you know how it is with music critics . . . .

MICHAEL: There's something, at least, you're darn good at. *(Pause. Michael feels that Benjamin is looking at him out of the corner of his eye.)* Boy, I'm all wet. It was really hot out there.

BENJAMIN: What direction did you come from?

MICHAEL: Pointe-Claire.[3]

BENJAMIN: Well! You really must be in shape to cycle all the way from Pointe-Claire to Outremont during the wee hours of the morning.

MICHAEL: You're right. I am in pretty good shape. I do a lot of sports.

BENJAMIN: Good for you.

(Pause)

MICHAEL: But you don't, though.

BENJAMIN: How can you tell that?

MICHAEL: *(trying to be facetious)* From the look of you . . . .

BENJAMIN: I simply don't have the time. As long as my fingers are in shape, that's all that concerns me. *(He waves his hand about in blithe insouciance.)* As for the rest . . . . *(He walks toward the piano and lights up a cigarette.)*

MICHAEL: *(in a mocking tone of voice, like a teacher upbraiding a student)* Tut, tut, tut . . . . *Mens sana in corpore sano!* I know some Latin too, as you can see. *Mens sana in corpore sano!*

BENJAMIN: *(becoming less aloof)* So you think I'm in that bad a shape?

MICHAEL: *(laughing)* Well, admit it . . . . You've got bags under the eyes, and you're no prize bodybuilder either. Whatever you are, you're certainly not in shape. *(more playful than censorious)* I bet you still smoke your full pack a day.

BENJAMIN: You've no idea how often I've tried to stop. But I just can't.

MICHAEL: Still take your five or six cups of coffee?

BENJAMIN: Yes.

MICHAEL: *(still joshing him)* I bet you like the booze too.

BENJAMIN: Occasionally.

MICHAEL: Cocktails before dinner?

BENJAMIN: Just the one.

MICHAEL: A dry martini?

BENJAMIN: A very weak one. A lot more martini than gin.

MICHAEL: A nice bottle of Bordeaux with each meal?

BENJAMIN: Make it a half-bottle.

MICHAEL: A V.S.O.P. cognac to cap the day?

BENJAMIN: Why not?

MICHAEL: And like the French, you like your sauces pretty thick?

BENJAMIN: How come you know all this?

MICHAEL: Just think back to the last meal we had together, at the airport: that's exactly the kind of meal you had. But let me tell you something: if I was the boss, that routine of yours'd change overnight. First, I'd get you to cut back on a lot of things, then force you to work out, get you on a bike, overhaul your lifestyle completely. . . .

BENJAMIN: *(disconsolately)* But life has so very few real pleasures!

MICHAEL: What's that you say? Are you complaining? You're making money hand over fist, traveling all over the world, seeing your name in the bright lights . . . .

BENJAMIN: Oh! Now that's not . . . .

MICHAEL: Will you listen to that! Here's a guy who's hounded by the most important newspapers in the world for interviews, who's considered the best Chopin interpreter today! Boy! Few people have made it as good as you in Quebec.

BENJAMIN: Sure. I know all that. But . . . .

MICHAEL: Tell me, what can be missing in your life?

BENJAMIN: Well, for one thing, I wouldn't mind being 18 today, like you.

MICHAEL: Do you think this is going to be the banner day of my life?

(Benjamin says nothing, conscious perhaps of having been too forward.)

What is it you want to say? Out with it!

BENJAMIN: Let's drop it.

MICHAEL: You're scared of growing old? *(Pause)* Why, for heaven's sake?

BENJAMIN: *(reluctantly)* Well, look at it this way. A 40-year-old body, well, tires fast. I didn't used to look much at old people before. But now I do . . . to see what I'm going to be looking like soon.

MICHAEL: Ah! Cheer up, man! I was just joking a while ago! You're not bad-looking at all! *(in a seductive tone of voice)* At any rate, to me you're darn good-looking for a man of 40. *(joshing him)* Those alluring eyes of yours, you've still got them! And would you look at that head of hair, with just the right little touch of gray. It makes you look, well, so suave, . . . and wise too. *(laughing)* Boy! I bet your girlfriends fall for it, *n'est-ce-pas?*

BENJAMIN: That's just the kind of compliment I detest receiving. It's the kind you address to people who've started to grow old.

MICHAEL: *(affectionately)* I didn't tell you that because you're growing old; I said it because I meant it . . . . *(Pause)* Funny, though. I never thought you'd blow a gasket, having to talk about your age. You grown-ups are really all alike. You were young once, and you had a ball. You've got nothing to complain about.

BENJAMIN: Young? I get the feeling that I've completely skipped that part of my life.

MICHAEL: Don't you remember having been 18 once?

BENJAMIN: Believe it or not, at your age there was no time for fun in my life. I'd spend 15 hours every day, hunched over the keyboard, practicing my scales, working away at numberless compositions by Chopin, Liszt, and droves of other composers. You see, I had to prove to my teachers, the journalists, even the sweet nuns of Vincent-d'Indy[4] (whose convent I had to live in) that I was in fact the young prodigy everybody wanted me to be. Today it's a bit late to make up for lost time.

MICHAEL: *(affectionately)* Well, all I can say is that if things work out for me the way they have for you, I'll have lived one hell of a nice life.

BENJAMIN: *(skeptical)* You really think so?

MICHAEL: *(deviously)* I know a person your age who gets much less fun out of life than you do.

BENJAMIN: *(sidestepping the allusion)* No doubt you do. *(Pause)* Well, that's enough talk, I'm afraid. I'm gonna have to get back to work.

MICHAEL: What a drag! I was starting to have fun.

BENJAMIN: We'll chat some other time.

MICHAEL: Why can't it be today?

BENJAMIN: I've just told you I've got lots of work to do.

MICHAEL: I don't believe this! It's my birthday today, and you can't spend one bloody hour with me! Think of how things were before: you always found time for me then.

(Benjamin glances at his watch.)

I suppose you're expecting somebody?

BENJAMIN: *(hesitating)* No, . . . not at all.

MICHAEL: That's it, isn't it? Somebody's about to show up here.

BENJAMIN: Well . . . .

MICHAEL: Your girlfriend? *(Benjamin does not respond.)* O.K. I get it. She's obviously more important in your life than I could ever be.

BENJAMIN: Good-bye, Michael.

MICHAEL: One hour, just one little hour!

BENJAMIN: No. Please leave! It'll be better for everybody all around.

(Benjamin gently pushes Michael toward the door, intending to shut it in his face.)

MICHAEL: *(obviously distraught)* Dad!

(Pause. Benjamin stops pushing Michael.)

There must be one hour in your life for me on my eighteenth birthday! You couldn't make me a nicer birthday present than that.

(Long pause. Michael dreams. He hears the sound of a waterfall.)

MICHAEL: *Why have you blindfolded me, Dad?*

BENJAMIN: *I want to surprise you even more.*

MICHAEL: *Are we standing next to the waterfall now?*

BENJAMIN: *Yes. You can have a look now. Happy birthday!*

MICHAEL: *Daddy! There's a horse there!*

BENJAMIN: *He's all yours. He's your birthday gift.*

MICHAEL: *You mean he's mine?*

BENJAMIN: *Of course.*

MICHAEL: *All mine?*

BENJAMIN: *All yours.*

MICHAEL: *I've got to mount him.*

BENJAMIN: *Easy now, I'll give you a hand. There we go.*

MICHAEL: *Hold me, Dad, I'm scared.*

BENJAMIN: *Don't be scared. He's really quite gentle. You'll learn how to mount him, and then we'll go riding horseback together.*

MICHAEL: *Daddy! I've never had such a nice birthday present in all my life.*

(The noise of the waterfall dies away.)

BENJAMIN: What is it you want with me?

MICHAEL: All I want is a chance to talk to you. That's all.

BENJAMIN: *(sighing deeply, then glancing again at his watch)* **All right. One hour. But not a minute more. Come in.**

(Benjamin finally shuts the door. There is a long, uneasy silence. Michael walks toward the piano and stands there, afraid to move. His father is still standing next to the door.)

BENJAMIN: Well, . . . go ahead and sit down.

(Michael sits on the piano bench. He says nothing.)

Do you want some coffee?

MICHAEL: No, thanks. Never touch the stuff. But I'd like another glass of water, though.

BENJAMIN: Would you prefer fruit juice? Maybe some orange juice?

MICHAEL: O.K.

(Benjamin walks toward the kitchen area. Left alone, Michael takes a good look around. Benjamin returns almost immediately with a glass of juice and a cup of coffee. Neither of the two says anything. They both seem at a loss for words.)

It's been ages since we spent one of my birthdays together.

(Benjamin nods his assent.)

Six years.

(A long silence)

Six years is a long time.

(Another long silence)

Do you realize we've seen each other four times in six years? A mere four times. Twice at the airport, in a hurry, between two flights; once in a dressing room with all kinds of people milling around us; finally by chance on the Montreal–Magog[5] bus. And that bus was so damn crowded, we couldn't even sit together. *(Pause)* I'm so happy to see you again. *(Pause)* If it's all right with you, . . . *(he says this in a very sheepish tone of voice)* since we've got this hour together, . . . I'd like to have a, well, . . . serious talk with you. After six years, I've got loads of things to tell you. Is that all right with you?

BENJAMIN: O.K. If that's what you want.

MICHAEL: But I'd like you to want it too! And I'd very much appreciate it if you brightened up a bit.

BENJAMIN: I'll try. It's just that, as you know, I'm pressed for time. *(Pause)* What do you want to talk to me about?

MICHAEL: I'm not sure just where to start.

(Pause)

BENJAMIN: You've got your college diploma now, haven't you?

MICHAEL: *(with a touch of pride laced with sarcasm)* Yeah, I got it about a month ago. As of early May, I am a graduate of the Mount Sutton Academy, the top-of-the-line school, I'm told.

BENJAMIN: Did the place agree with you?

MICHAEL: Yes and no. On the plus side, it's a darn interesting school. It's not like those public schools, with those thousands of kids milling about you. The profs are abso-

lutely first-rate, and there are loads of extra-curricular activities. *(sarcastically)* It must've cost you a bundle, but I'm
sure you got your money's worth.

BENJAMIN: You said "yes and no." What's on the minus
side?

MICHAEL: *(bitterly)* Maybe I would've preferred to stay in
Pointe-Claire. *(Pause. Then, somewhat reproachfully)* When I
had to start up high school, everything was in a shambles at
home. There was the divorce, and Mom having to work
longer and longer hours. And, to make matters worse, you
pull a disappearing act. Without quite knowing why, I
woke up one morning at granddad's, in Bromont. *(unable to
hide his bitterness)* Let's say things weren't as rosy as they had
been.

BENJAMIN: Uh...huh....

MICHAEL: When I was 13 or 14, all I seemed to be doing,
apart from studying, was sports, a lot of riding and a lot of
hockey. I was in the Granby[6] Midgets. We played in all
kinds of tournaments in the Townships, then throughout
Quebec. Granddad didn't much like that, let me tell you.
What snobs they are, really! Granddad claimed that that's
where I received my street education. And a darn good
thing I did! If it hadn't been for my buddies, there's a whole
slew of things I'd know nothing about.

BENJAMIN: Like what?

MICHAEL: Speaking like everybody else, swearing, telling
dirty jokes, cruising the girls, knowing how to defend myself. *(Pause)* When I look back at it all, I sure as hell can't
say they were the six nicest years of my life.

BENJAMIN: *(betraying increasing agitation)* Where do you go
from here?

MICHAEL: *(noncommittal)* I really don't know. To university, most likely. Everything depends.

BENJAMIN: Do you have some particular field in mind?

MICHAEL: Business administration, maybe.

BENJAMIN: *(not overly enthusiastic)* Business administration?

MICHAEL: Or maybe architecture. I haven't made up my mind yet. *(with pride)* What's remarkable, though, is just how good I am with figures. I've even been admitted to the University of Montreal's Business School.

BENJAMIN: *(rather tepidly)* Good for you! That's a darn good school.

MICHAEL: But before making up my mind, I'll wait for a reply from the School of Architecture. *(Pause)* What do you think I should do?

BENJAMIN: *(surprised)* Me? *(Pause)* Well, my first impulse would be to recommend architecture. I like the way it combines art and science.... Then I must admit that those business people.... But then maybe everything that has to do with art leaves you cold.

MICHAEL: You're wrong there. Art does interest me a lot.... O.K., not as a much as hockey or math, but it does interest me! Maybe you weren't aware of it, but at college I went in for the fine arts in a big way; I did a lot of painting there. I was particularly good at drawing. *(Pause)* I sometimes think, drawing and science, they're perfect for the architect, aren't they?

BENJAMIN: That's certainly my opinion too.

MICHAEL: Still,... I can't deny that business administration is also quite tempting. Mom would be so happy if I became a business manager. *(with a sudden burst of enthusiasm)* The Business School at the University of Montreal has started up a program in art administration. *(Pause)* I know, of course, that you've never really liked business people. *(Pause)* Yet Mom.... *(uncertainly)* Well, you loved her once....

BENJAMIN: I loved Mom the woman, not the business manager.

MICHAEL: A businesswoman.

BENJAMIN: *(appearing eager to sidestep the question)* How is she, incidentally?

MICHAEL: She hasn't changed a bit. *(with some bitterness)* She's working as hard as ever, buying loads of stores, traveling all over the place... *(pointedly)* like somebody else I know. I didn't get to see her much while I was at college. But I've been living with her since school ended. She's never there, though. Granddad had begun filling me in on her activities, because there was talk of me becoming her associate after university... on condition, of course, that I go into business administration.

BENJAMIN: *(becoming a bit testy)* So that, if you do exactly what they say, you'll come into all their assets, is that it? You'll be as rich as Rockefeller.

(Pause)

MICHAEL: Maybe I shouldn't tell you this, but things aren't all that hot between us. *(Pause)* Would you like to hear about it?

BENJAMIN: *(rather grudgingly)* If you wish.

(Pause)

MICHAEL: I get the impression she's not all that attached to me. It's hard to say. She just about totally ignores me. It's as if she had a grudge against me. Sometimes I get to thinking that maybe I'm responsible for... well, for what's happened between you two....

BENJAMIN: Your mother, you know, has never been a very demonstrative lady. Her work has always been... *(emphatically)* exceedingly important in her life.

MICHAEL: It's been that way for you too. *(Pause)* Why have you stopped coming to see me?

BENJAMIN: I never had the opportunity.

MICHAEL: I simply can't believe that. You've not made the teeniest little effort. *(Pause)* On my side, though, I did everything to get you to come. I've called you at least 637 times. You were never there. It was always that blasted answering machine of yours giving off the same blasted message. *(The following message could perhaps be aired at this point.)* "I'm sorry I'm busy just right now. At the sound of the beep, state your message, and I'll get back to you. Beep." Boy, have I left you a pack of messages! Beep! "Hi, Dad. Call me back, will you? I've got a few things to talk to you about." Beep! "Dad, listen, call me back, will you? I'd like to see you sometime." Beep! "Dad, would you please call me back!" Beep! "Dad, it's me again; I miss you so much." You couldn't have cared less.

BENJAMIN: Admit that I did care when your mother told me that our 13-year-old son had disappeared, leaving a note behind saying that he was going to jump off the Jacques-Cartier Bridge. Have you any idea what I felt at that time? And when I got wind of that story you concocted for your grandmother in order to be able to hide in her house for three days, the idea popped into my mind that your mother and I were going to pay dearly for our separation.

(Michael laughs. So does Benjamin as he resumes speaking.)

I suppose we can laugh about it today. But let me tell you, it wasn't funny then.

MICHAEL: Well, it wasn't funny for me either when you left. The worst, though, is that you never came around to bawl me out, as I was hoping you would. *(Pause)* You know, Dad, I think it's just great being able to talk about all this with you.

BENJAMIN: So much the better.

MICHAEL: I've been wanting to for a long time. This morning, I got up all the courage I could, then decided to go celebrate my eighteenth birthday in style: I'd pay my father a visit! I didn't want to call, or give you any advance warning. I'd just drop in, like I have. I admit I had a few butterflies. I wasn't at all sure what kind of reception I'd get. *(Pause)* I don't suppose that's something you'd like to discuss?

BENJAMIN: I would've preferred it if it hadn't been this morning.

MICHAEL: Well, for me, it was this morning or never. And it's stupid, but I don't know what else to tell you. I'm just so damned uptight.

BENJAMIN: Just say the first thing that pops into your mind.

MICHAEL: I simply can't get used to the idea that you've left. You've ruined my life by doing that. . . . You can't imagine how much I've suffered.

BENJAMIN: True, I did leave house and family. But you're not the only kid your age to have experienced that. And I certainly haven't left you poverty-stricken. Look at all I've had to pay to provide you with a first-class education.

MICHAEL: You're talkin' money!

BENJAMIN: I'm the one who paid for your sound system, your computer, your skis, your surfboard, your bicycle. And when I heard you were having problems adjusting to my departure, I got a psychologist to look into the matter.

MICHAEL: You're still talkin' money!

BENJAMIN: Then, you've got to admit that your mother and grandparents have taken the best care of you; at no time were you ever alone. You've always been well-housed, well-fed, well-dressed. What more could you have wanted?

MICHAEL: My father.

(Benjamin sighs deeply. There is a long interval of silence.)

I suppose you'd like me to go on again about myself?

BENJAMIN: If you feel like it.

MICHAEL: What more can I tell you?

BENJAMIN: I don't know.... But something a little more up-beat. *(almost lightly)* I got it: talk to me about your love life.

MICHAEL: I don't have any time for that at all, believe it or not. In the classics-math program, you're hitting the books all the time. My high standing at the exams, that's something I earned, let me tell you, especially during my final year. I had to work my butt off because I was aiming both at the University of Montreal's Business School and the

School of Architecture. I'm pretty sure there's a job down the line in both of those fields. And that's important! Many university graduates don't even have a shot at a job.

BENJAMIN: Tell me about your friends.

MICHAEL: I don't have any.

BENJAMIN: You must go to a few parties, now and then?

MICHAEL: Never. I hate parties.

BENJAMIN: Is that so! I've heard different from your mother on a number of occasions.

MICHAEL: You know how Mom is: she'll say anything. *(Pause)* Me, I've set my sights high....

BENJAMIN: *(half-jokingly)* I bet you want to be a good manager, have a wife and kids, a large house, an expensive automobile....

MICHAEL: *(firmly)* Why shouldn't I want all those things?

(Benjamin is rather taken aback.)

BENJAMIN: Well, ... if that's what you want, so be it! It's your life, after all.

MICHAEL: You see now how little you know about me. *(He waits. Then, as if he were imparting a secret)* But that doesn't close me off from passion.

BENJAMIN: Could you be more precise?

MICHAEL: *(elated)* I want to be frank with you. I'm head over heels in love!

BENJAMIN: But you've just said you had no time for the girls at all!

MICHAEL: *(with deliberate ambiguity)* Girls are not the only beings one can fall in love with!

(Benjamin immediately assumes that Michael has fallen in love with a boy.)

BENJAMIN: Is that so!

MICHAEL: And the whole thing's your fault.

BENJAMIN: Really!

MICHAEL: You must remember that nice present you gave me when I turned 10.

BENJAMIN: Yeah. That was Triumph.

MICHAEL: *(looking toward the painting)* Well, Triumph, Dad, is simply the handsomest horse in all of Quebec. *(He laughs.)* When I got him, I dreamt of becoming an Olympic champion, the country's master horseman; I'd make Triumph into the best jumper in the world.... Today, though, I want to keep him to myself, simply be with him.

BENJAMIN: *(almost inaudibly)* That's exactly how I'd imagined you'd be.

MICHAEL: Dad, you're the one to have given me the nicest present I've ever received.

(Benjamin walks toward the piano. Michael is lost in reverie. He hears the neighing of a horse.)

MICHAEL: *Hello, Triumph. I've come to see you, my friend. I've missed you, you know. I'm sure you must think I've got lots of work these days. Well, good buddy, you know how it is: if you want to succeed, you've no choice in the matter. But you know that, I'm convinced of it. Still, don't go thinking I'm forgetting you, my beautiful Triumph. Today I've got loads of time on my hands; you and I are going to have a ball. I'll check up, first, on how things are with you here; then we'll go trotting off towards the stream. You like that stream, don't you? We'll run, we'll walk, we'll play, we'll wash ourselves, and we'll dry out in the sun next to each other. How does that sound to you? Ah! I was sure you'd like it.*

(He hears the gallop of a horse.)

MICHAEL: Triumph, Dad, happens to be my best friend.

BENJAMIN: That was true of Hippolytus too.

MICHAEL: You mean the guy who liked horses?

BENJAMIN: You remember, then.

MICHAEL: You were always telling me those stories when I was a mere tot. Later in college, we had to read *Phaedra*. What a super play that was!

BENJAMIN: Think back to what Phaedra says while Hippolytus is training his horses:

> "Ye gods! Would I were seated in some forest gloom!
> When will I, through the noble dust,
> Perceive with mine eye a chariot flying towards the quarry?"
> et cetera, et cetera . . . .

MICHAEL: *(jokingly)* It's true I love horses, but I'm not at all keen on having what happened to Hippolytus happen to me. Think of it! Being dragged over the rocks by my horse, . . . worse still, being damned by my own father. Because . . . what was his father's name, again?

BENJAMIN: Theseus.

MICHAEL: Because Theseus, the father, wasn't at all happy to learn that his wife and his son ....*(Pause)* Isn't it amazing, Dad, how much you can get attached...! *(Pause. Michael is carefully picking his way.)* At least with Triumph I can be sure of one thing: *(pointedly)* He'll never leave me in the lurch, him; he won't dump me for some other person, him.

BENJAMIN: *(pretending not to have caught the hint)* I think you're darn lucky. A love story like that could never happen to a guy like me.

MICHAEL: *(with some bitterness)* You've made another choice.

BENJAMIN: *(The statement surprises him. He stops playing.)* What do you mean by that?

MICHAEL: *(still visibly bitter)* Music. I mean music. That's one thing, at least, you've always been faithful to.

BENJAMIN: To that at least?

MICHAEL: *(aggressively)* When it comes time to love, you're in it for the adventure, aren't you?

BENJAMIN: *(astonished)* Where in heaven's name have you heard that?

MICHAEL: Listen, Dad, I'm not your little boy anymore. Can we have a talk man to man? *(with ponderous emphasis)* I know damn well what kind of life you lead. I've heard about it again and again.

BENJAMIN: Oh, so that's it! Your grandfather and your grandmother too, no doubt. *(sarcastically)* Would you be so kind as to say what you "good" people consider to be my lifestyle?

MICHAEL: You're just a womanizer.

(Benjamin laughs derisively.)

I've got a scrapbook on you that thick. I've seen 'em all. Every shot of you is with a different girl. And you should read those articles!

BENJAMIN: You don't believe everything you read in the papers, do you?

MICHAEL: Are you going to deny sex has always meant more to you than love? Haven't you said that fidelity is a typically bourgeois fixation? It's one conquest after another, and not only in music, I'll bet. You score with the ladies too. Now isn't that true?

BENJAMIN: The parents-in-law have really been talking about me, haven't they?

MICHAEL: I need to know, Dad; I need to know if what I read in the papers and hear from my grandparents is true.

BENJAMIN: *(firmly)* It's all hogwash, Michael. Boy, how straight some people can be! *(Sadly, he begins to play a light tune. Then he looks up.)* True, I do get to meet famous women at all of my stops on the concert circuit, but they're friends of mine, that's all. *(despondently)* Only one thing matters to me now: my music. Aside from that, I eat, I drink, like everybody else; I have trouble sleeping ... and at rare intervals I'll make love.

MICHAEL: I'm glad to know there's nothing to all those rumors, and glad, too, the truth is exactly what I had imagined it to be.

BENJAMIN: *(looking up sharply)* And what had you imagined?

MICHAEL: You really want to know?

BENJAMIN: Yes.

MICHAEL: You won't laugh at me if I tell you?

BENJAMIN: Of course not.

MICHAEL: Achilles, Aeneas, Marco Polo.... Those are the heroes you talked to me about most often.... Well, for me you were exactly like them: great like them, tortured inside but strong. In your case, you conquered the world thanks to your talent. What gives you your power is music. A while ago, I reminded you of Hippolytus. Well, you... you're... what's the name you said his father had?

BENJAMIN: Theseus.

MICHAEL: Well, that's what you are, my Theseus. You win all your battles. But, to do that, you've got to be practicing hours on end, every single day. I should know; I've heard you often enough... and waited for you long enough when I was a kid. Cruising is something you don't have any time for. You've always got to be at the top of your form, ready for the toughest and most demanding audiences. Never for one moment did I believe them, Dad. *(Pause)* Still, I've got this nagging feeling that won't go away. I keep asking myself how a man like you—a man whose whole life is devoted to the musical exaltation of feeling, a man who plays Chopin and Liszt the way you do—I keep wondering how such a man could have spent six years of his life cut off from all love for another human being. It simply doesn't make sense to me. *(A long silence)* There is a woman in your life, isn't there?

BENJAMIN: Why should you think that?

MICHAEL: I don't know. But I feel her presence everywhere.

What kind of person is she?

BENJAMIN: Michael, that's not a subject I care to talk about.

MICHAEL: She's coming here this morning, isn't she? That's why you didn't want me to stay, isn't it?

BENJAMIN: Yes, I am expecting somebody. *(looking at his watch)* But we can spend a little more time together. *(Pause)*

MICHAEL: I missed you a lot, you know, during all those years.

BENJAMIN: *(moved)* Really?

MICHAEL: In spite of everything I heard about you, I never stopped thinking of you as my father.

(Silence. Benjamin is clearly moved.)

BENJAMIN: It wasn't any easier for me, Michael, to live apart from you.

MICHAEL: *(drily)* You don't say! If it'd been that hard, you wouldn't have disappeared from my life.

BENJAMIN: *(bitterly)* You mother....

MICHAEL: So it's Mother, is it? Let's explore that, shall we?

BENJAMIN: ...demanded and obtained by court order almost exclusive custody.

MICHAEL: From what I heard, you didn't contest that court order.

BENJAMIN: That's correct.

MICHAEL: Wasn't adultery the grounds for divorce?

BENJAMIN: Since you know, why bother asking me such a question?

MICHAEL: But the court had granted you some visiting rights. Why didn't you make use of them?

BENJAMIN: *(bitterly)* I didn't want to be beholden to some asshole of a judge, who knows virtually nothing about what binds people together, for the right to ... come and see my own son. Then, your mother, but particularly your grandparents, didn't make it any easier for me to see you. I chose, therefore, to wait until all those obstacles'd disappear. And now they have. You're 18 now, aren't you? You're your own man now? *(with deep feeling)* You've no idea how often I've thought about you during all those years.

MICHAEL: *(touched)* I'm happy you told me you continued at least to think about me. I couldn't help asking myself at times if that Theseus dad of mine had completely forgotten ... *(bitterly)* the little boy he had dropped.

BENJAMIN: Not in the least, Michael. It's exactly the opposite. I missed you terribly.

MICHAEL: *(obviously quite shaken)* It's nice to hear that. *(Pause)* Dad, ... I've got this .... But don't get sore at me if I put it to you.

BENJAMIN: Go right ahead. I'll see whether I need to get sore or not.

MICHAEL: I'd like to know EXACTLY why you up and left us.

(A silence)

BENJAMIN: Your question is badly phrased. You should've asked me why I left your mother.

MICHAEL: All right, I stand corrected. It wasn't just because you had had an affair with another woman?

BENJAMIN: I simply didn't love her anymore.

MICHAEL: *(explosively)* Baloney!

BENJAMIN: *(embarrassed and hesitating)* Love, you know, is not something you can turn on and off, like a tap.

MICHAEL: *(scoffingly)* So that's all there was to it!

BENJAMIN: We were hopelessly unlike each other, your mother and I. Her whole life is one long business transaction! We almost never got around to seeing each other. She had her work, I had mine; she'd fly off one way, and I'd fly off the other....

MICHAEL: I've heard that refrain before: out of reach, out of heart, right? Why don't you give me the real reasons? I'm not 12 years old anymore.

BENJAMIN: There are no other reasons. I simply didn't love her anymore.

MICHAEL: *(point-blank)* But she still loves you; she's always loved you. *(Pause)* If you saw that businesswoman of yours, you'd realize just how passionate a lady she is. That's the impression I get, at any rate. You should see her, Dad: almost everything she does or says shows how much she misses you....

BENJAMIN: I've no wish to hear anything about that, Michael!

MICHAEL: What you've got there is a woman who'll never be able to forget you.

BENJAMIN: Why do you keep harping on that, Michael? It's over between your mother and me.

MICHAEL: You should've tried harder to make a go of it.

BENJAMIN: Tried harder!

MICHAEL: *(with sudden intensity)* She would've forgiven you your fling, you know. You can't have left a woman who adored you . . . and *(emphatically)* abandoned your 12-year-old son . . . simply because the attraction wasn't as potent as before. I'm sorry, but that reasoning doesn't cut any ice with me!

BENJAMIN: Is that so!

MICHAEL: *(becoming more agitated)* You can put a relationship back together! There's more to it all, it seems to me, than sex and passion!

BENJAMIN: Is that really the case?

MICHAEL: What about friendship, understanding, attachment, fidelity. . . ? What about paternity too?

BENJAMIN: But what about when love dies . . . ? Your grandparents have stuck it out together, I know, though they've long since stopped loving each other. I can't do that. I've had to call it quits. *(He stops; then, in a tone perhaps too suggestive of paternal authority)* Listen carefully to what I have to say, Michael . . . .

MICHAEL: *(with scoffing emphasis on the word "Dad")* Yes, Dad.

BENJAMIN: . . . if those feelings you've just told me about are really genuine, you're going to become one of them: decent, respectable little bourgeois people who can think of nothing but their lawns and silverware.

MICHAEL: *(outraged)* So if I value fidelity I'll become like them? I'll become like them if I want to make my wife happy? I'll become like them if I want to have children I can love . . . children I'd take care of, at any rate?

BENJAMIN: Yes. If you do things the way your grandparents want, you'll end up being like them.

MICHAEL: You must really hate them!

BENJAMIN: I do. More than I can say. They stand for all that I hate most in life. *(passionately)* They're the people we've had to fight against in order to make it where we are.

MICHAEL: *(with equal vehemence)* But what about the people of your generation? You may not know it, but you've really screwed up the people of mine with your lousy little quiet revolution plus your newfound love of ass.

BENJAMIN: We can't have screwed up your generation the way they did mine, never.

MICHAEL: If you knew how big a gang we are in college, who are fed up with having to pay for your sexual high jinks!

BENJAMIN: But we've moved forward a little, at any rate! Your generation won't have to start from as far back.

MICHAEL: Moved forward! The kind of life we lead, you call that moving forward? Mother has beat it, or maybe it's Father. We've got to live with the mother of whoever or with the father of whoever. Then the male lover comes barging in, or maybe it's the mistress, with a slew of little brothers here, or little sisters there. How pleasant it would've been, really, to spend my adolescent years coddled by a mother and father who wouldn't have been liberated sexually maybe, but who'd loved each other and would've taken care of me and gotten me to think of doing things the way they did. Do you think your newfound sexual freedom was likely to make me happy?

(As if unwilling to hear more, Benjamin starts to play the piano. Michael yells at him.)

Goddam it! How I hate you at times! I'd done nothing to you! Answer me this: Why did you drop me like that? Why did you deprive a little 12-year-old boy of his father? A boy who's going to have to spend part of his life paying for a screwed-up adolescence because of a father who dreamt of making his prick king?

BENJAMIN: *(interrupting his playing)* I had to live my life, Michael.

MICHAEL: And what about my happiness?

BENJAMIN: You want to make me feel guilty about this, right?

MICHAEL: Don't try to deny, at any rate, that I've you to thank for the only thing that has really hurt me since the age of 12: your absence.

(A long silence. Michael hears children's voices. He sees himself back in school delivering a little speech in front of his classmates. He must be about 13.)

MICHAEL: *My father. My father's a concert pianist. He can't stay with me, because he has to travel all over the world to give his concerts. He comes to see me as often as he can, and that's when we get to do all sorts of interesting things together: we go see the Canadiens play, we go to the movies, we go eat in fancy restaurants, we go horseback rid-*

ing, and we do a lot of other things besides. My father often gets talked about in the papers, and I make sure to collect all the clippings. That's how I keep tabs on what he's doing. Last month, for instance, he won the Governor General's Prize. This is the photo of when he got the prize. My father will be spending the next holiday with me. I'll be 14 then. He's promised to take me to Europe. With my father I'll be visiting France, Spain, Italy, and Switzerland. It's wonderful having a father like I have, and I love him very much. Thank you.

(He hears the applause of the children.)

BENJAMIN: Michael, believe me, it wouldn't have been any better even if I'd been there. You've no idea how the situation had worsened between your mother and me. Sooner or later it would've affected you. We'll make up for lost time, you and I.

MICHAEL: Mom. Can anything be done about her?

BENJAMIN: I'm afraid not, Michael. It's been all over between us for six years. There's no point going on about that.

MICHAEL: You might think of doing it for me, even if you can't for her.

BENJAMIN: *(firmly)* No, Michael.

(A pause. Then Michael blurts out what follows.)

MICHAEL: You could at least do it out of gratitude to her.

BENJAMIN: Gratitude?

MICHAEL: Well, admit that you were lucky to meet a girl like her. *(Pause)* You didn't have a red cent in your pockets ....

BENJAMIN: True, thanks to her a little upstart from Saint-

Fulgence,[7] in the Saguenay region, was able to make his entrance into the kind of society that's closed to nobodies like him. From one day to the next, I suddenly found myself dining at the table of a Consul, no less. I started to meet ambassadors, politicians, artists....

MICHAEL: Not too bad a catch, eh, for a budding concert pianist?

BENJAMIN: I did genuinely love Odette. You can believe me on that.

MICHAEL: She was your first girlfriend?

BENJAMIN: Yes.

MICHAEL: You found her pretty?

BENJAMIN: Yes.... Our tastes complemented each other's.

MICHAEL: But you had to marry her, didn't you?

BENJAMIN: Yes. *(in a mocking tone of voice)* She'd made the mistake of talking to her mother about it. Well! A thing like that couldn't be allowed to happen in a fine, upstanding family of Outremont. I could either leave her and take the consequences, or marry her. But I would never have been able to bring myself to leave her in that condition. Besides, I loved her.

MICHAEL: But why all of a sudden stop loving her? What happened to make you do that?

BENJAMIN: I really can't say, Michael. It just happened; that's all. One day, I sort of started feeling differently about her.... I began feeling put out by the way she did things. ... She'd rent my halls, badger conductors or friends of the family into getting me to play a little solo here, a little solo there. I simply couldn't put up with her anymore. She'd become something like a walking cash register to me.

MICHAEL: *(reproachfully)* Dad!

BENJAMIN: When you stop loving, you'll look around for anything that'll justify your feelings. It's because of you, really, that it took so long for me to leave her. But the day came when I couldn't put up with her anymore. *(Benjamin starts playing the piano again. There is sadness in his manner.)*

MICHAEL: You're not upset, I hope, at my having been so direct?

BENJAMIN: No.

MICHAEL: I simply have to speak. I've kept that bottled up inside too long. And I need to be told the truth about all this. We can go on from here, can't we?

BENJAMIN: *(with spontaneous ardor, interrupting his playing)* From this day forward, we're free, aren't we, to establish the kind of relationship we want? If you'll let me, we'll go a long way together, you and I.

MICHAEL: I'd like that, . . . but I'm scared.

BENJAMIN: Of what?

MICHAEL: I'm scared of being . . . well, dropped again. It hit me hard when you left. Real hard. I was happy with you. Never in a thousand years could I imagine you leaving me; then, without any warning . . . you disappeared! I was only 12 years old; how could I understand? Now you see why I'm scared.

BENJAMIN: I understand.

MICHAEL: We were so happy together!

BENJAMIN: It's true, Michael; we did get along very well.

MICHAEL: Why, then, why did you leave?

BENJAMIN: I explained all that a little while ago.

MICHAEL: I get the feeling you haven't told me everything. Leave Mom, O.K., I understand, but leave me? What had I done to you? It's as if I didn't count at all in that whole story!

BENJAMIN: You couldn't be more mistaken!

MICHAEL: We had so much fun together! Boy, did we have a ball, yes or no?

BENJAMIN: Yes.

MICHAEL: Did we look at a slew of cartoons together, on TV!

BENJAMIN: Did we ever!

MICHAEL: I'd hate it so much when the babysitter arrived. That's when you'd start practicing and you didn't want to be disturbed.

BENJAMIN: I had to work, you know.

MICHAEL: I realize that now, but when you're just a kid.... Our best times together, I think, were during the summer. That's when you used to pass your summers at Bromont, in Mom's house. We'd be there alone, you and I, because Mom was working all the time. D'you remember those days?

BENJAMIN: I sure do. You found it really hard letting me rehearse.

MICHAEL: Really! Well, that's when Mommy would show up and whisk me away. It was so dull being with her! All we'd do together was jigsaw puzzles. I was so anxious for you to finish so that we could be together again!

BENJAMIN: We'd often go cycling.

MICHAEL: Swimming too in that little stream, remember?

BENJAMIN: We'd also go on picnics . . . .

MICHAEL: And you'd read me stories: about Achilles, Aeneas, Marco Polo. Then, when I turned 10, we started to go horseback riding together. We even took lessons, and I can remember you going off riding with me for whole days together. Evenings, you'd put me to bed, then go back to practicing the piano. Usually I'd fall asleep while listening to you play.

BENJAMIN: You're right. I remember it all now. *(Benjamin starts to play a piece full of languorous feeling, reminiscent of the kind of piece he used to play to put Michael asleep.)*

MICHAEL: Dad!

BENJAMIN: Yes.

MICHAEL: *(secretively)* Even nowadays I sometimes go to bed with my walkman, just to listen to you play before falling asleep.

BENJAMIN: Is that so!

MICHAEL: That's when I start thinking of the good times we had together. I was so happy with you, Dad, so tremendously happy! . . . But when everything collapsed, I was so unhappy that now I'm scared. I'd like it to be like it was, but I'm scared.

BENJAMIN: *(interrupting his playing)* Things have changed a lot since then, remember.

MICHAEL: But what is it that could have induced you to chuck all of that aside? What happened? Are you going to tell me someday?

BENJAMIN: You'd find it a very dull story, really, the story of a love gone haywire.

(Obviously disturbed, Benjamin starts to play a Chopin composition. A few moments later, Michael goes and sits next to his father. While listening to him play, he slips his arm around his shoulder.)

MICHAEL: Who are you thinking about?

BENJAMIN: Hippolytus.

MICHAEL: Don't think about him anymore. I'm here.

(Benjamin keeps on playing. Little by little, Michael's head settles down on his father's shoulder.)

I keep asking myself, could I be dreaming? I never thought I'd get this kind of a reception from a father who's got no end of conquests to his credit! Never did I think I'd be so close to you one day and *(Michael reaches over and kisses Benjamin on the cheek)* so happy being that way! *(softly)* Is it that way when you're with your father?

BENJAMIN: No!

MICHAEL: D'you still see him?

BENJAMIN: Almost never. Once a year I make that trek up to Chicoutimi.[8]

MICHAEL: And how is it when you meet?

BENJAMIN: Pretty cold. We've got nothing to say to each other. You'd think we weren't living on the same planet.

MICHAEL: D'you love him?

BENJAMIN: I respect him a lot.

MICHAEL: Would you've liked being closer to him?

BENJAMIN: *(sadly)* Yes, I would've liked that a lot, when I was young. I admired him so much! He won't ever have known what kind of person I was.

MICHAEL: *(drawing closer to his father)* Dad, you look so sad!

(Benjamin suddenly stops playing and stares directly at Michael.)

BENJAMIN: It's terrible having to live next to somebody you'd so much wanted to have loved!

MICHAEL: It could've happened to me too, you know.

BENJAMIN: *(bitter almost to the point of raging)* I got nothing from that man: not even a hug or a kiss, no tenderness at all. But I do remember the orders, the example, the work, the food. I really hate the people of that generation, Michael; you've no idea how much I hate them! I get the feeling I've spent all of my life trying to fend them off. And the worst is, it's not over.

MICHAEL: *(joshing him a little)* Well, we know how it is with you artists!

(Benjamin's hands strike the keyboard violently. Then a long silence ensues.)

MICHAEL: I'm sorry, Dad!

BENJAMIN: You just said something there that he would have said.

MICHAEL: Would you prefer it if I left?

BENJAMIN: Have you told me everything you wanted to tell me?

MICHAEL: No. I still haven't told you the real reason why I came here.

BENJAMIN: And what is that reason?

MICHAEL: Have we still got lots of time?

BENJAMIN: A little.

MICHAEL: Well,... before we start talking about that,... have I got time to take a shower? *(No response from Benjamin.)* I feel all hot and sticky. I don't feel comfortable at all.

(Benjamin hesitates. He glances again at his watch.)

I am asking a lot, aren't I? Would you like me to leave?

BENJAMIN: Yes.... I mean, no! I'll continue rehearsing some other time. Go right ahead. You'll find everything you need in the bathroom.

(Michael makes his way to the bathroom. In the loft, it would be behind a screen whose transparency would allow a viewer to follow Michael's every movement. Benjamin is clearly distraught; he is fidgeting uncontrollably. After a long interval he rushes to the tel-

ephone and dials a number. The spectators will remain unaware of the fact that there is nobody at the end of the line.)

Hello! It's me .... I want to tell you that you're dearer to me than anything in this whole universe, ... that without you my life is totally meaningless .... I know it's impossible, but I want to make love to you .... Yes, this very moment, right on the piano .... I've got this deep craving for you that gets me in the gut; I'm burning up ....

(The noise of the shower suddenly stops. The screen allows us to see Michael's shadowy figure drying itself. Benjamin is suddenly at a loss for words.)

Yes .... Yes .... Listen, if it's all right with you, we'll postpone today's meeting .... Somebody has just dropped in. ... It's my son .... We'll speak to each other later, O.K.? Bye! *(He replaces the receiver.)*

MICHAEL: *(still in the bathroom)* Was that her?

(Silence)

Thanks, Dad.

(Silence)

Dad! Did you hear me?

BENJAMIN: Yes, I did.

MICHAEL: I'd like to tell you the real reason why I've come here this morning.

BENJAMIN: Go right ahead!

MICHAEL: I've got this thing I'd like to propose to you.

BENJAMIN: What's that?

(Michael comes out from behind the screen with a towel wrapped around his waist.)

MICHAEL: I'd like it if we lived together.

(A long silence)

You've got this big apartment, and I'd have no trouble find-ing a little corner for myself. It's close to the university, so that I could make it there on foot. As for Mom, I'm sure she'd have no objections; she's never at home anyhow. Pointe-Claire's far from everything; you absolutely need a car. But Outremont.... *(Silence)* How does that sound to you?

BENJAMIN: No, Michael.

MICHAEL: *(somewhat piqued)* I see. *(Long silence)* Why?

BENJAMIN: Because it wouldn't work.

MICHAEL: Why wouldn't it work?

BENJAMIN: Well, ... your grandparents would be sure to refuse.

MICHAEL: Now listen! Don't give me a line like that! Find some other reason, if you want, but not that one. I'm not a kid anymore; I'm a grown-up. We can do what we want now; you yourself said it a while ago. *(Pause. Michael becomes more emphatic.)* C'mon, Dad, you and I'd get along famously together.

BENJAMIN: Michael, you're a great one for dreaming in technicolor.

MICHAEL: Well, that's another dream that's dropped into the drink. Am I going to have to dream only in black and white to satisfy you?

BENJAMIN: I say let's start with more manageable plans, O.K.? We could .... This summer, for instance, we could spend a whole week together, you and I .... Then, come the fall, we'd see each other more often, eat out, spend weekends together in the country....

MICHAEL: Dad, it's not a part-time dad I want, it's a full-time one, ... at least for some short period of time. It's not the moon I'm asking for, for heaven's sake! For six years I've had a never-there father; I've had my fill of that! Today, I want the father I had before he up and left. I couldn't be bothered about the other one. Listen, Dad, I'd like to live with my father. *(Pause)* We could learn to live together again, not the way we once did, but like two adults. We could try to understand each other, get to know each other better, help each other too. I'd take care of the apartment, and of the car too. Those are things I like doing; I did them all the time at Grandpa's. Dad, I'd like to live with my father.

(Pause)

BENJAMIN: It's simply impossible, Michael. I'm too often gone on concert tours; at home, I live out of my suitcases. And I'd like to make one thing quite clear: I refuse to jeopardize my career for anybody; it's too important to me. I'm booked for at least three years in advance, and I don't intend to make any changes there.

MICHAEL: I know all that, Dad. I'm not asking you to do anything like that. *(Pause. Michael attempts the following desperate ploy.)* Listen to this, Dad. I thought long about this plan before coming here today. It's been on my mind for months now. I wouldn't at all mind taking a sabbatical year between college and university.... My dream would be to, well, accompany you on your tour.

BENJAMIN: You're crazy, Michael!

MICHAEL: Let me finish! You'll see, it's not that crazy. I'm still young; I've got plenty of time to get through university! *(Pause)* I've often dreamt of being your manager....

(Benjamin laughs.)

Don't laugh,... it's true! I could help you ... plan your tours,... negotiate your contracts. Imagine how valuable an experience that'd be for me! Then there's the traveling: I'd get so much out of that! Think before you turn me down, Dad. Just for one year. This is no pipe dream.

BENJAMIN: I've already thought about it, Michael, and the answer is no.

MICHAEL: Boy, apart from your child support payments, you're one lousy excuse for a father.

BENJAMIN: Under the present circumstances, that's the best I can do.

MICHAEL: *(explosively)* The best you can do! As a father, you stink.

(Michael sinks once again into reverie. He hears the sound of a galloping horse growing fainter and fainter. He wakes up with a start, uttering a little cry. He speaks in a whisper.)

MICHAEL: *Triumph!... Look. Is that it?... I'm all sticky.... Is Dad still sleeping?* (He realizes that Benjamin is not there.) *Dad.... Where are you?... Triumph, tell me where Dad is. Has he left? He can't have left, because it's not light yet.* (Michael yells.) *Dad!... Dad!...* (He waits.) *Triumph, come here, my pretty Tri-*

umph, come here . . . . Easy, . . . easy . . . . Come right next to me . . . .
Don't be frightened, Triumph, don't be frightened; there's nothing to
fear, no harm will come to us. Don't you worry; Dad's not gone far.
There were those wolves, see, and he's gone to chase them far away. . . .
He's coming back right away; all we have to do is wait for him . . . .
I'll protect you; don't worry. Look, the sun's starting to come up,
we've nothing to fear now . . . . (Pause. Michael looks at his
stomach. He yells.) *Dad! . . .* (addressing Triumph) *Do you*
think he's angry? (He yells.) *Dad! . . . Come back, Dad!*

(Michael then comes out of the reverie, but he continues to mix
dream and reality.)

You're nothing but a damned abandoning father. You're the
most useless of all the fathers on this earth!

BENJAMIN: Hey! Not so loud!

MICHAEL: There's only one person who knows what kind of
father you are, and that's me. And if I feel like it, I'll yell it
out to all the world. *(yelling)* As a father, you're a total wash-
out, totally incapable, totally incompetent, . . . just like your
own father. *(Pause)* A father's of absolutely no use whatsoever. He's the kind of guy who's always gone but comes
back now and then, doles out some money, makes excuses
and is off in a flash. A father doesn't know the first thing
about what to do with his son, doesn't even know what a
son is. It's as if a guy like you had never learnt what it is to
be a father, what it is to love, really.

BENJAMIN: *(flaring up)* And where do you think I could have
learned that? Did my father love me, take me in his arms,
kiss me, touch me? Not on your life! My father, Michael,
never taught me how to love; the only thing I learnt from
him was how to intimidate others.

MICHAEL: Wouldn't you like that to change?

BENJAMIN: *(in a derisive tone of voice)* The real fathers, you know, are those that see their sons once in a while, to shake their hand and talk politics or hockey with them over a glass of beer. That's as far as I've been taught to go, as a father, and that's as far as I can go.

MICHAEL: Still, there was a time when you weren't that kind of a father at all.... You were a much better father than that.

BENJAMIN: It wasn't the same then. You were just a kid.

MICHAEL: What's that got to do with it?

BENJAMIN: When your son gets to be a certain age, you can't love him the way you did when he was a little kid.

MICHAEL: Just because he's gotten to be a bit older, then? Is that it?

BENJAMIN: There's more to it than that.

MICHAEL: No, I'm sure that's the reason. *(abruptly)* It's when he starts growing hairs on his balls and his prick gets stiff.

BENJAMIN: *(shocked)* Shut up!

MICHAEL: You may be a great artist, but you're just as great a bust as a father as all the others.

BENJAMIN: If you only knew how wrong you are, Michael!

MICHAEL: Then prove it to me! Accept my proposal!

BENJAMIN: I can't.

MICHAEL: Why can't you, for heaven's sake?

BENJAMIN: Let's can the whole discussion, O.K.? *(He returns to the piano and plays a tumultuous-sounding piece.)*

MICHAEL: *(yelling so as to drown out the music)* Will you stop playing that goddam piano and tell me why!

BENJAMIN: *(despondent)* Leave, Michael! Leave right away, or we'll hurt each other!

MICHAEL: *(subdued)* I'm sorry. That wasn't at all nice of me. I'll put on my things and go. *(He walks towards the bathroom.)*

BENJAMIN: *(interrupting his playing)* Just a second. *(Pause)* Don't leave. Stay a little while longer.

(Benjamin runs his fingers over the keys. Michael sits next to him.)

MICHAEL: I can be something of a pest, can't I? *(Pause)* Where are you now in your thoughts? *(Pause)* What scenes are you revisiting?

(Silence)

Are you standing on those Saguenay bluffs you used to bring me to, when I was a little boy?

BENJAMIN: Yes. It's brilliant sunshine. A horse on the river's edge is starting a slow ascent up the bluff. You'd swear he had just come out of the river.

MICHAEL: Is he alone?

BENJAMIN: No. Somebody's riding him.... *(He hesitates.)* Somebody I'm hopelessly in love with.

MICHAEL: Your girlfriend?

BENJAMIN: *(interrupting his playing)* I have no girlfriend, Michael.

MICHAEL: What do you mean, you don't have a girlfriend?

BENJAMIN: It's like I said; I don't have a girlfriend.

MICHAEL: Who's riding the horse, then?

BENJAMIN: A young horseman....

MICHAEL: What?

BENJAMIN: ...with flaming red hair.

MICHAEL: *(rising from the bench)* What's that you say?

BENJAMIN: You heard me.

MICHAEL: What kind of a joke is this?

BENJAMIN: It's no joke.

MICHAEL: Why are you telling me a thing like that, Dad? You've got to be putting me on!

BENJAMIN: No, Michael. What I'm telling you is the truth.

MICHAEL: You can't be telling me I've got a father who's....

BENJAMIN: Yes, your father's a homosexual, and you happen to be my son.

(Michael guffaws nervously while pacing to and fro.)

MICHAEL: *(with incredulous amazement)* Hey, guys! Would you believe that! I've got a faggot for a father! You're a barrel of laughs! Why d'you pull a joke like that on me?

BENJAMIN: So you don't want to believe me, eh?

MICHAEL: *(explosively)* If it's true, you're one hell of a scumbag!

BENJAMIN: *(rising from the bench)* Calm down, Michael!

MICHAEL: Don't you touch me! I'll knock you one that'll set your head rattling! I've already had to slug someone before; I won't hesitate to do it again. Last year, at college . . . somebody tried to come on to me . . . . He made me advances . . . . *(violently reproachful, in words seemingly addressed to his father)* I slugged the guy right in the kisser. . . . I've never been able to speak to him again . . . . Maybe you didn't know it, but the people at college who get caught doing those things are thrown out on their asses.

BENJAMIN: *(as if speaking to himself)* Even nowadays!

MICHAEL: There's nothing guys like that won't do! Once, when I was playing hockey, the team got hold of a dirty magazine. All the action was in public toilets, and it involved only men. I found the whole thing . . . disgusting, if you want to know. *(Pause)* I certainly wouldn't like to be told that my father goes playing with his and foreign pricks in the toilet.

   (He walks towards the bathroom. He is seen dressing. On coming out, he strides purposefully towards the door.)

So long, I'm out of here. The only thing I can tell you before I leave is that, if what you said is true, then you'd better hightail it to a shrink quick!

BENJAMIN: I've been to see some already.

MICHAEL: And?

BENJAMIN: Three wanted to cure me; the fourth one taught me how to feel good about myself.

MICHAEL: *(scathingly)* But how have you been able to accept that you'll never live a normal life again?

BENJAMIN: Normal?

MICHAEL: I mean exactly that. Never to have a wife anymore, not even a mistress, kids, a home.... When you go out, for example, let's say to a reception, you get to meet a lot of people who know you. What d'you do then? *(with a sudden flash of insight)* Now I see it! All those ladies you're always being photographed with, they're just a front, aren't they?

BENJAMIN: No, Michael; they're really friends of mine.

MICHAEL: But what if they'd want to ... what if they'd want to ... go to bed with you?

BENJAMIN: *(quietly)* I can tell you, at any rate, that it never finishes with me being "slugged in the kisser."

MICHAEL: I don't understand.... I'd never have thought somebody could have a father who loves men.

BENJAMIN: *(trying to be facetious)* Don't you go worrying; it doesn't run in the family.

MICHAEL: *(sharply)* If it did, I'd know about it. *(Pause)* But how... how does it happen my own father's turned gay?

BENJAMIN: I've always been that way.

MICHAEL: Since you were a kid?

(Benjamin nods.)

Boys more than the girls?

BENJAMIN: It depends on when. Sometimes yes, sometimes no.

MICHAEL: This simply can't be! I can't get it through this head of mine that I've been... how do you say that?... by someone who was gay. When you and Mom made love, you must've wanted her. You must've loved her. You couldn't have been a homosexual at the same time you were doing that!

BENJAMIN: Yes, Michael, I was a homosexual when I married your mother, when I made love to her, when you were born, and when the three of us were living together.

MICHAEL: Buy why? Have you ever asked yourself why?

BENJAMIN: *(flaring up)* Of course I've often asked myself why! I even spent far too much time asking myself why. I don't know why, Michael; I don't know and I don't want to know anymore.

MICHAEL: If you knew all of this when you married Mom, why did you go ahead with it? You must've known it couldn't work out, that you'd make her miserable. Why did you marry her, for heaven's sake?

BENJAMIN: I loved Odette at that time, and it felt good being with her.

MICHAEL: Does she know this?

BENJAMIN: Yes.

MICHAEL: *(sharply)* How did she take all of this?

BENJAMIN: She also was bitter about the whole thing, at first. She felt she'd been taken in, manipulated. But after a while, she realized I had really loved her, that I hadn't acted out of malice. Maybe she hasn't forgiven me, but I'm sure she understands. As for your grandparents, well, they capitalized on Odette's pain. They had their lawyers settle everything: the divorce on grounds of adultery, the child custody arrangements, the alimony, everything. *(sarcastically)* One thing, though, they kindly consented not to disclose—without consulting with me about it, of course— to save my career, they said, to prevent your life from being messed up, and especially to nip scandal in the bud . . . that thing was the gender of the person whom the adultery had been committed with.

MICHAEL: Because you'd cheated on her with a guy?

BENJAMIN: Yes.

MICHAEL: How did they find out?

BENJAMIN: Listen, Michael, it's hard for me to go into all of this. There must be other things we can talk about.

MICHAEL: Not on your life. If I'm to understand, it's important I know everything. I've got to know the truth.

BENJAMIN: Well, you won't find the truth all that appealing. Are you sure you want to know more about this?

MICHAEL: Yes.

BENJAMIN: Even if what you hear disgusts you?

MICHAEL: Yes.

BENJAMIN: It was your grandmother who first found out about it. She was reading about a police raid in the newspaper.... It described... Michael, are you sure you want me to go on?

MICHAEL: I'm certain to hear about it, one way or another.

BENJAMIN: *(in a quiet tone of voice)* What she read about was a police raid on some public toilets.

(A long silence)

MICHAEL: Don't tell me that you too, you do that in the public toilets! That's just awful!

BENJAMIN: Why?

MICHAEL: You're not going to try to defend yourself, are you?

BENJAMIN: You wouldn't understand that? Where I went, you don't give a damn whom you screw, so long as you get to screw somebody!

MICHAEL: But that prick of yours is deep in shit, Dad!

BENJAMIN: Stop it, Michael! I said, stop it!

MICHAEL: But they're shit, Dad, plain, unadulterated shit, all those people who go screw in public toilets.

BENJAMIN: That's not true, Michael. I also saw there what could've passed for images of my own father: defeated fathers, sad-looking, confused, vulnerable.... I'll always remember the contemptuous look your grandparents gave me when they stuck that newspaper article under my nose. Shit.... I bet that's all I was to them too. Your grandmother was fit to be tied. Your grandfather, though, didn't say a blasted word. *(Pause)* At the divorce hearing, I obviously had no choice but to accept all their conditions.

MICHAEL: What about your father?

BENJAMIN: Him? Well, if he'd known about it....*(Pause)* I was 9 years old at the time. He was in the swing with my uncle Roger. Some people in the village had caught one and roughed him up a bit. I can actually remember Dad saying this: "If I found out one day that my son has gone faggot, I'd take my shotgun and let 'im have it both barrels."

MICHAEL: So you'll never tell him?

BENJAMIN: It makes no difference anymore. But for many years, let me tell you, I was pretty damn anxious to see him die; yes, that's what I wanted, to see him die.

MICHAEL: Why's that?

BENJAMIN: I get the feeling he's never forgiven me for making a career out of playing the piano. For him, piano was for sissies; at home only the girls cared about the pee-AH-noh. There was something else I had to do, maybe, to redeem myself, to prove to him I was a man who could love a woman and father children. My father, you know, is not any different from all the other fathers who've never held sons in their arms, because they're afraid they might find the experience pleasant.

MICHAEL: *(very aggressively)* So, Dad, you were anxious to see your father die....

BENJAMIN: *(suddenly aware of the import of his remarks)* All right, let's stop all that!

MICHAEL: I'd like something like that to happen to you, too. I don't know anymore how much I hate you.

BENJAMIN: I'd really like to stop that!

MICHAEL: D'you still go into those toilets?

BENJAMIN: No. *(Pause)* Not since I've had a . . . lover, at any rate.

MICHAEL: Because you've . . . .

BENJAMIN: Yes, I've got a lover.

MICHAEL: Is that so! Then I've got a . . . stepfather? Is that how I should call him?

BENJAMIN: For heaven's sake, Michael!

MICHAEL: Who's the guy?

BENJAMIN: What's the point in asking that?

MICHAEL: Who is the guy?

BENJAMIN: Michael!

MICHAEL: D'you love him?

BENJAMIN: *(with some hesitation)* Yes.

MICHAEL: How long's this been going on?

BENJAMIN: Eight months.

MICHAEL: Eight months.

BENJAMIN: Eight months.

MICHAEL: I'm just about to freak out, I think.

BENJAMIN: We can stop here, if you want.

MICHAEL: I'd like to know a little bit more, if you don't mind. Tell me, who is this guy?

BENJAMIN: *(exasperated)* Martin Lapalme. Anything else you'd like to know?

MICHAEL: Martin Lapalme!

(Benjamin says nothing.)

But that guy's my age! He's only 18! *(pacing in a highly distraught manner from the door to the piano)* He must think he's going to bed with his father! What school does he go to, him? Who does his assignments? His dad and mom: do they know anything about this?

BENJAMIN: Whether it's Martin Lapalme or somebody else, Michael, it's no business of yours whom I choose to live my life with.

MICHAEL: *(forcefully)* Right on! You prefer being nice to some damn...faggot than to your own son. *(at the top of his voice, with tears streaming down his face)* What a filthy bunch of bastards you are! As for you, you're just a lousy ass licker! Jesus, am I going to have to go faggot to get you to love me? What's that guy got that I haven't, for shit's sake, that makes you give him everything I've always wanted while I get only the leftovers? I suppose it's because you can grab his cock, isn't it? *(thrusting his pelvis forward)* Well, go ahead, damn you, play with my cock if you need that to love me.

(Benjamin retreats to the piano.)

BENJAMIN: Leave, Michael!

(Benjamin begins to play.)

MICHAEL: *(yelling so as to drown out the music)* I'm not leaving 'til I've had my say. That'd be letting you off the hoook, wouldn't it? I've got other things to say, if you don't mind. You want to know why I came here? It was to see my father. But that dear father of mine has dumped me, just as he's dumped my mother. That fine gentleman doesn't come to see us, doesn't write, tells us fuckall about what he's doing. You wanna know why? The fine gentleman can't spare the time; he's too busy licking the asses of kids my age! No wonder he can't take care of us, or find time to love us! I ask you, what kind of father are you, to show so little interest in what happens to me? You're really a prize pop, you know! I've spent six whole years waiting, hoping you'd return, watching for the mailman every day. I've looked into every goddam newspaper, hoping to see your face, built dreams as big as all outdoors where you and I'd be happy together, only to be told by the fine gentleman that he refuses to have anything to do with me because he's gone faggot! Well, I won't buy it. So long.

(Michael exits quickly, slamming the door. Benjamin sits stunned a moment, then makes a frenzied attempt to execute a complex musical phrase. The last few chords ringingly betray his agitation.)

BENJAMIN: Not you too! You're not going to stand me up too! *(He starts playing another, softer-toned passage, and is heard addressing the music.)* Come back.... Come back.... Now there!... There's nobody here, nobody but you and me. I'm yours, yours alone. You can take up all the room, if you want. We'll build a high wall around us, and keep everybody else out.... Ah! That's just fine.... Be nice to me.... Caress me.... Beautiful! *(He suddenly interrupts his playing and slams his foot against the piano leg.)* For shit's sake! You're not exactly my idea of a great lay! *(Greatly agitated, he paces back and forth. Then, stopping suddenly, he yells at the top of his voice:)* Martin!... *(Hoping to calm down, he lights up a cigarette. Then he walks up to the photograph of the horse.)* So you won't buy it, eh?... Well, that's your hard luck! I'm crossing you out, Michael. You've got to take me as I am, or not at all.

(He walks back to the piano, intending to play. Addressing the piano)
He's coming in.... He's standing there, next to the door,
with the sweat pouring down.... *(to Martin)* Your dad's
well?...You've certainly grown since I last saw you....
You're almost a man now.... *(to the piano)* Boy! Is he ever
nice-looking!... *(to Martin)* Are you in a hurry? Maybe
you'd like a beer or a cup of coffee before leaving? *(to the piano)* I don't want him to leave.... There's something about
him,...his voice, the way he acts.... I'll get him a beer....
We're just there, the two of us, staring at each other, trying
to think of things to say.... *(to Martin)* You're gonna make
me blush.... You must have a lot of other idols besides me.
... *(to the piano)* That's when he asks me to.... *(to Martin)*
Of course. I'd be happy to. Come sit next to me...Now
what would you like to hear?... *(to the piano)* A whole
bloody concert, if that's what he wants, so long as he stays!
(to Martin) Would you be a great romantic too? *(He plays in
seductive tones, wooing Martin. He throws fetching glances at him
and smiles coquettishly.)* You've got really nice hair.... I've always liked people with red hair. They're people with real
passion in them. *(to the piano)* He's shaking a bit, just a tiny
bit. He's staring at my hands.... *(Benjamin impregnates his
playing with a palpable sensuality. And when he speaks, his voice is
quavering with emotion.)* He's staring at me now. He's breathing harder. I can feel his breath on my cheek.... I turn to
look at him. His mouth is right next to mine.... *(He abruptly
stops playing and yells out at the piano.)* You're damn right. On
you, right there. And what's that to you? *(He walks up to the
painting of the horse.)* If you can't hack it, go find some other
wall to hang on! *(He then addresses his father's photograph.)* Why
are you all hot and bothered about whom I make love with?
Go get that gun of yours! Blast away! I've known for ages
now you'd never be able to do it. *(Walking back to the piano, he
begins playing a tempestuous musical phrase.)* Listen, George,
your son Martin's going to be 18 in a few months! *(He plays
the same phrase over again.)* Even at that age, you can be aware
of that, you know. *(He repeats the same phrase.)* Let 'im live his
own life. You can't turn the clock back to 1950, to that col-

lege in Chicoutimi! And you can't ask him to put his desires on hold the way I had to during I don't know how many years, simply because I thought there was nobody else like me! *(He is still playing the same musical phrase, but less forcefully. In bitter tones, since he is addressing the piano while continuing to play)* Thanks, George. Thanks for not calling the police. Thanks for our long-lasting friendship. Thanks for that little bit of consideration you still have for me. Thanks for my career. I promise you, I won't see him again. *(He starts playing a more gentle tune.)* I've at least been able to find out that he loved me.... *(He laughs briefly.)* Believe me, I'm not the kind of guy who would've told anything like that to my father! That Martin has got all kinds of guts.... Or maybe he was just being candid.... A nice kid, really.... *(Pause)* A mere kid! *(At the word "kid," he slams his hands against the keyboard. He then stands up and starts pacing agitatedly as before. Stopping next to the piano, he wraps his arms around it.)* I beg of you, love me. There's only you; you're all I've got in this world. Everybody else's left. *(He stops, then looks resentfully at the piano. He looks toward the door and addresses Martin.)* You will come back, won't you, Martin?... When? That's fine, Sunday, Sunday morning early. *(Benjamin plays a very romantic air. There is a change of lighting in the apartment, indicating a lapse of time. It is now late afternoon. The doorbell rings. Benjamin makes no move to answer it. It rings again. He decides to press the intercom button.)* Who's there?

MICHAEL: *(on the intercom)* It's Michael. *(Pause)* I've come back. *(Pause)* Can I?

(A long silence. Benjamin presses on the entrance button, then walks back to the piano. When Michael walks in, they look at each other for a moment. Then Michael runs up to his father. They embrace.)

MICHAEL: Dad! You must take me in, or I'll go off the deep end for sure. I'm alone, completely alone. I need you, Dad. I've no idea what to do with my life. Mom? She's a stranger to me. And as for my grandparents, they're driving me crazy. There's nobody I feel good with, except Triumph. *(Pause. He is crying.)* As for that other thing, well, I don't care. It's fine with me whoever you go out with.

BENJAMIN: It's better that we don't.

MICHAEL: I'll be able to take it, Dad. That part of your life, that's your business, not mine. We'll pull a nice big black curtain over it and I'll forget all about it.

BENJAMIN: It's too late.

MICHAEL: What do you mean?

BENJAMIN: You don't see us making a threesome out of it, do you?

MICHAEL: Because....

BENJAMIN: We made an arrangement 15 days ago.

MICHAEL: *(gently remonstrating)* Liar! *(Michael walks up to Benjamin and speaks to him gently.)* Hey, it's me, your son, Dad, nobody else.

BENJAMIN: Michael, Martin's not my son; he's my lover.

MICHAEL: I'm the one who needs you, Dad. I'm the one who's alone. I'm the one whose life's on the rocks.

BENJAMIN: You can't take Martin's place.

MICHAEL: *(holding back, trying to speak as dispassionately as possible)* Dad, Martin Lapalme left six months ago with his parents; I know all about it. *(There is a long pause.)* What's the point of you lying to me, Dad? There's nothing between Martin Lapalme and you.

BENJAMIN: *(musingly)* He never did come back.

MICHAEL: Put all that behind you, Dad. The whole story's fiction, and quite frankly I'm damn glad it is. *(There is a long silence.)* It's clear your life's no bed of roses, is it, Dad? I can't get over the things we'll come up with to hide from the others just how miserable we feel! You can't imagine all the crap I used to tell my chums on the hockey team! I had them believing I had a girlfriend in Pointe-Claire, who I'd come lay every weekend. Boy, just to impress those guys, have I screwed a lot of those Granby girls! *(He laughs, with some bitterness. Then there is a pause.)* How do you think we can manage, you and I, to love each other and to cut out the crap? How do the others do it?

BENJAMIN: They've made up their minds to respect each other. What they want to give each other is, well, esteem, admiration, pity, other things like that too, for all I know.... They do what they have to do.... They protect each other, give each other money when they're lacking some.... They buck each other up, watch over each other's interests.... They go out on a limb for each other.... They may even die, some of them....

MICHAEL: Is that really the case? What is it about me that, when I talk of loving my father, I'd like it to mean more than that? *(Pause)* I mustn't be normal, really.

BENJAMIN: What would that be... for you?

MICHAEL: I don't know anymore. I'm all mixed up. *(Pause)* We'd have to live it. To try it. I've got to make a kind of leap from the time I was a kid to right now. The only problem, though, is, there's no telling what comes after that. It's a total blank to me. What about you?

BENJAMIN: I'm not any better than the others are at inventing. I do what's been done before.

MICHAEL: *(walking slowly toward the door)* We've reached a deadlock, I think, and I'm not sure we'll be able to see eye to eye someday. The only thing clear to me now is that you don't want me to move in with you. *(Pause)* What's worse, I'll never have known whether you hate me or love me.

(Michael walks slowly out of the door, but Benjamin speaks just as he is about to close it.)

BENJAMIN: I love you, Michael. *(A long silence)* Young Hippolytus on his horse, galloping through the countryside: that's you. That image's locked into my brain, and it springs out at me . . . before my every concert.

MICHAEL: What's that? During those five or six seconds you're concentrating before starting to play, you're thinking about me!

BENJAMIN: Yes. *(Pause)* What's more, you're even more marvelous in the flesh.

MICHAEL: What d'you mean?

BENJAMIN: *(with obvious reluctance)* I find I've got the handsomest son on earth.

MICHAEL: *(seizing the opportunity)* If that's the case, why couldn't you and I go off together, you, like the Theseus of old, off to conquer the world; me, your son, a kind of latter-day Hippolytus, eager to help you do it?

BENJAMIN: I'm too scared.

MICHAEL: Scared?

BENJAMIN: The horses'll bolt, and you'll tear your flesh on the rocks.

MICHAEL: What are you trying to say?

BENJAMIN: What I'm saying is that I'm scared to...love you.

MICHAEL: But I'm your son!

BENJAMIN: You don't understand. I'm scared to be with you, to live with you, to travel with you.

MICHAEL: Why?

BENJAMIN: Michael, let's stop this discussion right now! I can't go on!

MICHAEL: Why are you afraid of me?

BENJAMIN: If things were to be the way you say.... If we were to be together all the time, close to each other.... *(There is a very long pause.)* If I started to love you too much, to crave more than...to....

(Benjamin is crying; he tries in vain to continue speaking. Meanwhile Michael tries to make sense of what his father has just said.)

MICHAEL: You want....

BENJAMIN: Don't say it!

MICHAEL: You want me.... You want to go to bed with me.

BENJAMIN: *(pleadingly)* Enough, Michael! *(There is a long pause.)* I've never wanted to hurt you. I simply loved you too much. I had to leave.

MICHAEL: Is that it! So that's why you left!

BENJAMIN: Yes.

MICHAEL: Because you ... wanted me.

BENJAMIN: Yes.

MICHAEL: But I was 12 years old!

BENJAMIN: Yes.

(A long silence)

MICHAEL: You left in the middle of the night. I'll always remember it. We'd decided we'd go off romping on horseback during the night. We had made a little wood fire, I remember. It was hot, really hot, that night. We had played for hours with Triumph.

BENJAMIN: Those days are long gone, Michael. Maybe you should leave now; I think we've said everything we had to say. You see now why you can't come and stay here.

MICHAEL: Then we lay down, one next to the other, on top of our sleeping bags, because it was so hot. I remember I'd gotten Triumph to lie right next to us to protect us. I suppose I was scared of wolves or coyotes. Then I fell asleep. When I woke up, it felt all sticky. It was the first time. I didn't know what it was. It scared me.

BENJAMIN: It was normal; you were 12 years old.

MICHAEL: You did something to me that night; I know you did, and that's why you left. Tell me what it was. I want to know!

BENJAMIN: Somehow I couldn't sleep. It was hot. I walked around a good part of the night. That's when I decided to go away.

MICHAEL: But didn't you come back to lie down at some point?

BENJAMIN: You were tossing restlessly on the bag. Suddenly, you turned completely towards me; you were still sleeping.

MICHAEL: What happened then?

BENJAMIN: Your penis was stiff, and it was up against my thigh.... You were breathing heavily....

MICHAEL: Go on!

BENJAMIN: I stroked it gently.... *(A long silence)* You came almost immediately. I got up and ran off in a panic.

MICHAEL: I was only 12. You knew what you were doing, at any rate. I'm grateful you left.

BENJAMIN: I don't know how I made it back to Montreal.... I got stinkin' drunk,...then went and hid myself in the toilets.... A police raid,...the station,...the interrogation.... It was as if I was trying finally to get punished! I made up my mind it was over, that I'd never be the one to hurt you.... I turned to my work to forget,...to music,... only to music....

MICHAEL: Can you love me now, today, without wanting me? Can I be only a son to you?

BENJAMIN: *(staggered)* I don't know, Michael. There are others in the same boat as I am who can; I know that for a fact. But in my own case, I really can't say. For me, loving is desiring too. I'd be the most fortunate man in the world... but also the unhappiest...if we were to become lovers.

(A long silence. Michael stands next to the door.)

MICHAEL: I'm 18 now, Dad; I can make up my own mind. So, when you don't feel so bad about it....

(He waits a moment, as if in expectation of some response from his father. The light fades out.)

CURTAIN

∽

NOTES:

[1] Benoît in the French original.

[2] Outremont is a very affluent borough on the Island of Montreal.

[3] Pointe-Claire is a predominantly English-speaking town on the outskirts of Montreal, approximately 15 miles from where Benjamin lives.

[4] Vincent-d'Indy is a famous school in Outremont.

[5] Magog is a small town in the Eastern Townships situated some 80 miles from Montreal and close to the town of Bromont, where Michael's grandparents live. In Bromont live some of the wealthiest families in Quebec. It is a well-known ski resort and equestrian center.

[6] Granby is a small town in the Eastern Townships, adjacent to Bromont.

[7] Saint-Fulgence is a little fishing village on the shores of the Saguenay River.

[8] Chicoutimi is an industrial town close to St-Fulgence on the Saguenay.

Jean-Claude van Itallie

ANCIENT BOYS
a requiem

Author's note: This edition of "Ancient Boys" is an early one.
A further version is being used for production.

in loving memory
of Ira

JEAN-CLAUDE VAN ITALLIE was born in Brussels, Belgium in 1936 and raised in Great Neck, Long Island. He graduated from Harvard in 1958. Van Itallie divides his time between Boulder, Colorado, where he teaches at the University of Colorado and Naropa Institute, his farm in northwestern Massachusetts, and New York and Princeton universities, where he teaches.

His trilogy of one-act plays, *America Hurrah*, was hailed in the United States as the watershed off-Broadway play of the 'sixties. A political play, it ran for two years at the Pocket Theatre in New York City and was performed at the Royal Court Theatre in London. It received the Vernon Rice Drama Desk Award, was translated into French, Dutch, Japanese, and many other languages, and continues to be produced all over the world.

Van Itallie was the principal playwright of Joe Chaikin's Open Theater. His early short plays include *I'm Really Here, Almost Like Being*, and *The Hunter and the Bird*, which premiered on Danish television. Van Itallie wrote for the Open Theater what has been called "the classic ensemble play," *The Serpent*. *The Serpent* opened at the Teatro degli Arti in Rome in 1968 before touring Italy, France, Switzerland, and Holland and returning to New York to win a *Village Voice* Obie.

Van Itallie was one of Ellen Stewart's original LaMama playwrights; his plays *Motel* and *Interview* premiered there. *Motel* and van Itallie's *War* were part of LaMama's first European tour.

Van Itallie has written musicals with composer Richard Peaslee, including *The King of the United States*, and *A Fable*.

In the 'seventies, van Itallie wrote his frequently produced new English versions of the four major plays of Chekhov.

Van Itallie was a long-time student of the Tibetan teacher, Chögyam Trungpa Rinpoche; his play *The Tibetan Book of the Dead*, a classical but contemporary poetic and theatrical ensemble version of the text, with music by Steve Gorn, was first produced at LaMama in New York City in the early 'eighties. *Paradise Ghetto*, his play based on the Nazi detention camp for Czech artists, was first produced at Actors' Alley Theatre in

Los Angeles in the fall of 1987. His 1985 translation of Jean Genet's *The Balcony* was commissioned and first produced by the American Repertory Theatre in Cambridge, Massachusetts. In the fall of 1988, van Itallie directed it at New York University. *The Traveller*, his full-length play about a person recovering from aphasia, was first produced at the Mark Taper Forum in the spring of 1987 and was seen in the fall of that year at the Almeida Theatre in London, starring David Threlfall. His short monologue play written with and for Joe Chaikin, *Struck Dumb*, received its premiere production at the Taper Two in Los Angeles in the spring of 1988 and is playing in cities in the United States in the fall of 1989.

Van Itallie has often written for public television, including a film on Picasso, *Picasso, A Writer's Diary*. He has been the recipient of grants from CAPS, The National Endowment for the Arts, and the Rockefeller and Ford Foundations and was twice a Guggenheim Fellow.

Van Itallie has recently been performing in a dance-theater piece he co-conceived with the choreographer Nancy Spanier on the subject of aging. *Ancient Boys* will be produced at La-Mama in November, 1989, and at the University of Colorado in March, 1990.

CHARACTERS

LUKE, *in his forties, is trim and attractive, wearing jeans, a flannel shirt, and a good-looking lightweight sport jacket. He does not have a moustache.*

SHERRY, *in her thirties, is dressed all in contemporary black except for bright red lipstick and red tights.*

DANNY, *in his thirties, evidently a dancer, wears neatly pressed designer overalls, a gingham shirt, and bright new sneakers.*

CHRIS, *in his twenties, is a blond body-builder.*

REUBEN, *in his thirties, is thin, dark-haired, intense, and charismatic.*

TIME
August 1984

PLACE
Reuben's loft, Manhattan

(At the back of the stage is the large slide screen. The projection on the screen is now of an apartment on New York's upper West Side in the early 1980s. Objects are neat: a candle; large books on art, magic, and the movies; a jar of colored pencils; some crystals; beautiful new and antique tools.

Below the screen is the main playing area, which will serve as several remembered locations. In the playing area are a draughting table and a contemporary stool; an old wooden wheelchair with an old velvet cushion; a couch; and a low table on which there are light switches, a cassette player, a slide projector, and the phone. An eating table and two chairs are to one side.

The friends—Sherry, Luke, and Danny are there now—sit near the front of the stage, facing the audience; each has a phone beside him or her. It is as if they are watching the slides and events that actually take place behind them.

The music heard from the cassette player is Cole Porter singing Cole Porter, at a fairly low volume. The friends are drinking champagne.

Until Reuben's entrance, we will see the following slides in succession:

> *Fred and Ginger dancing*
> *Actual color close-up of Saturn's rings*
> *Cole Porter's face*
> *Greek bust of Emperor Hadrian's lover*
> *Wicked witch and flying monkeys—still from the film* The Wizard of Oz
> *Stonehenge*
> *Danny sticking his tongue way out*
> *Interior of La Scala opera house*
> *Michelangelo's Adam from the Sistine Chapel*
> *The Great Pyramid*
> *Romantic close-up of Sherry's face in a red hat and veil*

Sometimes the next slide comes on by itself; sometimes one of the friends changes it by remote control.

DANNY: *(speaking to the other friends, but looking out front)* The watershed event in our mutual puberty was to be flown to New York to see a crappy musical which we both adored: *Destry Rides Again*. It started me dancing, and he built this exquisite model of the set.

(Chris enters. He seems awkward and ill at ease. He nods at Luke, who gets up and embraces him. Sherry does the same.)

LUKE: *(who knows him, to Chris)* Hi. Sit down. We're just talking about him.

DANNY: *(impressed by Chis)* Hi, I'm Danny. Reuben kept us in airtight compartments, didn't he? Ruby rules, I guess.

CHRIS: Hi. *(Chris sits. There is a phone next to him too. Several slides go by.)*

SHERRY: *(pouring champagne for Chris)* Most of my men friends are gay, but my relationship with Reuben was different. It was always different. From the start I told myself: face it— he's queer, and you're attracted to him. Not quite from the start. Ours was the first class at Princeton with women in it. So I was insecure. He and I laughed a lot, a little hysterically. People enjoyed us together: we were champagne buddies. Til one day in my room he suddenly got mad, I don't know why—he put on his funny kid's khaki jacket with the hood and left school. Dropped out. Said that was enough formal education. I didn't see him again for six years. If I don't have a cigarette I'm going to die too, right now.

(She changes the slide. She lights a cigarette, takes one puff, and puts it out. She changes the slide again, then, seated, continues.)

All right—what happened is he freaked because I got him to bed. It was the end of our sophomore year. It had taken me all that time. And he tried, he really did. He was polite, he was very polite, he was even funny. But in the end he just said, "There are too many ghosts, Sherry. I can't get past the ghosts." He said he was sorry. Now, don't any of you say it can't be done. That was how I found out. Six years later when I was Girl Fridaying on Broadway, I go to see *A Little Night Music*, and there at intermission—da dum: big recognition scene. At two in the morning after a lot of expensive caffeine on 57th Street, it's settled: we're not lovers, we're soulmates. At three in the morning he brings me home to see his slide show. So after that I started sending over people to see his work, so he could earn some money.

LUKE: The first time, and every time I saw him with his slides, it was—the same. He'd slowly flip through what I didn't even know before were the crazy archetypes of my soul. They were also his personal tarot images. He was like a serious child playing, a young priest exquisitely performing fierce Mysteries at Eleusis, or on Atlantis. Afterward he'd be smiling, and my eyes would be tearing. It didn't matter where we were. He could take us anywhere. It was acid without acid. He was the purest artist I ever met, and the most personal. He must have learned over a lot of lifetimes. I remember after the first visit I ended up dazed on the street, with a red rose in my hand.

(Behind the friends, Reuben enters the playing space. There is a magnetic intensity about him, and a lightness. He wears black pants, a white collarless shirt, and sneakers. He casually lays a board against the wall. Throughout the play he will keep adding to this pyramid of found boards and brooms. He puts on a cassette of big-band music, lies on the couch, picks up the phone, and dials. Sherry's phone rings. She picks it up.)

REUBEN: *(on the phone to Sherry—he has a slight Southern accent)* They're ashamed of me, Sherry.

SHERRY: *(on the phone to Reuben)* I'll be there in two shakes.

> *(They hang up. Reuben puts on a slide of a pig's face. Sherry gets into an evening coat. Reuben takes black-tie accoutrements out of elegant store boxes and half-heartedly puts them on.)*

SHERRY: *(to the others)* We loved shopping together. We could have both been fashion designers. But by the time I got to his place . . . .

REUBEN: Sherry, I don't want to go.

SHERRY: Why not?

REUBEN: *(imitating his mother)* "Honey, ah'm counting on you. Your Daddy and ah *need* to be proud of our boy. All your Daddy's business acquaintances are gonna be there." *(He drops the accent.)* Sherry, she thinks I'm going to wee-wee right on the floor of the Rainbow Room.

SHERRY: *(revealing a bottle of champagne)* Inducement?

REUBEN: To wee-wee? They want to show me off. I have to play macho. I have to play a success.

SHERRY: *(pouring champagne)* So?

REUBEN: *(self-disparagingly)* So?

SHERRY: My son the artist. Why not?

REUBEN: Because they want my son the *famous* artist. They want proof. You've gotta show written proof. That's the rules. They don't care what I do—I could juggle turds, if I got a good review. They could show the review to their friends: "Look, it says he's the greatest turd juggler in the world. He's going to Hollywood. My son the successful turd juggler." We're going to have to strut a lot of style to get through this evening, Sherry.

SHERRY: So? *(She sings from* My Fair Lady. *)* "I said to him you did it, you did it. They said you were romantic, and so damned aristocratic, and *you* did it."

(They both drink the champagne.)

Cheers. What's that? *(She is asking about the slide.)*

REUBEN: Close-up: a pig. On the nine hundred bucks for this nifty mufti I could I live for two months. *(He changes the slide.)* Grasshoppers fucking.

(He puts on a Strauss waltz. She helps him with the black tie, admiring the result.)

SHERRY: Oh, swoon, Fred.

REUBEN: I'm hysterical. How come you want to go out with me?

SHERRY: Because the rest of the world terrifies me. With you I take off my armor. You make me feel soft. "You make me feel so young."

REUBEN: Yeah? You know you look gorgeous?

SHERRY: *(posing, pleased)* Yeah?

REUBEN: Yeah, you do.

SHERRY: Aw, you're just saying that.

(Reuben switches the slide to a stereopticonlike view of the interior of the Schonbrunn palace ballroom in Vienna and adjusts the lights. He turns the music up and bows to Sherry. She curtsies to him. They waltz around the room elegantly and pose as if they

themselves were in a film. The slides are close-ups of Sherry in ro-
mantic poses, a close-up of Garbo, one of Dietrich, a slide of Fred
and Ginger dancing, and slides of Noel Coward and Gertrude La-
wrence.)

REUBEN: "Big romantic stuff, this."

SHERRY: Noel Coward.

REUBEN: You got it.

(Reuben spins off into the bedroom. Sherry returns to her seat.
Slide of a human skeleton wearing a baseball cap and ribbons.
Duke Ellington music plays as the slide changes, showing the
skeleton in different poses. Danny waits a moment before
speaking.)

DANNY: The week before his Bar Mitzvah, in his attic, I
finally got up the nerve. We were sitting by a trunk full of his
mother's clothes. I put on a black cloche, and I whispered
to him: "I think I'm homosexual." "Well, of course," he
said. "We're both fairies. Who didn't know that?" We tried
holding hands, but we felt silly. To be gay in Richmond,
Virginia in the early sixties meant hoarding dirty maga-
zines and dreaming of New York. We did dress up, though.
His mother caught us once. And last time we did it we were
thirty.

CHRIS: *(interested)* Yeah?

(Reuben enters from the bedroom, carrying an ironing board. He
carefully props a cheap full-length mirror on its side on top of it.
He clips a couple of lights to the mirror and puts two battered sty-
rofoam wig stands on the ironing board. Danny goes into the main
playing area and off into the wings. Reuben puts on a slide of Judy
Garland in Easter Parade *and a cassette of the same. Reuben is*
always controlling his environment as a theatrical space—
managing objects, slides, and music. Danny comes back in,
wearing a cheap woman's wig.)

REUBEN: *(exaggerating his southern accent)* Honey, you take that right back to 14th Street. You look like a West Side Highway trollop. Is that what you want to look like?

DANNY: *(stepping back)* You can be a real pain, Ruby. You know that?

> *(Reuben laughs. Danny stands by the door brushing out the wig, trying to make it more presentable. Reuben sits at the makeshift dressing table.)*

DANNY: *(to the others)* It was eleven. I had come from rehearsal. It was snowing. This was his old apartment on West 70th—overheated like old brownstones used to be. Almost everything in it he'd found on the street. We—he had made this plan for the full moon in February.

REUBEN: Why not?

DANNY: 'Cause I'm not a transvestite.

REUBEN: Neither am I. So what?

DANNY: Each to dress up like . . . .

REUBEN: Not just any woman—the woman you'd most want to be if you were one. *(He calls.)* Get your ass out here, Girl.

DANNY: We'd been shopping for weeks—to surprise each other. *(He comes further into the room.)*

REUBEN: *(seeing him in the mirror)* Put your face on before your wig.

DANNY: Shit, Man.

(Danny takes off his wig again. Reuben puts it on one of the wig stands. He changes the slides. Now we see portraits of famous women: Eleanor Roosevelt, Lillian Russell, Virginia Woolf, a statue of Aphrodite, Queen Alexandra, George Sand, Pocahontas, Carole Lombard, a Japanese geisha, Marilyn Monroe, and Queen Victoria. The music is more baroque. Danny sits at the make-up table. Reuben helps him apply make-up.)

REUBEN: Seriously, Danny-boy, do you want to look like a slut?

DANNY: Yeah. A little.

REUBEN: Me too. But just a hint.

DANNY: "Hint of slut." That's a good name for a lipstick.

REUBEN: *(applying rouge)* And a little "ruby rougette."

DANNY: Can you see this on the "Today" show?

REUBEN: No, Danny, this is too serious for the "Today" show.

DANNY: Well, it could be a board game: "Gender Fuck." A sort of reverse strip poker. Women add a moustache or something, and men maybe a stocking each time they lose on the dice.

REUBEN: Why don't you talk it over with your father. Maybe he'd invest.

DANNY: *(serious)* How come you wouldn't design Clay Lawford's show?

REUBEN: Because I'm allergic to cigar smoke. Hold still or I'll make you look like Liberace.

DANNY: So bossy.

REUBEN: *(picking up the shoes Danny brought)* Here.

(Danny starts taking off his trousers.)

No!

(Reuben covers his eyes, pointing offstage.)

"Surprise me," Diaghilev said. I want a revelation.

(Danny grabs his stuff and dances with a leap into the bedroom. Reuben goes to the refrigerator and pulls out a bottle of champagne.)

You know what Chekhov's last words were?

DANNY: *(from offstage)* What?

REUBEN: "Give me some more champagne."

DANNY: *(calling from the bedroom)* I'm having trouble with the skirt. At the back. Hold on.

REUBEN: *(as if at the window, looking out at the snow)* They've taken the city away. There's just us.

DANNY: *(calling)* I'm ready.

REUBEN: *(leaping into action)* Minute.

(He turns on a small spotlight with which he can follow Danny and changes the music to Gershwin's "An American in Paris." Slide of the Eiffel Tower. Danny makes an entrance in a white pleated skirt, blue angora sweater, white wedgie shoes, and a wig the same color as his hair. He dances a wild dance while Reuben takes snapshots of him. When the dance is over Reuben applauds.

then turns the lights out momentarily. He puts on a cassette of Haydn, with sudden chords, and a slide of Magritte's painting of an apple with the words 'Ceci n'est pas une pomme' under it. When Reuben turns the spot on again, he is under it. He wears a discreet but dazzling dark-blue and silver silk blouse from the 'thirties and a wig in his own hair color, with added gray in it— long and straight, parted in the center. He wears white gloves and carries a purse. He still has his trousers on.)

DANNY: *(really impressed)* Wow. I mean wow.

REUBEN: Ah am a 'thirties woman. I haven't got the skirt yet.

DANNY: You look like a lesbian.

REUBEN: Ah suppose if ah were a woman I'd be just exactly that, wouldn't ah?

DANNY: Oh, God, I know who you look like.

REUBEN: Who's that, pray tell? *(He pulls a pair of glasses from his bag and hangs them around his neck on a black ribbon. He checks the effect in the mirror.)*

DANNY: Your mother.

(Reuben drops the glasses, then takes a quick look at Danny through them.)

REUBEN: *(angry)* Playtime is over. Little no-neck monsters got to go home.

DANNY: Ruby, I'm sorry. But, I mean, what's so strange? Do I look like mine?

REUBEN: *(checking him out)* Maybe. A little. When she was going out to play tennis with her boyfriend.

DANNY: *(looking in the mirror)* Really?

REUBEN: *(taking a breath, straightening himself up, really changing his persona into his mother's rather frightening one)* "Just what the hell do you children think you're doing? Get the hell out of my clothes this instant!"

DANNY: Oh, my God. Eerie!

(Danny stares at Reuben, who really looks and speaks like someone who could be his mother—we get an impression of her in this way.)

REUBEN: "Ah am worried about you, Ruby. Ah am. Get out of my clothes *this instant*, do you hear? This instant. You look disgusting. You little boys look like—. Ah can't tell your Daddy. Ah'm too embarrassed. Ah can't look at you." *(He turns away, then spins back.)* "Take those clothes off! Off! Ah want you to put everything back exactly where you found it. Everything. It was a bad dream and we've forgotten it. And ah want you to march right downstairs and play like boys."

(They burst out laughing. They make faces in the mirror, Reuben sticking his tongue out. They pull off the wigs. Danny wraps himself up in a blanket and goes to the window. Reuben turns off the music and the lights. He wraps a corner of Danny's blanket around himself. They are silhouetted in the snowy light from the window. A champagne glass breaks onstage.)

SHERRY: *(who has dropped hers)* Sorry.

LUKE: I'll get it. *(He kneels to pick up the pieces of glass.)*

CHRIS: You'll cut yourself. I know where the dustpan is.

(He gets it and deals with the glass. Danny returns to the others. Reuben has disappeared into the bedroom.)

LUKE: He could have told me we were on the moon, and I would have been happy to be there.

(Luke walks toward the door of the apartment, knocks, and waits. Reuben arranges the lights and slide frame. Slide of two Buddhas. He opens the door for Luke. They embrace. They are warm and a little courtly toward each other.)

REUBEN: Hi, Luke.

LUKE: Hey, Rube. I'm sorry I'm late. I—.

REUBEN: It's okay. You're always late. But we've only got six minutes. *(He sets a stopwatch.)*

LUKE: Til what?

(Luke takes off his shoes. Reuben puts them away.)

REUBEN: Luke, I want you to write a letter for me.

LUKE: Sure.

REUBEN: Here: sit on your birthday throne.

(Reuben reveals some velvet and silk cushions on the floor with a canopy against a wall, a throne for Luke. Luke settles into it.)

LUKE: Feels like the right place.

REUBEN: And here. *(He hands Luke a rubber ball attached to a flexible rod attached to a handle on which he has tied a couple of elegant ribbons. Slide of a jeweled Fabergé egg.)*

LUKE: Thank you. What is it?

REUBEN: *(demonstrating, hitting himself with the ball)* ...along the shiatsu meridians. When I was in the shop in Chinatown the woman said: "That's for old men—keeps them young." I said, "I know. I'm seventy."

(They laugh. Reuben looks at the time on the stopwatch.)

Five minutes and thirty-three seconds.

LUKE: Til what?

(Reuben alternates the slide of the Buddhas with a slide of a snapshot of himself and Luke, arms around shoulders, smiling.)

LUKE: *(pleased)* Ha!

(Reuben adjusts the slide frame so it's as open as possible. Slide of a close-up of Luke's face, then a slide of Luke's astrological chart. Reuben alternates the two.)

REUBEN: Picture of the stars at your birth: your astrological chart. Your chart is the shape of your mind, Luke. *(Reuben uses a long pointer to point to the different planets on the screen.)* When you were born, Mercury and the sun were in the Gemini part of the sky. Twins. A double point of view—the artist. Perspective. But the planets form a cross—your cross to bear in this lifetime, Luke. Gives you energy: you can hop from one element to another, but you've got to learn stick-to-it-iveness.

LUKE: What's the letter you want me to write?

(Slide of stars in deep space. Music: Bach. To the slides, Reuben adds colored lights: a light show. Another slide of deep space, predominantly green. Slide of Jupiter. Music: Beethoven.)

REUBEN: Jupiter. Big. Benevolent. Expansive—full of gas. Everybody has people who are like the different planets in their lives. You're my personal Jupiter.

LUKE: Full of gas? Your farter? As in "farter and martyr"?

(Beautiful slide of Saturn and its rings. Music: Wagner.)

REUBEN: This is my "martyr": Saturn, the time-keeper.

LUKE: She's beautiful.

REUBEN: And she constricts—like her rings. She's done it again, Luke. Martyr's written one of her letters. *(He takes on his mother's accent.)* "Your father and I are worried about you, dear. We're getting older. What's going to happen to you? Shouldn't you go back to school? Get a degree in law. You know your father and I'd be happy to subsidize that. Honey, you've *tried* your own thing. You say you don't want to come home and live in Richmond, but ah'm so worried about you." *(He drops the accent.)* That's a wild phrase: "Ah'm so worried about you." What are you supposed to do with "Ah'm so worried about you"? It makes my stomach turn. *(Reuben checks the time on the stopwatch.)* Now. *(He puts on a slide of Uranus, and Tibetan chants.)*

LUKE: What?

REUBEN: Uranus takes eighty-four years to go around the sun—a lifetime. At—this instant... Uranus is exactly opposite the place it was the moment you were born.

LUKE: You mean—this is the middle of my life?

REUBEN: Astrologically speaking, ... yes.

(Music: Bing Crosby singing "Happy Birthday." Reuben kisses Luke on the cheek.)

LUKE: What am I supposed to do?

REUBEN: Start thinking how to die right. Want some chamomile?

LUKE: I probably need some, now I'm on the downhill slope.

(Reuben turns the music off and goes to the stove to make tea.)

REUBEN: I need something stronger. I need marijuana. Do you want any?

LUKE: No, thanks. Not anymore now. I'm too old.

REUBEN: I talked to her on the phone last week: she was chocolate syrup. Now Spider Woman again.

LUKE: Reassure her.

REUBEN: What do you mean? *She* should reassure *me*.

LUKE: No. Turn the tables. You be the parent.

REUBEN: *(handing him a pad and pen)* Write it for me.

LUKE: *(not writing)* "Dear Ma, thanks for your concerned letter. I was moved to receive it."

REUBEN: That's certainly true.

LUKE: "It's good to know you're in the world worrying about me."

(Reuben laughs.)

REUBEN: That's too much, Luke. She's smart enough to play bridge and mah jong.

LUKE: What does she look like?

REUBEN: A petite Doris Day grown old. My father treats her like a glass doll. But basically, she's Kali, Luke. She pretends things aren't happening to her, like children. She had her insides taken out when she had cancer, and she said she felt cleaner afterward. I think she feels everyone should have their insides taken out. Insides are dirty.

LUKE: *(continuing to plan the letter)* "I have been thinking a lot about what you said, Ma. And I want you and Dad to know that though I'm committed to being an artist, I believe in having my feet on the ground."

REUBEN: What does that mean?

LUKE: "Keep your feet on the ground and your head in the stars." Teddy Roosevelt. I thought it might have a sort of subliminal presidential ring.

REUBEN: *(honey jar in hand)* Do you want any honey, Honey?

LUKE: No. Yes. One spoonful, please.

REUBEN: Will you write it for me?

LUKE: A rough draft, maybe. You'll have to add the personal touches.

REUBEN: I sure am enjoying your birthday party. *(He hands the tea to Luke.)*

LUKE: I must have done something right to land up on this throne in the middle of this lifetime.

(Luke returns to his seat with the others. Reuben puts on music from the St. Matthew Passion. He lies on the couch and dials his phone. All the friends' phones ring. Groans from everyone.)

SHERRY: The late-night calls!

(More groans.)

LUKE: He was a phone Scheherazade—I hate the phone.

DANNY: I never dared hang up.

(Reuben speaks to Sherry on the phone.)

REUBEN: I'm not feeling so good, Sherry.

SHERRY: Shall I come over?

REUBEN: No.

SHERRY: Did you like Clay Crawford? He asked if you have a union card. I lied.

REUBEN: I don't want to work for Clay, or any other grown-up, Sherry.

SHERRY: Why not?

REUBEN: I couldn't be spontaneous. She'd hate what I did, and so would I.

SHERRY: You need a job. Pat's offering.

REUBEN: I need a job, but I don't want one. Except in the movies. Can you get me a job designing spaceships?

(Reuben hangs up, then dials Danny, whose phone rings.)

REUBEN: Hi, it's me. Listen to this:
   A guy is getting drunk in a bar, and he says to the bartender, "I'll bet you four hundred dollars I can bite my right eye." The bartender thinks he's crazy, so he puts his money down, and the guy pops his glass eye out of its socket, bites on it, and the bartender has to give him the four hundred dollars.
   So the bartender is real mad, and he watches the guy get-

ting more smashed and playing pool with his friends.

Then the guy comes back to the bar. He says, "I'll bet you four hundred dollars I can bite my left eye." Now, the bartender saw him play pool so he knows he's not blind, so he says, okay, this guy is a nut, but he puts his money down, and the guy takes out his fake teeth and bites his left eye.

So the bartender is real mad, now and sad, 'cause he owes the money to the cash register. Then the guy comes back really plastered and says to the bartender: "Hey, do you want to make your money back?" And the bartender says, "What now?" The guy says, "Look, I'll bet you nine hundred dollars if you slide a glass from one end of the bar to the other, that I can piss in that glass and not get one drop on the bar." Now the bartender knows this cannot be done even by a guy who's sober, so he sees a chance of getting his money back, and he takes the cash out of the cash register, and the other guy puts his cash down too, and he stands on top of the bar and takes his peter out, and says, "Ready?" And the bartender slides the glass down, and the guy pisses all over the bar. The bartender is really happy to get his money back even if it is a little wet, and the guy goes back to his friends playing pool.

Later the guy comes up to the bar for a drink, and the bartender says to him, "You were ahead. How come you blew it all?" "Oh," the guy says: "Don't worry about me. I bet my friends over there I could piss all over your bar and you wouldn't bounce me."

DANNY: That's great. I bet you heard that at the Saint. How was it?

REUBEN: A lot of people were interested in me. I have Mercury on the Ascendant this week.

(He hangs up and dials Luke, whose phone rings.)

REUBEN: *(talking to Luke)* It was such an honor. I was overwhelmed. I felt I was in one of her old films. Madam sat bolt upright in her chaise longue—black lace dressing gown with a big red satin ribbon at the bosom, Tibetan lap dog in her lap, and me at her feet. A perfect Velasquez, and she knew it. I want to marry her, Luke. I'm free. So is she. It doesn't matter that she's seventy-eight, does it?

LUKE: *(wanting to get off the phone)* Listen, Rube....

REUBEN: *(anticipating him)* I have to get off the phone now, Luke. Bye.

(Reuben hangs up and dials Chris.)

CHRIS: Hello.

REUBEN: Come over here. I need you.

(Lights dim as Reuben walks off the stage.)

CHRIS: *(getting up)* He had picked me up at the Saint. I had never seen anybody like him there before. I had never seen anybody like him, period. Suddenly there was this funny little thin guy, staring and staring up at the ceiling. Sure, there are stars on the ceiling, but who's staring...? *He* is.

REUBEN: *(returning now in black leather trousers and a silk shirt, standing in the playing area, looking up)* There's Mars. It's redder. Or should be.

CHRIS: *(to the others)* I don't know how he knew I was there. He didn't look at me. And there was all that rock playing. *(He speaks to Reuben.)* What?

REUBEN: *(pointing)* Mars.

(Reuben looks toward Chris and smiles. Chris has stood up by his chair. He moves slowly toward Reuben, as if hypnotized by him.)

CHRIS: He was nuts, obviously. So obviously I couldn't resist. I'm curious. He gave me his address and told me to come by in an hour. I've always loved fairy tales. And he was an elf.

(In the apartment, Reuben hurriedly but carefully prepares the slides, puts on Fellini movie music by Nino Rota, pulls a bottle of champagne from the refrigerator, puts two old thick goblets next to the bottle on the old trunk that serves as a coffee table, lights the candle next to that, and burns some incense. He turns the mirror around, makes a face at himself, and turns the mirror back. He dims the lights.)

CHRIS: I was actually scared. I didn't know what I was going to see. I swear to God.

(Chris is silhouetted in the door.)

REUBEN: Hello, Mars.

CHRIS: And I almost turned around and left. *(to Reuben)* Hi.

(Chris looks around the apartment. Reuben watches him with pleasure.)

This is your place? *(to the friends)* Dumb. It was dumb. But what was I going to say?

REUBEN: You want to give me your jacket?

CHRIS: Yeah, sure. *(He wears a very tight T shirt underneath.)*

REUBEN: And your boots?

CHRIS: Huh? No, no, I'll keep them. *(to the friends)* He was not my type at all . . . not even to hustle, . . . but something in the way he looked at me was sexy.

(Reuben flips on a slide: a room in a Borgia palace.)

Jesus!

REUBEN: Would you like some champagne? *(He pours some for Chris and himself.)* Palace of the Borgias.

(He hands Chris his glass, which Chris takes unnoticingly.)

CHRIS: Thanks.

REUBEN: It's not poisoned.

CHRIS: *(not quite comprehending, but drinking)* Oh, yeah. It's good. Is that a real place?

REUBEN: As real as "The Saint."

(Slide: stone wall in a dungeon. Strange devices on the wall.)

CHRIS: Is this your hobby?

REUBEN: My work. Why don't you take your shirt off?

(Chris starts to do so, fast, awkwardly.)

Would you do me a favor?

CHRIS: I *am* doing you a favor.

REUBEN: Take your shirt off real slow. Listen to the sound of the fabric against your skin.

(Chris smiles.)

CHRIS: You are too much.

(Reuben turns the music up. Chris very, very slowly takes his T shirt off, pulling it over his head and swaying his hips slightly. Reuben sits and watches.)

You like that, don't you?

(Reuben nods. Chris puts out his hand with his goblet in it. Reuben pours more in his glass. Chris sprawls on a chair, displaying his body. Reuben unabashedly looks at it as they speak.)

REUBEN: Where are you from?

CHRIS: Jersey City.

REUBEN: Your father's a truck driver?

CHRIS: My father's a butcher.

REUBEN: And you handle the meat?

CHRIS: No more. I did.

REUBEN: What do you do now?

CHRIS: What do you think I do now?

REUBEN: I can guess.

CHRIS: I bet you can't.

REUBEN: Movie star?

CHRIS: I'm a nurse—that is, I'm studying to be a p.t.—a physical therapist.

REUBEN: So you know what these are? *(He hands Chris a pill box.)*

CHRIS: *(inspecting the contents of the box)* Downers?

REUBEN: *(taking one)* Quaaludes. Have one.

> *(He hands Chris his wine glass. Chris hesitates a moment, then drinks down the pill with the wine. Reuben changes the music to the St. Matthew Passion again. He swallows his own pill.)*

CHRIS: I must really trust you—a funny little thin guy I met in a disco. *(He puts his arm around Reuben's shoulder and squeezes.)*

REUBEN: *(mildly)* You're hurting.

CHRIS: I'll make it better, then.

> *(He kisses Reuben's arm, slowly working his way up to where the rolled-up silk shirt meets the flesh. Reuben is holding out his arm very stiffly.)*

You don't like that, do you?

REUBEN: I like it.

CHRIS: Your arm is stiff as a board.

REUBEN: I said I like it.

CHRIS: Hey. Why don't you tell me what to do.

REUBEN: Excellent. Sit down.

> *(Chris sits. Reuben kneels to pull off Chris's boots.)*

CHRIS: Everything under control?

> *(Reuben stands.)*

REUBEN: Lift me up, Mars, slowly.

(Slide: a starry night. Reuben has arranged the frame so that the slide covers as much of the back wall as possible. Chris, standing behind Reuben, his hands on Reuben's hips, slowly lifts him straight up in the air.)

REUBEN: *(in the stars, looking up)* Higher. *(after a moment)* Higher.

(Chris puts him back down.)

REUBEN: I liked that, Mars.

(They look at each other a moment. The lights and music go out in the apartment.)

CHRIS: *(returning to his seat with the others)* I know that's the moment he liked best. When we got to bed he was uncomfortable. He had an okay body, but he didn't like it.

LUKE: I was driving him to my house in Vermont, and we hit this humongous jam on I-95, so we got out of the car and sat in the grass by the side of the New England Thruway. I picked dried grasses. So, of course, I began to sneeze because I'm allergic in the springtime.

(Luke and Reuben are in the playing area. Luke is as if gathering tall wild grasses. He sneezes.)

REUBEN: Luke—Chris is not my lover.

LUKE: *(sneezing)* So what?

REUBEN: Will you write him a recommendation for a scholarship?

LUKE: *(sneezing)* A scholarship to what?

REUBEN: Physiotherapy. Whatever nurses do. Hey, looky, Luke, the whole world has stopped. It feels wonderful, doesn't it? Like before they invented the motorcar.

LUKE: *(sneezing)* Yeah.

REUBEN: Are you going to keep gathering those grasses?

LUKE: *(sneezing)* Just a few more cat tails. *(He sneezes.)*

REUBEN: You'll sneeze all day.

LUKE: *(sneezing)* I know I'll die of greed. But they're so beautiful. *(He sneezes again.)* I can't help it.

REUBEN: Well, then pick a few for me.

> *(Reuben is climbing something high behind Luke.)*

Remember our Chinese lifetime, Luke?

LUKE: *(sneezing)* No.

REUBEN: You were a plump Buddhist monk, always sneezing.

LUKE: I remember. You were a tall old Taoist dressed in black with a white goatee.

> *(Reuben is slowly lowering an apple on a thread toward Luke's head. Luke is sneezing and gathering his grasses, not noticing.)*

REUBEN: We walked from town to town, doing healings. I performed magic tricks, and you wrote love poems for people. Write me a love poem now, Luke. *(Reuben is now, unseen by Luke, on top of a chair behind Luke, as if it were a tree.)*

LUKE: *(improvising, still sneezing, picking grasses)*
            Two ancient boys
            By the side of the road
            Playing with fire—

(Luke suddenly sees the apple dangling in front of his face. He looks up at Reuben.)

Ha!

(They both laugh.)

REUBEN: *(singing from his perch)*
            I'm the top, I'm the Mona Lisa,
            I'm the top, I'm the Tower of Pisa....

(He swings down, more sober.)

What is it in this lifetime's not working out, Luke? Right here on this land where we're sitting, in Mamaroneck, gay native Americans were the tribal medicine men. We tended the fires in a healing circle. We weren't hunting or having children, but we had an important function, Luke. We played a part in society, just like we did in China. We should still be making ceremonies. That's our job.

LUKE: *(eating the apple)* But that's just what you do.

REUBEN: I feel like that jerk in the Bible who was given a hundred talents. At the end of his life he said to God, "Look what I did with those hundred talents. I buried them to keep them safe. Aren't I good boy?" *(sadly, after a moment)* How come, Luke? *(He passes the apple back to Luke to finish.)*

LUKE: These are dark times. Ever since the nineteenth century, people believe the world is solid, without spirit. They think they don't need medicine men. They think science has conquered disease, and everyone is immortal.

REUBEN: But we've been around, Luke. There've been other dark centuries. What happened this time, to us? To me?

LUKE: Not enough mother's milk, or too much mother's milk, maybe—or both.

REUBEN: Both?

LUKE: Speaking for myself, she loved me too much, like I was part of herself. Then, when she began to sense what she'd done—she denied there ever was that kind of relationship. "She loves me, she loves me not...." A variation on child abuse. Some variations are more virulent than others.

REUBEN: The fault may be in my mother's milk, Luke, but what do I do about it now?

LUKE: A good therapist? I know one or two in the world. That's enough.

REUBEN: Not for me, Lukey. I don't trust words enough. There's no magic for me in analysis. And even if some wise guy did manage to spear my devil, Luke, it might turn out my devil was my angel, and then where would I be? I have to do it myself. I'm a healer. Healer, heal thyself. A wounded healer is the best kind, they say.

(Reuben leaves the stage. Luke puts on an apron and cooks by the eating table.)

LUKE: At the farm he'd insist on sleeping in the schoolhouse out back. The night before Thanksgiving, at one in the morning while I was cooking, he appeared in the kitchen, pale, like a scared Little Prince. I didn't know what to do for him.

(Reuben comes in quietly, wrapped in an old quilt.)

REUBEN: Who is Ganymede?

LUKE: Ganymede?

REUBEN: I need to know right now.

LUKE: He was a beautiful boy Zeus fell in love with. Zeus flew to earth as an eagle, snatched Ganymede up in his claws, and carried him up to Olympus, where he made him his cup bearer.

REUBEN: I just saw him. He visited me.

LUKE: Zeus, or Ganymede?

REUBEN: Ganymede. I woke up, because there was this blinding light in the room. I could just make out his wings. I've been dreaming about Ganymede for days, but this is the closest he's come.

LUKE: Sounds terrific.

REUBEN: No, Luke, it was horrible. That's why I came to you.

LUKE: To begin with, sit down. How do you know it was Ganymede?

REUBEN: His name just came to me. But I don't know what he wants. When I was ten, I dreamed I was waiting in a railroad station with enormous birds. I was scared. The birds were bigger than the train. I'm scared of Ganymede, Luke, but I have to go back to him tonight and find out what he wants.

LUKE: *(feeling Reuben's forehead)* I'll make you some "Sleepy-time" tea.

REUBEN: I want coffee. I have to have *something*.

LUKE: Do you think Ganymede is Chris?

REUBEN: No.

LUKE: You said I was like Jupiter. Jupiter was Zeus in Greece. Are you worried about me and Chris?

REUBEN: No. This is about me, Luke—not you. If you're feeling guilty about something, it'll be in your dreams, not mine. Anyway, I told you it's okay. He and I aren't lovers.

(Luke gives Reuben coffee.)

REUBEN: *(sighing)* There's no point being gay, Luke, is there? The competition. It's impossible. It's like two male plugs. It doesn't work.

LUKE: Here.

(Luke drinks herb tea and wraps himself in another quilt. They sit at the kitchen table.)

REUBEN: Would you be gay if you could choose?

LUKE: I don't get to choose. So I want to enjoy.

REUBEN: AIDS is like one of the Biblical plagues, Luke. Alzheimer's is another. They're warnings.

LUKE: Of what?

REUBEN: Something to do with the planet. We are the earth, Lukey. We're her consciousness. When we're sick, she's sick. If the earth dies because of our pollution, it'll be earth suicide. The hole in her ozone is the biggest cancer of all. And it's there because we just can't stop ourselves obsessively, compulsively using hairspray and air conditioners. *(He seems agitated again.)* We're out of control, like a wild, horny teenager in the cockpit of spaceship earth.

LUKE: When I was in my twenties, I wasted energy for years cruising around the Village. And I usually ended up picking up at least one guy every twenty-four hours. I'd bring him back to my apartment. Sometimes we didn't even speak until afterwards. And once—I remember I was cooking a piece of liver when I had this flash—I realized I was getting away with murder: spilling my seed, as the Bible says.

REUBEN: In autopsies of people who've died of AIDS, they've discovered the thymus gland is all shriveled.

LUKE: What is the thymus gland?

(Behind them on the slide screen, as if they were drawings Reuben had made, appear sketches of a man seated cross-legged, with glands and chakras of different colors.)

REUBEN: It's the sex clock which regulates when you reach puberty. It's right near the heart. Edgar Cayce says the thymus gland is the heart chakra. We're misusing heart energy, Luke. It's a question of love. Not just gay men—the whole society. We're misusing heart energy.

LUKE: AIDS is a physical disease, Rube. It comes from a virus. We know that much.

REUBEN: A virus is a teeny thing, Lukey, if it even is a "thing." The physicists are tracing the paths of such minute particles now that they don't even know anymore if what they're looking at is matter or energy. They're naming what they think they see as "truth" and "joy." And they say that just by observing these things or these energies called truth and joy, they may be changing them, or even inventing them. So how physical is a virus? We may not find a physical cure for AIDS until we learn what AIDS energy means. And why it's happening now.

LUKE: And why to gays especially?

REUBEN: It isn't to gays especially in Africa. But I don't know—maybe we're the chosen people, like the Jews: maybe we're chosen to be especially smart, creative, and responsible—to be medicine men—and if we don't live up to that, and we misuse our heart energy.... I don't know, Luke. Anyway, whatever it is, "gay" doesn't work for me personally. I've had it.

LUKE: *(laughing)* So what are you planning to do about that?

REUBEN: I don't know yet.

LUKE: Does it make so much difference—man–man, man–woman?

REUBEN: To me it does. Mostly, I prefer women. They're emotionally smarter. And for another thing, I'm not attracted to a man—I'm attracted to men—all the time. I obsess about them. I can't help it. I'm going back to New York tomorrow—I'm lured by available men. They're like sirens to me. I'm serious.

LUKE: Tomorrow? Tomorrow's Thanksgiving. There's this dead bird here. I don't even eat meat. We're going to spend Thanksgiving together. That's what you said.

REUBEN: I'm sorry, Luke. I can't. I have to go to New York. I can't stay here one more day. I need the city.

LUKE: But you said you weren't feeling well. City's no place to be if you're not feeling well.

REUBEN: I'm sorry, Luke. I have to go.

LUKE: So, go.

REUBEN: I'm sorry. It has nothing to do with you. You know that.

LUKE: Yes. But that doesn't make me feel any better.

REUBEN: You and I could have slept together before we became friends.

LUKE: What do you mean? We were friends right away.

REUBEN: If I ever sleep with anybody I'm close to, it'll be you. I love you. But I don't sleep with my friends. I just sleep with—not even men—with parts of men: thighs in denim, an ass in chaps, a big chest....

LUKE: Ditto. Ditto. I've tried to get away from all that by vowing I'm not sleeping with anybody I don't have a feeling for. So I end up not sleeping with anybody. Anyway, listen. Take care of yourself.

REUBEN: I do take care of myself. That's how come I'm here with you now.

(He stands up. They embrace.)

I have to go back to Ganymede now, Luke. I have to find out what he wants. I'm scared.

(The lights fade. Luke sits down again with the friends.)

LUKE: Back and forth: city and country—Dr. Jekyll and Mr. Hyde—Mr. Feelgood, Mr. Feelbad—fleshpots and drugs alternated with "Sleepytime" tea.

DANNY: When I'd come back from touring, I'd call him. He'd say, "I've been traveling too, Danny boy—in Afghanistan." Standing joke: "How was Afghanistan?" "It was okay."

(Slide: Michelangelo's David. Reuben comes out from the bedroom of his apartment. Chris gets up to join him, taking his shirt off.)

REUBEN: *(straightening his clothes)* I'm sorry.

CHRIS: Hey—it's okay. Don't worry about it.

REUBEN: I must be getting to like you too much.

(Reuben changes the music: Bach. He changes the slide: pre-Columbian surgical tools. He adds to the pyramid. He starts whittling a piece of wood. Chris watches what he's doing, crouching beside him.)

I saw this man in black leather, down by the Bethune Street pier. I was turned on by him.

(Sherry, at her seat, puts her hands to her ears. Slides of the East and West Village, New York, and of the old Hudson River piers.)

We didn't speak. I followed him a few blocks to Washington Street. I knew he knew I was following him, but he didn't let on. I slipped into his building after him and followed him upstairs. He unlocked his door and went in, leaving the door a crack open, like by accident, only it couldn't have been an accident, I told myself. I could hear him moving around. I was scared, too scared to push the door open and go in. I stood outside his door for five minutes at least, wondering if I dared go in, or if I should leave. Finally, I hear two women coming up the stairs, laughing. So I just went in. He looked at me. Very stern. No words. It was terrific. Then suddenly in this high voice, he says, "I know you. I was in your apartment. I saw your show." That finished it for me, Chris. It was just another sexual disappointment. Pass me that saw.

(Reuben focuses a light on a piece of wood he is preparing for the pyramid. Chris finds the small saw and passes it to Reuben.)

CHRIS: *(pointing to the pyramid)* What is that?

REUBEN: A pyramid. *(He changes the subject.)* I've always wanted a 24-hour nurse, Chris—A sailor nurse, like the little tsarevich had in *Nicholas and Alexandra.* If I got sick, would you take care of me?

CHRIS: Sure.

REUBEN: Here, sand this. *(He hands Chris a dowel to sand and a piece of fine sandpaper.)* Any pyramid, the one in Egypt or this one, is built to precise dimensions for high-energy gathering and concentration. On Atlantis and in Egypt a pyramid was used as an initiation vehicle, like a spaceship. *(He readjusts what Chris is doing.)* Slow. Slowly. You want to sand, not scratch.

CHRIS: *(as he continues sanding, speaking to the friends)* I had a job-job selling silver balloons near the Plaza. For hours in the cold he'd sit on a bench near me. When business was slow, he'd buy a balloon, examine it, then let it go, and stand and watch it until it was out of sight. Like he'd stood watching the stars at the Saint. It made other people watch, and it made them buy balloons. *(addressing Luke)* Luke, I asked him once if it was okay if I went up to visit you in Vermont.

LUKE: *(very interested)* What did he say?

REUBEN: *(still working, but angry, to Chris)* No. Absolutely not. That place is for *me.* I forbid you to go see Luke.

(Chris gets up and returns to his seat. Lights fade slowly on Reuben as he continues working meticulously.)

LUKE: Oh, my God. That's why you never came....

CHRIS: Yeah.

LUKE: It was as if an invisible beast had him by the throat—a leopard, maybe. When he called last August, it was a perfect day. I had to come in from the vegetable garden to get to the phone. *(Luke stands to answer his phone.)*

REUBEN: *(on the phone in his apartment, lying on the couch)* I just came back from the doctor, Luke.

LUKE: My hands were full of moist earth—I was trying not to get everything dirty.

REUBEN: *(on the phone to Luke)* I went with Sherry.

LUKE: As I listened to his voice, I was squinting at a postcard of the Piazza San Marco in the rain pinned in front of my desk, my eyes getting used to the indoors.

REUBEN: I have it, Luke.

LUKE: I felt at a distance, as if he were speaking to me through a long, dark tunnel.

REUBEN: The doctor said he'd make some lab tests. But he was almost certain.

LUKE: How can he tell?

REUBEN: I've had swollen glands for months. And now I have red things on my arms. I have Karposi's sarcoma, Luke.

LUKE: Oh, God. I—I'm sorry. Is there pain?

REUBEN: I've been feeling bad for a long time. It's not worse.

LUKE: I'll come down.

REUBEN: No, I'm coming up to you. There's a lot of things you have to help me figure out. But listen, Luke—.

LUKE: Yeah?

REUBEN: Don't tell anybody.

LUKE: No?

REUBEN: Promise me.

LUKE: Okay.

REUBEN: I'm not even going to tell my parents til I know what I'm going to do.

LUKE: Are—what kind of danger are you in?

REUBEN: Well, it's not the pneumonia kind. I don't know enough to explain it yet.

LUKE: 'Course not.

REUBEN: He wants me to start treatment in three days.

LUKE: What kind of treatment?

REUBEN: Chemotherapy.

LUKE: Shit. Do you want that?

REUBEN: The doctor expects that's what I'll do.

LUKE: Is he gay?

REUBEN: I think so. He was nice to me, anyway.

LUKE: How can you do chemotherapy and come up here?

REUBEN: I don't think I want those chemicals in my body, Luke. We have to figure it out.

LUKE: When are you coming?

REUBEN: In the morning.

LUKE: Okay. Ruby. . . .

REUBEN: Yeah?

LUKE: I'm with you.

REUBEN: You have to be. I can't do it alone.

(They hang up.)

LUKE: I'm blown away. There's this literal pain in my heart. Did I say the right things? Was I loving enough? Did it sound like pity? I feel guilty: he's dying and I'm not. I go outside. I can't make it fit. Here's all this August sunlight, the trees, the fields. Everything is different because of the phone call, but nothing is different. The spade is just where I left it. I remember how much Ruby hated working in the garden. I don't love it much myself. Why do I bother?

(Luke moves into the main space, which is now his kitchen in the country again. Reuben sits at the table. Luke is holding a pamphlet.)

I picked this up at the post office. They air expressed it. *(He reads aloud from the pamphlet.)* "There is no proof that any case of AIDS has ever been cured by conventional methods. Chemotherapy takes a terrible toll on the body and mind. The techniques suggested here may or may not be successful for everyone, but applied mindfully their effects can only help."

REUBEN: I don't like their style either, Luke. What do they say to do? Read the specifics.

LUKE: There are sections on herbs, massage, and fasting-and-diet.

REUBEN: I need a clinic. I want somebody to take care of me completely.

(Luke puts a sheet around Reuben's neck and places a mirror in front of him.)

I need someone to tell me what to do.

(Luke starts giving Reuben a haircut.)

Do we have to do this with a mirror?

LUKE: Yes.

REUBEN: Are you afraid you'll catch something from my hair?

(Luke doesn't answer.)

I don't want red things growing on my face, Luke. Anyway, you can't use my eating utensils. What if you knew you could never kiss anyone again on the lips: your kiss might be the kiss of death.

LUKE: We'll make a list of leads, okay? Everyone who knows anyone who knows anything.

REUBEN: Never have sex with anyone *ever?* I'm a pariah.

LUKE: All gay men are pariahs now. Especially to each other.

REUBEN: Do you have an answer for everything?

(Luke just continues cutting hair.)

LUKE: I think I know how you're feeling. I'm sorry.

(Silence from Reuben.)

Look. We'll find the right clinic, if you want that.

REUBEN: And you know, of course, who's going to have to pay?

LUKE: When are you going to tell them?

REUBEN: Do you mind my being in your schoolhouse, Luke? Using your sheets?

LUKE: I think I'm going to punk your hair.

REUBEN: You can shave it off if you want to. I'd like to look like a concentration camp person. Speaking of which, how is your book coming?

LUKE: I need to go to Israel again and look up some stuff on Jews who denied their Jewishness during the War. "Coverup"? I think that's my title. Do you like it?

REUBEN: I want you to call Edward for me.

LUKE: Edward who?

REUBEN: The psychic.

LUKE: *You* call him.

REUBEN: Just tell him you have a friend—.

LUKE: What do you mean? He's a psychic!

REUBEN: *(pulling the sheet off himself)* I don't want anyone feeling sorry, and I don't want anyone turned off. *(He throws the chair on the ground. He picks it up.)*

LUKE: Ruby, there are other gay men with AIDS.

REUBEN: Victims. We are called AIDS victims. I don't want to be a victim. I don't like the word.

LUKE: People With AIDS is the name of a gay support group.

REUBEN: I'm not a support group kind of person, Luke. Okay?

LUKE: Okay. Do you want some carrot juice? *(He holds up a bag of large carrots.)*

REUBEN: I'm allergic.

LUKE: Shit. I forgot. There's a local woman here who cured herself of cancer with carrot juice and cloverleaf tea.

REUBEN: I don't want chemotherapy.

LUKE: Good. I'm glad.

REUBEN: I need a doctor—one who talks our language.

LUKE: Shall we make the list now ?

REUBEN: I have to go to bed, Luke. I'm on a roller coaster. My energy goes up and down. Goodnight.

(Reuben leaves.)

LUKE: *(to the others)* It was four in the afternoon. About eleven he got up again.

REUBEN: *(returning)* Where's my dope?

LUKE: In the bread drawer. Rube, dope affects the immune system.

REUBEN: Is there any beer?

LUKE: So does alcohol. *(He looks in the refrigerator, pulls out a beer, and opens it. He sighs.)*

I bought it for you.

REUBEN: Thanks. I'm going to watch TV. Goodnight, Luke.

LUKE: 'Night.

REUBEN: *(turning back)* Want to watch the late show?

LUKE: Sure. What's on?

REUBEN: *(talking like Bette Davis) Dark Victory.*

LUKE: Come *on.* You're kidding.

REUBEN: Yes.

(They both laugh.)

I'll just sit here. Sleep well, Luke.

LUKE: You too, Rube.

REUBEN: Yeah. *(Reuben sits in the dark in front of the TV, flipping the channels with a "remote" stick. Eventually the light goes out on him.)*

LUKE: *(returning to his seat)* A famous San Diego cancer clinic told us they couldn't take people with AIDS because it upset their staff. I went with Ruby to the best-known AIDS doctor in New York, and he suggested experimental treatment. Ruby didn't like him and said he didn't want to be a guinea pig. We finally found an M.D. Ruby found human who was also an herbologist. He prescribed a macrobiotic diet. Ruby tried it, on and off. He couldn't stay on the diet. I did consult Edward the psychic. Edward was sympathetic but said he didn't have much hope. I didn't tell Ruby that. It stunned me. It was the first time I felt Ruby might really die. I told him Edward also said he had to make up his mind to live. *(Luke is back in his seat.)*

SHERRY: Meanwhile, back in New York, when the dust had settled, it was obviously time to tell Mommy and Daddy. He directed the event like a play.

(She joins Reuben in the central area, which is now his apartment again. Slide of Cole Porter. Music: Tibetan bells, low volume. The pyramid is more advanced.)

SHERRY: *(continuing, to Reuben)* I told her what you said: to call back in three hours. *(She looks at her watch, an elegant contemporary one.)* It's two hours and fifty-five minutes now.

REUBEN: Tell me what she said again, exactly.

SHERRY: *(carefully)* I asked them not to comment but to digest, and to phone you in three hours. Your father was on another extension. She talked. He didn't. *(Sherry glances at her watch again.)*

REUBEN: He never does.

SHERRY: I said, "The biopsy was positive." I thought they'd understand words like that.

REUBEN: They know about AIDS. It was on "Sixty Minutes." We watched it together, in fact, though we never talked about it. And they know I'm not a hemophiliac, so the cat's out of the bag at last: I'm Haitian. *(He does a quick Latin American step.)*

SHERRY: I told them you were not in immediate danger.

REUBEN: Thanks, Sherry. You're a sport. Remember that old expression: "a sport"? As in, "Would you like a sport of tea?"

SHERRY: Shall I leave the room when the phone rings?

REUBEN: No!

SHERRY: Well, then, I'm going to have some coffee, thank you. *(She pours herself a cup. Reuben already has one.)*

REUBEN: She's going to want to come stay with me in New York. I know it. She's been waiting to pounce for years. Remember when she sent me that cancer questionnaire? She wanted me to send my blood to a hospital in Virginia. She's a vampire. I need some more coffee.

(He holds out his cup. Sherry pours.)

SHERRY: You're aware this is a no-no.

REUBEN: I'm aware that everything I like is a no-no. Coffee has always been a no-no for me. It gives me the runs. It always has. So what? I'll die sitting on the john, like Noel Coward. Listen, when they ask, "What can we do for you, Darling?" I'm gonna ask for money. I'll tell them my cure is going to be work, but I need financial help for that. How does that sound?

SHERRY: Good.

REUBEN: What time is it?

SHERRY: *(glancing at her watch)* Any moment.

REUBEN: I can't wait for this to be over.

(The phone rings. Reuben recoils and indicates Sherry should answer. She complies.)

SHERRY: Hello. This is Sherry. *(She looks at Danny.)*

DANNY: *(remembering)* Oh, my God.

(He picks up the phone.)

Sherr? Hi, Sherry. It's Danny.

SHERRY: Hi, Danny. Long time no see. You sound on top of the world.

(Reuben indicates to Sherry that he doesn't want to speak to Danny.)

DANNY: I am; I am. I've got news. Where's Ruby?

SHERRY: Incommunicado right now. So, what's the news?

DANNY: I have a part in *Buns*.

SHERRY: *Buns?*

DANNY: The new Clay Crawford musical.

SHERRY: I thought it was *Cheeks*.

DANNY: They changed it to *Buns*, and I'm in it.

SHERRY: Great! Let us know when the previews start.

DANNY: Yeah. Tell Reuben I called.

SHERRY: Oh, sure. Bye, Love.

DANNY: Bye.

> *(They hang up.)*

DANNY: *(to the other friends)* And I was ticked 'cause he was too busy to talk!

SHERRY: *(to Reuben)* Aren't you going to tell him?

REUBEN: No.

SHERRY: Why not?

REUBEN: He's too young.

> *(Even Danny laughs.)*

SHERRY: Look, I really don't think I should be here.

REUBEN: Stay, Sherry.

SHERRY: Just to the other room.

(She blows him a kiss from the bedroom door and leaves. He looks in the mirror for red spots, which he does not find. He turns the mirror to the wall. He puts on "Pavanne for a Dead Princess." He starts to dance to it. He starts to call Sherry back in.)

REUBEN: Hey, Sherry——. *(He halts, terrified, as the phone rings.)* Oh, God . . . . *(He stares at it, as if paralyzed. After three rings he goes purposefully to the control table, turns down the music, and picks up the phone.)* Hello. Yeah, Ma—it's me. I'm all right. Yeah, really. I'm okay, Ma. It's not . . . the worst kind. I look like I always do. I love you too. Both of you. I'll give you the name of the doctor, Ma. Talk to him. The best? He's the best for *me.* I'm going to be fine, Ma. Really. *(He begins to cry.)* I'm sorry. I'm sorry this had to happen. *(continuing, catching himself)* Listen, I want to cure myself through work. I don't want to worry about money. Can you help me? Some of the bills'll be on the insurance, but——. Thanks, Daddy. That makes me feel better. Because I don't *want* to come down there, Ma. Sure, you could . . . , but just for a couple of days. I want to see you, but I need to handle this myself. I have good friends, Ma. They'll help me. Yeah, Sherry's wonderful. No, I agree. I'm not telling people. What should you tell your friends when you come up here? I don't know. Tell them I'm having a party. I have to hang up now. I'm sorry. I'm really sorry this had to happen to you. Please try to forgive me.

(He hangs up. He is very shaken up. The lights fade on Reuben in the central area. Sherry has returned to the group of friends.)

SHERRY: From the bedroom I could hear him crying. I didn't go in right away. I don't think he wanted me to.

(Sherry's phone rings. The lights are up on the central area. Reuben is finishing putting on white pants with a loose turquoise shirt and white vest. He is holding a cordless phone. Eventually he sits in his old wheelchair, with the front extended to form a chaise. The space is now Reuben's new loft. All the objects in the room are

the same, including the unfinished pyramid, but the whiteness of the lighting gives a sense of the large size and the spaciousness of the new loft. The slide is of a wide Mark Rothko painting with soft, colorful, broad horizontal stripes.)

REUBEN: They're gone. I'm exhausted. They can't come again. Not a third time. Tell them, Sherry.

SHERRY: Tell them yourself, Beautiful.

REUBEN: I'm not going to answer the phone anymore— unless you or Luke ring three times, hang up, and call back.

SHERRY: Noted.

REUBEN: *(using his mother's voice)* "Honey, how about if ah come live in the other bedroom?" *(back to his own voice)* I told her you're going to stay here.

SHERRY: Okay. *(Reuben hangs up and gets up to rearrange the loft.)*

LUKE: *(to Sherry)* I'm glad you were there. I went back and forth to Jerusalem for my book, and when my brother had a stroke, I was with him while he was in the hospital, and I was worried that Ruby was feeling abandoned by me.

(Luke pulls up the modern chair he has been seated on to join Reuben. Reuben puts a large, clear uncut crystal on the trunk in front of the couch, and Luke puts a red rose he has brought into the old bottle. Reuben uncovers a board with the Japanese game of "Go" in progress—played with small, smooth black and white stones. Reuben puts on Bach harpsichord music, loud and clear, and beautiful slides of a Tibetan Buddhist monastery in a high mountain region.)

LUKE: How are you feeling this minute?

REUBEN: Lousy.

LUKE: Pain?

REUBEN: No, . . . just lousy. *(He plays the "Go"game, taking out some of Luke's white pieces.)*

LUKE: What does the doctor say?

REUBEN: For three months now, he's been giving me herbs and medicines—.

LUKE: Which you take?

REUBEN: Mostly. I had a test last week. When he told me the results in his office, we cried together. A lot more lesions inside. I'm going on a trip, Luke.

LUKE: Do you want to come back with me to Israel?

REUBEN: Too far. I just need to get out of New York. And Sherry needs a holiday. We're going to the airport on Sunday and pick a plane.

LUKE: "Pick a plane" sounds good.

(Reuben gathers some black pieces from the "Go" board. Luke adds some white stones.)

REUBEN: Luke, why stay alive? I can't tell anymore. I've forgotten.

(Luke is alert.)

LUKE: Do you need a list of reasons? I think it's obvious.

REUBEN: It's not obvious to me. *(He puts down black pieces on the "Go" board.)*

LUKE: You're not thinking straight. That's part of the disease. Things look gray.

REUBEN: Yeah.

LUKE: You need to fight.

REUBEN: Why?

LUKE: Remember Dylan Thomas: "Rage, rage against the dying of the light." Even for survivors in concentration camps it was never a question of *why* stay alive, but *how*. Life is precious, Ruby. Short and precious. You must know that better than I do.

(Reuben picks up the crystal.)

REUBEN: *(looking at the "Go" game)* I get confused, Luke. Which is white's territory, and which is black's? Which is forward—death or life? I'm really not sure.

LUKE: *(touching Reuben)* Don't disappear, Rube, please.

(Luke kneels by Reuben's chair. Reuben caresses Luke's head.)

REUBEN: I think I've done everything I can do in this body, Luke. It's worn out. There's lots more I need to learn, but I think my teachers are out there. *(He gestures toward the outside and smiles.)* You remember Goethe's last words? "Light—more light."

(He moves to another part of the loft and picks up a couple of smaller crystals. He puts a small white spotlight on what he's doing. With careful attention, he wipes a pitcher and a bowl. He places the crystals in the bowl. He slowly pours water over them. We hear the sound of the water hitting the stones. When he has finished pouring the water he picks up the crystals, holds them near his ear, and knocks them gently together, making small clicking

sounds, which the whole audience hears clearly. Reuben remains serious a moment, seeming to listen to the echo of the stones. Then he smiles.)

LUKE: *(returning to his seat)* I felt so awkward, because I couldn't find any words to make him want to live. And somehow he made me feel peaceful.

(Slide of the Grand Canyon. Sherry gets up and enters the main space.)

SHERRY: We ended up at the Grand Canyon. We trekked down to the floor of it to listen, as he said, to what it was like four billion years ago.

(There are insect sounds and, underneath these, East Indian drum music, quiet but insistent. Reuben and Sherry stand on the stage as if listening to and looking at something very ancient. They speak after a time.)

Isn't that a bit extreme?

REUBEN: I *feel* extreme. I'm angry. Good and angry. I have AIDS, and they want to lock me up in an institution. She wants to put me behind bars.

SHERRY: She's worried about you. She's your mother.

REUBEN: I need to free up my energy from her, Sherry, so I can go exploring. I need control—over my life, and my death.

(The music is angry, and the slides are of horses and cowboys rushing.)

They *gave* me the money, didn't they? It's mine. I want to control it. I want to write my own will. I want you to come to Richmond to see the lawyer with me, and I won't even tell them I'm there. I need to cut the umbilical cord, Sherry.

SHERRY: Okay. We'll go.

(The music subsides. Insect sounds are heard again. A new Grand Canyon slide: very beautiful, intensely red, taken at sunset.)

(continuing, after a moment) You know what she's worried about, don't you?

REUBEN: Yes, I do. "Ah'm worried about you." She's always been worried about me. She thinks I'm going to do myself in. I believe she planted that idea herself when I was too young to know what contract I was signing. Probably when I was in her lap, a year old, and we were out in her rose garden in Richmond, with all that precious wisteria around the gazebo. She took advantage of my extreme youth. "Honey, the world out there is a terrible and a dirty place. If you leave here, you'll be so sorry. There's simply nothing out there. If you leave here, you might as well kill yourself. Honey, outside our garden there's just nothing."

(There is a short silence as they continue to stand, listening to the insect sounds.)

SHERRY: Promise me something.

REUBEN: What?

SHERRY: If you ever decide to really do that, warn me.

REUBEN: *(mischievously)* I'll give you an hour's notice. Is that enough?

(Reuben turns off the Grand Canyon slides. Sherry returns to her seat. Reuben stops the insect sounds and the drum music. He puts on dancey show music and, lying on his chaise, phones Danny.)

REUBEN: *(on the phone to Danny)* Hey, Danny-boy. How's the "sunshine in the meadow"?

DANNY: *(angrily, into the phone, to Reuben)* Where've you been?

REUBEN: *(cheerfully)* Afghanistan.

DANNY: I've been trying to reach you for *days*. I need to see you.

REUBEN: Then haul your ass over here.

(They hang up.)

DANNY: *(to the others)* I can't believe what I said when I came in.

(Reuben greets Danny, embracing him.)

DANNY: Don't kiss me on the lips.

REUBEN: *(shaken)* I wasn't going to.

DANNY: I have to sit down.

REUBEN: What are you saying?

DANNY: Not me. Tommy died last month in the hospital in San Francisco. And David was diagnosed yesterday. . . .

(Danny breaks down. Reuben is encouraging him to continue to cry.)

I'm so scared.

REUBEN: Just cry.

DANNY: I'm sorry. . . .

REUBEN: It's good. Crying is better than anything except coffee. *(He goes to get coffee.)*

DANNY: *(feeling better, looking at Reuben, meaning it)* You look terrific, you know.

REUBEN: Yeah? Thanks.

DANNY: You really do. You've lost weight. And your face is glowing. Are you working out?

REUBEN: *(giving him coffee)* A little meditation.

DANNY: You even have a tan. Maybe you really have been to Afghanistan.

REUBEN: *(lightly, but meaning it)* Dere ain't nuffin in dis world, except to love each other, Danny. That's a fact.

DANNY: *(suspiciously)* You haven't found God, have you, Reuben? You're not a born-againer?

REUBEN: Who—li'l ole me? *(He does a couple of soft-shoe steps.)*

DANNY: *(relaxed enough to get hysterical again)* Henry's the sixth I know. Feel my glands. Are they swollen? I've begun to think if this were the last year of my life, what would I do. I hardly touch anybody anymore, but it's probably too late. I keep expecting I'll wake up and the nightmare'll be gone. More likely I'll wake up and every person I know will be gone, and me too—or maybe I—.

REUBEN: Look *(He activates the slide carousel so that a series of Danny dancing stills comes on.)*

DANNY: *(pleased)* Hey!

REUBEN: Here. *(He gives Danny the crystal. The Danny slides start alternating with shots of the Himalayas.)*

Tell me what it feels like.

DANNY: I dunno. Heavy? It's getting warmer. That's my hand, though.

REUBEN: Whenever you want, just hold it.

DANNY: You're giving me this crystal?

REUBEN: Now——.

(He indicates Danny should dance for him, which Danny does, eventually leaping out of the center area carrying the crystal. The music continues, and Reuben continues half dancing around his loft.)

DANNY: *(to the others)* One week ago. *(He's angry.)* Then he leaves me—like that!

(Chris gets up and enters the space.)

CHRIS: I did the unforgivable, didn't I? I dropped in.

(Reuben turns up the music, does a couple of quick steps for Chris, then falls into his arms backwards like a ballerina.)

CHRIS: Hey, feeling good, are we, Little Buddy?

REUBEN: Yes, Mars.

CHRIS: Mars today? Not the sorcerer's apprentice?

(Reuben nods.)

I passed my last exam. I'm a real live physical therapist.

REUBEN: I always thought you were. Let's break out the bubbly.

(Reuben gets a bottle of champagne from the refrigerator and pulls out the same two goblets he had the first time he met Chris. Chris is inspecting the loft.)

CHRIS: Hey, this is almost finished.

(He indicates the pyramid. Reuben offers the pill box. Chris picks out a pill and holds it up, smiling.)

Where have we seen such a rare jewel before?

(Reuben pours out champagne into a goblet. He switches the music to the St. Matthew Passion.)

REUBEN: You look real good to me today, Mars. Maybe you could unbutton your shirt a little—now you're a physical therapist.

CHRIS: *(smiling)* You mean slowly, so I can hear the fabric against my skin?

(Chris unbuttons his shirt very slowly for Reuben, opens it, and slowly slips it off. He performs a subtle movement to show off his chest to Reuben. Reuben flips a switch, which puts Chris in a scarlet spotlight. Chris is a few feet from Reuben. He turns slowly and lets his pants fall, revealing small red underwear. He moves slowly, sensuously, and continuously, offering Reuben several views of his body. Reuben is mesmerized. Suddenly Reuben lets out a loud sound, expressing pain and fury. He knocks the goblet from Chris's hand.)

CHRIS: Hey!

(Reuben turns the lights back to normal. Chris is stunned.)

What gives? *(He sees Reuben's face.)* Hey, Little Buddy, what's the matter?

REUBEN: I'm sorry. Go home, Chris. I'll clean up the mess. *(Reuben has a determined expression. He adds a last touch to the pyramid.)* I have something to do.

(Chris picks up his clothes, slips into them, and returns to where his seat is. The friends remain facing front.)

CHRIS: I guess what he was doing was saving me from himself.

SHERRY: He was saving himself from himself. He had to keep control.

DANNY: Aw, shit, he was scared of dying, scared of the pain. Aw, Ruby. . . .

LUKE: Keep on dancing out there in the cosmos, Ruby. . . .

(Reuben performs what he does now with quiet determination:
He picks up and puts away Chris's goblet.
He turns off the music but leaves the slide on.
He unfolds a straw mat, which he places on the floor underneath the pyramid.
He places candles around the pyramid.
He arranges the lighting on the pyramid so that the pyramid has sharp shadows, like bars.
He lights the candles.
He pours champagne into the remaining goblet.
He pulls out a pill bottle, looks at it for a moment, then gulps down as many pills as he can at a time until the bottle is empty.
He puts the bottle and the glass on the table.
He goes to the table to jot down a note.)

REUBEN: *(writing)* I'm sorry. I have to go now. Mama, please forgive me.

(He slips into the see-through pyramid, and, from the inside, pulls the last piece into place.
He puts a crystal on his forehead. We see him on his back, his arms folded across his chest.
The lights fade on him.
The friends remain still for a moment, facing the audience.
Lights out.)

∽

PREFACE
Liliane Wouters

THE LIVES AND DEATHS OF MISS SHAKESPEARE

Translated from the French by Anne-Marie Glasheen

To Henry Chanal

LILIANE WOUTERS was born near Brussels in 1930. A teacher for over thirty years, since 1980 she has been able to devote herself full-time to writing. Along with Françoise Mallet-Joris, Wouters is probably one of the last Belgian writers of Flemish descent to write in French. Her first collection of poems, *La Marche forcée* (1954), was awarded the French "Prix de la Nuit de la Poésie" by a jury that included Louis Aragon and Jean Cocteau. Subsequent books of poetry followed, including *L'Aloès* (1983), a nearly complete collection of her poems. Her first play, *Oscarine ou les Tournesols*, was produced in 1964; *Vies et morts de Mademoiselle Shakespeare (The Lives and Deaths of Miss Shakespeare)* was produced in 1979. Among her other plays are *La Porte* (1967), *L'Equateur* (1985), *Charlotte ou la Nuit mexicaine* (1989), and a play about teachers, *La Salle des profs* (1983)—the most successful Belgian stage work of recent years. A member of the Belgian Academy of French Language and Literature since 1985, Liliane Wouters has also translated the works of Flemish and Dutch poets and edited anthologies. She is presently writing a series based on *La Salle des profs* for Belgian television.

ANNE-MARIE PONCELET GLASHEEN was born in 1945 of an English mother and Belgian father. When she was three months old her father took his family back to Belgium, where they lived for six years. In England she lived in the Midlands, where she finished her basic education, and then she went to Lancaster University for a degree in French and English. At Exeter University in 1978, Glasheen started researching the post-war developments in Belgian theater and translating the plays of the country's contemporary dramatists. Her translations include Jean Sigrid's *Angel Knife*, which was produced in Brighton and at the 1982 Edinburgh Festival; René Kalisky's *On the Ruins of Carthage*, produced at the 1983 Brighton Festival; and Paul Willems' *It's Raining in My House*, which was recently produced in the United States, at Creighton University. Her collection *Four Belgian Playwrights* was brought out in 1985 by John Calder in the theatrical magazine *Gambit*. While continuing to translate plays, Glasheen also teaches French and English.

CHARACTERS

WILLY-ANNE SHAKESPEARE
HER MOTHER
HER FATHER
AGATHA I, II, III, IV
NEMESIS
CATHARSIS
WALPURGIS
PSORIASIS
RICK O'SHEA. in turn:
           Doctor, Mother Superior, Journalist,
           Patron of the Arts, Mrs. Putiphar, General,
           Psychoanalyst

The action takes place on a square or a park corner. Willy-Anne's statue is supported by the four goddesses: Nemesis, Catharsis, Walpurgis, and Psoriasis.

A light mist clears slowly. The gradually increasing song of birds and rustling of leaves can be heard, as well as the sound of voices: adults' and children's. They can be given shape as silhouettes in the park but must remain "unreal." The goddesses, on the other hand, are very real, very concrete.

VOICES:—Who's that over there?
—Where do you mean?
—There.
—I think it's Shakespeare.
—Do you only think it is, or are you sure?
—I only think it is; I'm not sure. It might be François Coppée or Sully Prudhomme.
—No, it is Shakespeare.

NEMESIS: Any likeness to a well-known historical person is purely coincidental.

CATHARSIS: Of course, the name Shakespeare is very common.

* * *

VOICES:—Shakespeare now, well, well.
—It's a statue of Shakespeare.
—When did it live?
—What?
—The statue.
—What?
—The statue.
—A long time ago.
—What, even before Granny?
—A long time before Granny.
—Is the person still alive?
—No, of course not; people never get that old.
—Looks very young.

WALPURGIS: He's not so stupid, that one, is he.

PSORIASIS: Wait til he grows up.

*   *   *

VOICES:—So Shakespeare is dead.
        —Of course.

(Silence. We can hear the statue's heart beating.)

*   *   *

VOICES:—Listen, Leo.
        —Hey, Daddy, what's that?
        —What's what?
        —That, that noise.
        —I don't know. Don't ask silly questions.

CATHARSIS: If you listened carefully, you'd realize it's the
sound of a heartbeat.

*   *   *

VOICES:—Daddy, it sounds like a heartbeat.
        —Look. For a start, it's a statue, and secondly, Shake-
        speare is dead.
        —But, Daddy.
        —Be quiet.

NEMESIS: Of course it's a heartbeat. How could you expect a
heart that beat so much to stop?

WALPURGIS: Not counting the nights it beat twice as fast.

NEMESIS: Not counting that you should never count.

CATHARSIS: Neither wealth, nor stealth, nor faces, nor ages.

WALPURGIS: Neither love words nor ordinary words.

PSORIASIS: Nor the running after words.

WALPURGIS: Nor the feeding off words.

PSORIASIS: Nor the living for words.

CHORUS: Nor the writing!

(The heartbeat gets stronger and stronger.)

VOICES:—Why is its heart beating, Daddy? It is its heart beating, you know.
—I've already told you not to ask silly questions.

NEMESIS: You're the silly one; everyone else has understood
that a poet's heart doesn't die in the ordinary sense of the
word.

*   *   *

VOICES:—What's a poet?
—What's it for?
—Nothing.

(The heart stops. Silence.)

*   *   *

VOICES:—What was the statue's name?
—I've already told you: Shakespeare.
—Yes, but what else?
—Isn't that enough, then?
—The other name?
—The first name?
—Oh, the first name? I think it was William.
—Willy-Anne?
—Come, come, now. It was a man.
—Really?
—William or Willy-Anne?
—Oh, what does it matter!

—Come on, then! Was it a man or a woman?
—A poet.
—He was or she was?
—You're beginning to get on my nerves.

CATHARSIS: The love sonnets were dedicated to boys.

PSORIASIS: She was a woman, then!

WALPURGIS: You don't know the first thing about it.

CATHARSIS: Well, the Mona Lisa was a man.

NEMESIS: So you think ending up in the wrong body is funny!

PSORIASIS: I protest! She was very happy in hers.

WALPURGIS: How do you know?

CATHARSIS: Did she tell you?

PSORIASIS: Of course I know; of course she told me.

(Nemesis, Catharsis, Walpurgis, Psoriasis, chanting.)

> Body received without knowing
> Body returned without wanting
> Body on credit, body borrowed
> Body with forbidden tomorrows.
> Body, precious puppet, gentle ornament.
> Center of all desires
> Through which pleasure discovers bitterness.

(Sound of a crying baby. Rick O'Shea/Doctor gives the baby to the mother.)

RICK O'SHEA / DOCTOR: Here is your son, Mrs. Shakespeare.

MOTHER: You mean, my daughter. She looks like a boy, but she's a girl. And I so wanted a son! I'd even decided to call him William.

RICK: But you still can. Call her Willy-Anne.

MOTHER: Willy-Anne! There's no such name!

RICK: There will be! There is now. Willy-Anne. Not bad. Not bad at all. You'll see; you'll be happy. Girls are so much nicer. You'll be able to soap her, scrub her, dress her up, brush her, polish her, wax her.

MOTHER: Boy or girl, the fact is I never wanted either.

RICK: Ah, well, the wine is drawn, it must be drunk. Even if it does taste like vinegar.

MOTHER: It all happened one day in April. The woods were full of daffodils.

RICK: I see.

MOTHER: I wasn't on my guard! I'd been brought up to think that babies were found under cabbages!

RICK: I see only too well.

MOTHER: And now here she is, born, Willy-Anne.

RICK: You've got to take life as it comes.

MOTHER: What shall I do, what will become of me?

RICK: When God sends the sheep, he also sends the fleece.
    (Exit.)

(Nemesis, Catharsis, Walpurgis, Psoriasis, chanting)

> She came out of her mother's womb, colorless and clothesless, dripping water and blood. Like everyone, she came out head first, or was it bottom first? Oh, we've forgotten. Never mind. A baby born with a caul on its head; does it have a sex? Yes, two rather than one; which? which? We don't know; who will know; she was born yesterday, tomorrow, 413 years ago in England, in Furstenberg Square, on the Pincio, Unter den Linden. Ah, she came into the world, born from never into always—or for a little while at least, no one knows. No one knows anything.

(Silence)

(Light)

(The statue comes to life.)

WILLY-ANNE: It all began one day, but which day? Before this day I was not. Before this day, there was nothing, nothing I can remember, although it was all here. Or so I've been told. And I believe it. The world revolved before us, and it will continue to revolve after us. But while we're here, how different it is! Am I really here? It would seem so. There are only two possibilities: life or death. It is accidental that I breathe, but intentional that I continue to breathe. I have only to say no. Shall I continue to breathe? To breathe in, to breathe out, in, out, in, out. Air in, insults in. Air out, life salts out. For why, for whom?

NEMESIS: The moment has come for me to show myself. It is time for me to descend from my pedestal. Look at me. Really look at me. Deep into my eyes. I am Nemesis. Avenging Nemesis. The wicked fairy of mythology. All those who bear the sign return to me. You bear the sign. So here I am.

WILLY-ANNE: I haven't asked for anything.

NEMESIS: The good fairies have gone; they've given you their gifts, haven't they? Now let me give you mine. Nemesis, distributive justice. Fortune, misfortune. You will know them all.

WILLY-ANNE: Give me time to think, to decide.

NEMESIS: To decide what?

WILLY-ANNE: Whether I want to be Shakespeare.

NEMESIS: You have no choice!

WILLY-ANNE: Not even a bit ?

NEMESIS: No. You have the right to end the game when you want to, that's all. But if you play, it will be with my dice.

WILLY-ANNE: But supposing I fancy a quiet life. Supposing it's security I need.

NEMESIS: It might be.

WILLY-ANNE: What then?

NEMESIS: The good fairies have been and gone. They have given you too much. I can't leave things as they are.

WILLY-ANNE: Yes!

NEMESIS: No! Too much, I say. Out of their own pockets. Too much. How many of them were there?

WILLY-ANNE: Six.

NEMESIS: Six? What folly! Wait, let me count: Adela, Asphodela, Hirondella, Haridella, Mortadella and Tired'aila. Is that right?

WILLY-ANNE: Yes.

NEMESIS: What folly!

WILLY-ANNE: I don't think it was.

NEMESIS: Of course you don't. Egoist!

WILLY-ANNE: Nothing is too good for me. To think that death is waiting for me somewhere!

NEMESIS: Just listen to that!

WILLY-ANNE: If my time here is to be no more than a lie, then I want the best possible deal.

NEMESIS: Huh! She gets better and better!

WILLY-ANNE: One day I shall have to die. To die.

NEMESIS: Everyone has to die.

WILLY-ANNE: Yes, but they don't think about it all the time.

NEMESIS: Anyway, your godmothers did. They gave you everything. Well, nearly everything.

WILLY-ANNE: Not really. No more than anyone else gets. But the slightest thing fills me with wonder. For example, I can't get over the changing seasons. The falling leaves, the bursting buds . . . .

NEMESIS: Huh!

WILLY-ANNE: My heart that beats, and time that flees.

NEMESIS: Huh!

WILLY-ANNE: The moment that everything stops. The moment that everything starts again.

NEMESIS: Huh! *(Pause)* Huh!

WILLY-ANNE: I'll need at least a thousand lives!

NEMESIS: You will have them. And you will pay dearly for them. I shall make sure you are well equipped. There is after all such a thing as justice. Dis-tri-bu-tive justice! Let's see, now, what did they give you? Adela?

WILLY-ANNE: Youth.

NEMESIS: Seventeen at heart all your life? Very well, then, I shall make you seven dozen in your head. Asphodela?

WILLY-ANNE: Friendship.

NEMESIS: Hirondella?

WILLY-ANNE: Escape. Dream. The call of the wild. No earth sticking to the soles of my shoes.

NEMESIS: Nice present. *(Pause)* Haridella?

WILLY-ANNE: The satisfaction of work well done.

NEMESIS: I recognize the old nag in that! What about Mortadella, Mortadella, stuck with cloves, pitted with garlic...?

WILLY-ANNE: Love.

NEMESIS: I knew it would be that! I knew it. I would have bet on it! She still doesn't understand. She never will. Incor-ri-gi-ble! Love! The tingle of pleasure! The fingers up and down the spine! The wonderful clouds! Your Adam's apple rising, your solar plexus falling! 40,000 volts! 100 degrees Centigrade! 212 degrees Fahrenheit! The second movement of the Brahms Sextet! Memories so happy they break your heart! *Mon âme la nuit!* Love...love, passion, fashion, affection, affliction, annihilation. *(Pause)* My poor little dove. I suppose you were pleased?

WILLY-ANNE: Very.

NEMESIS: And that you even thanked her?

WILLY-ANNE: Yes.

NEMESIS: Thank you, thank you very much, a great big thank you.

WILLY-ANNE: Yes.

NEMESIS: Well, you deserve a good hiding. Huh! I'm not surprised Tired'aila came along too. She gave you poetry, no doubt. It's what she always gives. Only in desperate cases, mind you. PO-E-TRY. So, you accepted, I suppose?

WILLY-ANNE: Yes.

NEMESIS: Don't always answer yes. It's irritating. Well, we are in a nice mess. And what can I give you after that lot?

WILLY-ANNE: I don't need anything else.

NEMESIS: But I must give you something. I must. *(She concentrates. Beginning to chant)*
When the scales of justice are level,
When gifts are two-sided weapons,
When the pendulum swings between sweetness and bitterness, heat and cold, good and evil,
What else can I give you, but want.
Want, the incurable wound.

The sore with stubborn edges.
Want, want.
You will always be hungry for more bread,
Thirsty for different water.
And you will never be more hungry
Than when the bread is taken from you.
And you will never be more thirsty
Than next to a dried-up spring . . . .

(She rejoins the chorus.)

* * *

MOTHER: We did our best. We brought her up well. She never wanted for anything. Ever.

FATHER: Well brought up, that's right!

(Voices of Mother and Father, more or less alternately)

—Don't put your finger up your nose.
—Stand up straight.
—Say good morning to the lady.
—Eat your soup.
—Say good-bye to the gentleman.
—Don't eat like a pig.
—Eat your salad.
—If you wet your bed again, I'll rub your nose in it.
—Don't stand around daydreaming.
—Eat your meat.
—Don't read all the time.
—9½? Why not 10? Why not 11? You must get 11 out of 10 next time!
—Don't dirty your pants.
—Shut up and eat.
—Eat.
—Eat.
—EAT!

WILLY-ANNE: *(She is busy writing, then raises her head.)* I am Shakespeare. I am Shakespeare.

(Exit.)

MOTHER: She was, after all, a child like any other.

FATHER: Not quite.

MOTHER: She didn't cry at night, perhaps?

FATHER: She used to scream.

MOTHER: No louder than any other baby.

FATHER: Louder.

MOTHER: Not as loud.

FATHER: Louder. She drove me mad.

MOTHER: If only you'd been her father....

FATHER: Aren't I her father?

MOTHER: How should I know!

FATHER: But I thought....

MOTHER: Yes, me too. I always think. Anyway, I suppose you are. I'm not sure. There were so many daffodils around that day. *(Pause)* How should I know?

FATHER: You're her mother, aren't you?

MOTHER: If only I could be sure!

FATHER: But, you, you....

MOTHER: I'm sure they swapped her at the hospital. Mine was a boy.

FATHER: But she's got your nose!

MOTHER: So, what's a nose!

FATHER: Really!

MOTHER: Any daughter of mine would have loved ribbons. She would have had ballet lessons. She would have spent hours in front of the mirror.

FATHER: Yes, that's true.

MOTHER: She would have been thrilled at seeing her breasts growing.

FATHER: That is indeed true.

MOTHER: She was furious when hers grew. They didn't grow together either. The left one grew before the right one did.

FATHER: The left, of course, the seat of the heart.

MOTHER: She refused to wear the lovely dresses I made her.

FATHER: And I must admit, you do sew well.

MOTHER: And did you ever see her play with a doll?

FATHER: She dreamed of owning a huge stallion.

MOTHER: Was she ever interested in boys? She didn't even think about them.

FATHER: Only when she wanted to be like her friends.

MOTHER: She was totally indifferent to men.

FATHER: To everyone, in fact.

MOTHER: Not always! Not for long! There was a time.

FATHER: At that time.

MOTHER: And she wanted to go to the convent.

FATHER: She would have set fire to it.

MOTHER: She slept with her rosary.

FATHER: No, it was a statue of St. Cordula.

MOTHER: She denied herself all sorts of pleasures, for I don't know what reasons.

FATHER: She tried to die before she'd really lived.

MOTHER: It didn't last long.

FATHER: Right now, she's fighting to live before she dies.

MOTHER: Even so, you still sent her to that boarding school.

FATHER: She was the one who wanted to go.

(Willy-Anne enters in her nightdress.)

RICK O'SHEA / MOTHER SUPERIOR: This is the first time a pupil has ever come into my office wearing only a nightdress. The first time I have been disturbed after nine o'clock at night. The first time someone has disregarded the curfew. The first time that I, Mother Mary of the Agony of Gethsemane, have seen a pupil come before me, by the light of the moon while the rest of the community is asleep. The first time since I became a novice, that is to say, in the year of the beatification of the blessed Cordula, when the magnolia in the garden was in full bloom though we had thought it to be infertile. Infertile. Why aren't you in your bed? Lying on your back? Arms crossed? Why have you left the door open? Draughts! Draughts! The Devil comes in with draughts. Shut that door. Better still, take some Holy Water. What do you want? What's so urgent? There aren't many things that can't wait until morning. Speak, Willy-Anne.

WILLY-ANNE: I am Shakespeare.

RICK: So? What next? There's nothing new about that.

WILLY-ANNE: But *I* am Shakespeare, and no one seems to realize it.

RICK: Prove it, then.

WILLY-ANNE: That's what frightens me.

RICK: Prove it, I said. All we want is to believe you.

WILLY-ANNE: Christ did sweat blood in the Olive Grove, didn't he?

RICK: Yes. We have three drops of it here, in the chapel. What are you getting at?

WILLY-ANNE: He did say "Let this cup be taken from me," didn't he?

RICK: Yes. Before giving in to the divine will. Why?

WILLY-ANNE: If Christ was frightened, how do you think I feel?

(Horrified, the Mother Superior dismisses Willy-Anne with a wave of the hand.)

WILLY-ANNE: I am Shakespeare and no one seems to realize it.

RICK: Not only Shakespeare, it would seem, but Christ too. Who does she think she is? We'll have to lick her into shape. All we need is a bit of planing, scraping, pruning, filing, kenivering. We'll get rid of all protrusions, anything unusual, so that she can be popped into a box, stored in a drawer. We'll shorten her if necessary—a thumb, an elbow, a head. We've managed it with tougher ones than this one.

> WALPURGIS: You don't know the nature of the blood coursing through her veins.

> PSORIASIS: I do. I made it.

RICK: Education. Nothing like it. Training horses in the ring. Fleas in a box. Banging nonstop at the same piano, the same nail. If your hand sins, cut it off. If your feet take you too far . . . .

> NEMESIS: Only I know how far she'll go, and no one will hold her back. But it won't be along your paths.

> CATHARSIS: Plane. Scrape. File. Prune. Kenive. Your methods are worthless compared to mine. You'll get nowhere, whereas I shall.

(Willy-Anne is once more before Rick/Mother Superior.)

RICK: Again! This is getting to be a habit! You have to come down from the dormitory in a crocodile. You are always trying to get your own way. Yesterday you fainted. You rolled down the great staircase. Your spirit should not leave your body without warning. It is only polite.

WILLY-ANNE: Just one word to help me sleep. One word to warm this convent. It's so cold here.

RICK: It must be cold. The cold keeps ideas where they belong, fixes them there, lifts them. Heat softens them and gives rise to different ideas.

WILLY-ANNE: Just one word.

RICK: While on earth, never amass a treasure where the moth and the worm might devour it, where the thief can drill through and steal it. Do not give your heart to another human as vulnerable as yourself. Put your trust in God, Willy-Anne.

WILLY-ANNE: God draws me to him like a magnet. Pastures green and hills flowing with milk and honey.

RICK: Good.

WILLY-ANNE: In your pastures green, you made me rest. With your waters clear, my thirst you quenched.

RICK: Very good. Very good.

> WALPURGIS: Chat away, my dear. You haven't yet experienced the soft air of a balmy evening, the cool wind of dawn. The trembling at the sight of a certain person approaching. Your knees becoming weak, your thighs clammy. You haven't yet sighed "Ahh" in someone's arms.

WILLY-ANNE: Ahh. Ahh. *(Pause)* Agatha!

RICK: What did you say?

WILLY-ANNE: Agatha.

RICK: Agatha? Who's Agatha?

WILLY-ANNE: What did I say?

RICK: You said "Agatha"!

WALPURGIS: *Exactement!*

WILLY-ANNE: I don't know anyone called Agatha.

NEMESIS: You will! Oh, you will!

MOTHER: Who would have thought she'd ever become Shakespeare? We didn't bring her up to be like that. We never had any books in the house.

FATHER: Yes, we did; there was the dictionary.

MOTHER: At seventeen months she could read it upside down. At fourteen she knew it by heart.

FATHER: You're exaggerating.

MOTHER: By heart. Even I've remembered bits of it. "You're trembling, Bailly," one of his assistants said. "Yes, my friend; it's because of the cold," he replied.

FATHER: Impudence, more impudence, always impudence.

MOTHER: Show my head to the people; it is worth seeing.

FATHER: I am looking for an honest man.

MOTHER: You?

FATHER: No, not me. Diogenes.

MOTHER: Suddenly happy, he exclaimed "Grouchy." It was

Blücher.

FATHER: Madame Bovary is me.

MOTHER: You?

FATHER: No, not me; I can't remember who it was.

MOTHER: Weep like a woman for the kingdom you were not
man enough to defend.

FATHER: But it does move!

MOTHER: Just another minute, Mr. Executioner.

FATHER: Noli me tangere.

MOTHER: What are you saying?

FATHER: It was in the appendix.

MOTHER: Concedo.

FATHER: Dixi.

MOTHER: Doctus cum libro.

FATHER: Ex cathedra.

MOTHER: E pericoloso sporgersi.

FATHER: Man spricht Deutsch.

MOTHER: Mister Livingstone, I presume?

WILLY-ANNE: If you think that it is with that gibberish that
one becomes Shakespeare....

MOTHER: What is it, then; what is it, then; what is it, then?

WILLY-ANNE: *(She is alone in a sort of semiconscious state. She speaks the following twice, the first time groping, searching for the words; the second time, confidently.)*

> I wake. No. I think.
> I am awake.
> Another mimics
> The gestures I make.
>
> I speak. In my ear
> The voice: This is you!
> It lies. I run clear
> The other has my roof.

PSORIASIS: She's losing consciousness for nothing. They are wondering why her spirit is leaving her, just like that, all of a sudden.

NEMESIS: They don't know. They cannot know.

PSORIASIS: And these sudden unexplained bouts of fever. The doctor says it's because she's growing. My foot!

WALPURGIS: Is she still going through her mystical period?

CATHARSIS: I'm afraid she'll never get over it completely.

WILLY-ANNE: Let—this—cup—be—taken—from—me.

CATHARSIS: This is where I intervene, dearest one. Nothing will be taken away from you. You will be made to drink it all up. The full measure brimming over, until you throw up.

WILLY-ANNE: I don't want to!

CATHARSIS: I'll hold your head over the basin, I'll stick my fingers down as far as your epiglottis, you'll throw up your soul, you'll throw up your entrails, you'll throw up.

WILLY-ANNE: No, no, no!

CATHARSIS: Then I'll fetch clean handkerchiefs, and cool water, and very gently, I'll wipe your mouth. I'll give you water, in tiny sips; you'll look around surprised, astonished at still being alive.

WILLY-ANNE: No!

CATHARSIS: Yes! Clean handkerchiefs, cool water, water that washes everything, that washes away everything. Clean water that washes away all marks, water—three drops on your forehead. Sleep, little one, sleep. Get better, gather your strength; you'll need it. Life seems long with minutes and seconds, the hour we spend waiting, but short when time passes or has passed. Here you are, dead. Yes, for the first time, but not the last. Dead. I am here to help you breathe again, to help you draw breath, carefully, with difficulty. Three drops on your temples, on your mouth. Water. The sac of water we had lost, searched for; that we return to, curl up in, are reborn from. And how many beings are there in one, and how many existences between the nappy and the shroud? *(Change of tone)* What about me, then? What will you do with me? What's to become of me? I am the leech sucking out your blood to turn it into ink. I am fat, pregnant with your works, with your emptiness. No, no, don't wake up yet. No, no; if you open your eyes, deliver me, with your words . . . .

RICK O'SHEA / JOURNALIST: Willy-Anne Shakespeare, what made you take up writing? *(seeing the scene)* Oh!

CATHARSIS: Throw up, my angel, throw up. Let me be thin again. I am as swollen as a leather bottle; you must empty me. Each time you write, I shall get thinner.

RICK: It only goes to prove that poetry remains a mystery to us. Yesterday I interviewed the Pythia of Delphi. Yes, the Pythia. There she was, seated on her stone. And do you know what she said to me?

CATHARSIS: *Ta gueule! (rejoining chorus)*

RICK: Oooh! *(Pause)* Who would have thought it? And I was talking about the Pythia, no less. Really.... Everything is going to the dogs. I suppose you believe in God?

(Exit.)

WILLY-ANNE: I believe a door is either open or shut. The tragedy is that it shuts as soon as the wind gets up.

> CATHARSIS: *(rejoining the chorus)* It's terrible how fat I've become! It's time young Shakespeare came to help me. *(to Nemesis)* Have you got any plans for her? What have you got in store for her?
>
> NEMESIS: Nothing much. The odd daily chores. The odd meeting. The odd affair of the heart.
>
> CATHARSIS: What about me, though; what's to become of me?
>
> NEMESIS: Don't worry!
>
> PSORIASIS: If I follow....
>
> WALPURGIS: You must. What would we do without you?

PSORIASIS: Really!

CATHARSIS: With a good deal of revulsion, I have to admit that we still need Psoriasis!

PSORIASIS: Thank you!

NEMESIS: Silence, Ladies!

CATHARSIS: Make sure she's strong enough. Not everyone who wants to can be Shakespeare.

PSORIASIS: I've given her sturdy loins.

WALPURGIS: That suits me too.

CATHARSIS: You're just a sex maniac!

WALPURGIS: Sex won't be one of her weaknesses.

PSORIASIS: Which sex?

WALPURGIS: It makes no difference.

CATHARSIS: Sex maniac. You really are a sex maniac.

NEMESIS: Silence, Ladies.

CATHARSIS: We'll be quiet. We'll be quiet. But I would like to get thinner.

NEMESIS: Silence, Ladies!

WILLY-ANNE: The first time I saw Agatha was in Egypt, in front of a Mastaba. She was stroking a male ibis her father Putiphar had given her. We met every day after that.

AGATHA: Willy-Anne!

WILLY-ANNE: Agatha!

AGATHA: Willy-Anne! You're all there. Eyes. Lips. Hands.

WILLY-ANNE: Agatha! You're all there. You're complete! Lips. Hands. Eyes.

> WALPURGIS: They won't go any further than this, not this time.

> CATHARSIS: And what about me in all this?

> NEMESIS: One thing at a time.

WILLY-ANNE: What's happening to me? Oh! I feel like kissing the Sphinx, climbing the Great Pyramid, crossing the desert, going up the Nile.

AGATHA: What's happening to me? Oh! They'd talked to me of love. "You'll find love," they said. I believed them. I searched everywhere. I tried them all. Blond, brunette, and others. Bald and tall, curly-haired and short. Men, of course. Love was a man as I was a woman. And here I am, Willy-Anne.

WILLY-ANNE: Do we chose whom we love?

AGATHA: What do we love? A face—your face? A voice—your voice. Silence—your silence. We love everything. I love everything .

WILLY-ANNE: We can't imagine what it will be like, so it's a real surprise when it hits us.

AGATHA: And you end up losing your head and your heart.

(Mrs. Putiphar appears. The parents run up to look at her.)

RICK O'SHEA / MRS. PUTIPHAR: I was talking about it to Nefertiti only yesterday. Don't buy any more shares, my dear, I
said, not in the present climate. Bricks, bricks, it must be
bricks. A little flat in Luxor XV, or a maisonette—better
still. Doesn't Akhenaton agree? Don't tell me he wants a
Swiss chalet on the outskirts of town! Gstaad in February
maybe, but... or near Pontresina at the beginning of
March—although it has become rather downmarket now!
I'm more interested in winter sports in Peru! Timbuktu!
Caramariboo! When my daughter Agatha settles down,
then perhaps.... She's still only a child at the moment.

MOTHER: *(to Father)* Willy-Anne! Too young? Your niece has
just got married and she's eighteen months younger than
Willy-Anne. So....

FATHER: Willy-Anne is in no hurry. She's happy to stay at
home.

MOTHER: At home! What do you mean at home! She's always out.

RICK: Youth must have its way. And I'm sure my Agatha
isn't wasting a minute of it.

MOTHER: If only I knew where she went. She comes, she
goes, as quiet as the grave. She never says a word.

RICK: As far as that's concerned, I have no fears. Agatha
tells me everything. I know everything that goes on inside
her, to the remotest corner of her heart.

MOTHER: Nothing, nothing, nothing, nothing. I'm losing
my daughter.

RICK: As I was telling Nefertiti, what we sow, we must reap.

MOTHER: What have I done to deserve this!

FATHER: You've nothing to reproach yourself for, my dear.

MOTHER: We did our best, didn't we?

FATHER: We did our very best. Anyway, she hasn't turned out so badly.

RICK: Too young, yes. But female to the ends of her fingernails, to the tips of her breasts. A hundred percent female, the complete woman from the day she was born.

MOTHER: I told the doctor, she should have been a boy.

FATHER: What else could she want? She's got everything she needs.

MOTHER: You don't see anything. You don't want to see.

RICK: What do I see? Are my eyes deceiving me? Is that my daughter at the top of Mykerinos, or is it the top of Chephren? No, it's the top of Cheops! Perhaps it is time to marry her off? I hope, at least, that he is a young man of good blood, related to the eighteenth dynasty. A young exec, a top civil servant, a graduate? *(seeing Willy-Anne)* Looks O.K. I wonder who it is? *(She looks harder.)* More the artistic type. Never mind, she might get over it.... *(Pause. Suddenly seeing properly)* Oh, hell! It's a girl!

WILLY-ANNE: *(to Agatha)* My desert rose, my star-encrusted papyrus!

AGATHA: My honeycake, my desert antelope!

> CATHARSIS: Tumble down, you waves of stone.
> If you were not my lovely
> I am Egypt's Pharaoh
> His sister-wife, his army
> If you are not my love alone.

WALPURGIS: Lovely! Lovely! Who's it by?

CATHARSIS: Apollinaire. I wonder when young Shakespeare will give us something like that?

WILLY-ANNE: Agatha....

CATHARSIS: All the time she keeps muttering "Agatha" and rolling the whites of her eyes, I carry on, getting fatter!

AGATHA: Face. Voice. Silence. I'm in love.

RICK: It's not possible.

WILLY-ANNE: Silence. Voice. Face. I'm in love.

RICK: I must be dreaming!

WILLY-ANNE: I must be dreaming.

AGATHA: The top of Cheops. Forever, perhaps.

PSORIASIS: You can tell it's the first time. She said: forever.

WILLY-ANNE: Forever?

RICK: Stop that now! Stop it immediately!

AGATHA: For-ever.

RICK: Enough! Enough!

WILLY-ANNE: No, not yet, not already.

AGATHA: I'm in love for the first time. Not already.

RICK: Cut! Cut!

WILLY-ANNE: So this is the soft air of a balmy evening, the cool wind of dawn? So this is it?

AGATHA: I shall remember the top of Cheops all my life.

WILLY-ANNE: We've only spent one night there, only one night, and I haven't been able to decide the exact color of your eyes.

RICK: Cuuuuuuuut!

(Blackout. Exit Agatha.)

WILLY-ANNE: *(writing)* The second time I saw Agatha was at the foot of a fortified castle. She was on horseback and had a falcon on her wrist. I thought she would have been doing a tapestry.

CATHARSIS: She's mistaking her for Penelope.

WALPURGIS: Undoing and redoing are also work.

CATHARSIS: Who said that?

WALPURGIS: Mao-Tse-Tung.

PSORIASIS: I thought he said: work, and work carefully.

WALPURGIS: No, that was Teilhard de Chardin.

NEMESIS: Ladies, I beg of you.

WILLY-ANNE: A falcon on her wrist! And I who am so frightened of birds!

PSORIASIS: Yes. I can't understand that phobia.

NEMESIS: We'd better mention it to the analyst.

WALPURGIS: I'd rather mention it to a confessor.

PSORIASIS: It amounts to the same thing.

WALPURGIS: Except that a confessor doesn't charge for his services.

NEMESIS: Ladies!

WILLY-ANNE: It was a beautiful day in May. The grass and leaves were pubescent. The buds were budding, the clouds clouding, the birds birding. A painter was fixing onto his canvas a thousand little flowers. Me-ti-cu-lous-ly.

(Enter Agatha.)

NEMESIS: The ground quakes beneath your feet. The Flemish soil trembles and the tall poplars bend beneath the sea breeze.

WILLY-ANNE: Agatha, I think we've met before.

AGATHA: Willy-Anne. I do recognize you; I think we must have spoken to one another once.

WILLY-ANNE: I'm not sure that we spoke, but I'm sure we knew one another.

AGATHA: It was, but I know not where, in a time gone by.

WILLY-ANNE: Wasn't it on the banks of the Nile, or was it on the banks of the Tagus?

AGATHA: There's something familiar about your face, something about your voice.

WILLY-ANNE: And yet, you've changed.

AGATHA: And yet, you're different. Do you think we could again?

> WALPURGIS: You could, oh, you could. If you only knew how you could again and how many times you could again.

> PSORIASIS: The same body and yet a different person.

WILLY-ANNE: Let's run away together. A long way away.

AGATHA: I was searching for India but discovered America instead.

> PSORIASIS: But America hadn't been discovered then!

> NEMESIS: It doesn't matter; be quiet.

> PSORIASIS: But I can assure, America hadn't been discovered.

> NEMESIS: Ssssh!

WILLY-ANNE: Shall we sail from Bremen or from Bruges?

AGATHA: We're not sailing from anywhere. We'll just climb the highest tower we can find.

> PSORIASIS: Why are they so mad about heights?

> CATHARSIS: I can see you've never been in love.

WALPURGIS: Far from prying eyes and horrified looks.

CATHARSIS: Far from herself. She's still running away from herself.

WILLY-ANNE: Can you see the villages of stone lace, the bridges, woods and trees of cross-stitch?

AGATHA: I can see far into the distance,
I can see very clearly.

WILLY-ANNE: Can you see sand dunes and waves on the horizon?

AGATHA: I can still see,
I can always see.

WILLY-ANNE: Can you see the clouds beneath our feet?

AGATHA: No. I can see no more.

WILLY-ANNE: Look at me instead, then.

AGATHA: Willy-Anne . . . .

CATHARSIS: Here we go again! Didn't I tell you? She's frightened. Nemesis, my sister, we'll never make anything of this girl.

NEMESIS: The time is not ripe.

CATHARSIS: Up above the clouds and waves! As if poetry could be written up there. Get a hold on your life, little one; get a hold on your life.

NEMESIS: The time is not ripe!

CATHARSIS: But I'm becoming obese!

NEMESIS: Patience.

CHORUS: What a lot it takes to make a poet!
Moonless nights , moonlit nights,
Moments wasted, moments squandered,
Seasons waiting, harvests sleeping,
Days maturing, dying, rotting.

(During this time, Agatha is leaving Willy-Anne very slowly.)

CATHARSIS: Faster! Faster!

NEMESIS: Patience!

PSORIASIS: Patience!

WALPURGIS: Patience!

(The three together)

In—the—blue!

WILLY-ANNE: I don't care whether it's blue or grey, as long as I find Agatha again. Where is she?

WALPURGIS: At the foot of a fortified castle. No, at the top of the highest tower.

WILLY-ANNE: That was where I lost her. In one day, I found her and lost her again.

PSORIASIS: That day lasted six months!

WILLY-ANNE: Six months! It couldn't have been. It went so quickly. Time spent with her is timeless. Time without her stands still. Oh, my little pearly-nailed Egyptian.

WALPURGIS: I thought we were in Flanders.

WILLY-ANNE: My lady of the manor, seated at the second window of the seventh tower.

PSORIASIS: Ah! We were in Flanders.

WILLY-ANNE: Between the pillars of the temple, on the banks of the Father-River, watched by the eyes of Horus. Predatory bird. Face of desire.

WALPURGIS: It is Egypt after all. I can't follow what's happening.

WILLY-ANNE: Distaff in one hand, you spin; watching the road made dusty by the crusader' war chariots.

PSORIASIS: She's mixing everything up!

WALPURGIS: You must admit, she's covered quite a distance.

WILLY-ANNE: Pearl of Amenophis, my lady of the flaxen eyes.

RICK O'SHEA / MRS. PUTIPHAR: C-U-T!

(Nemesis, Catharsis, Walpurgis, Psoriasis, chanting)

Cut, cut, she's been skinned, she's raw, she's done to a turn, leave her alone now. Cut, cut, will she take the final plunge?

She's lost consciousness; she can't see properly anymore. And yet, without knowing it, little by little, she's moving forward. She dies, she dies, and then it all starts again.

* * *

FATHER: I've thought it over again and again, and I still don't understand.

MOTHER: She goes off on some journey to God knows where; she comes back with a face like death and never stops talking about someone called Adele or something like that....

FATHER: Agatha.

MOTHER: Agatha, that's right. She cries for a week and then spends three weeks covering pieces of paper with black scrawl.

FATHER: It's as if her blood were secreting ink.

MOTHER: Her blood or her tears?

FATHER: Does she cry in front of you?

MOTHER: No, but I hear her. And I've read what she writes about it.

FATHER: And?

MOTHER: "Who would have thought the human body contained so many tears?"

FATHER: Yeah.

MOTHER: It's very odd, you know. Why does she want to write? No one else in the family has had that illness.

FATHER: No, nor the other one.

MOTHER: Which other one?

FATHER: Do I go around looking at men?

MOTHER: We're normal people.

FATHER: *(after a pause)* There was cousin Julius.

MOTHER: Caesar?

FATHER: No, not that one.

MOTHER: Oh, the one who was Pope.

FATHER: Whose friend painted ceilings.

MOTHER: That's right.

(Pause)

There was that foreigner as well.

FATHER: A foreigner? In our family?

MOTHER: Yes.

FATHER: There are no foreigners in our family.

MOTHER: Oh, yes, there are.

FATHER: Oh, yes, so there are. There was that Greek woman who lived on an island.

MOTHER: I've forgotten what her name was.

FATHER: So have I. Never mind. It doesn't matter.

MOTHER: Are you sure she was like that?

FATHER: Yes, quite sure. *(Pause)* But she did love a man as well.

MOTHER: Are you sure?

FATHER: Yes, lot of women and one man.

MOTHER: Why, to see what it was like?

FATHER: No, no; she really loved him.

MOTHER: Willy-Anne too.

FATHER: Willy-Anne too? What do you mean?

MOTHER: Don't tell me you didn't know?

FATHER: Well, I am telling you. Really, I didn't know. Who was it?

MOTHER: Oh, honestly. . . .

FATHER: Who was it?

MOTHER: It was so long ago now. . . .

FATHER: Well?

MOTHER: You should know, after all. *(Pause)* It was that great patron of the arts, your boss.

> *(Rick O'Shea as a patron of the arts enters, dressed in his ceremonial academician's uniform. Father is helping him get dressed. He passes him his two-pointed hat, his medals, etc. The whole of this scene must resemble a kind of ballet.)*

RICK O'SHEA/PATRON OF THE ARTS: Now for the order of St. Francis of Sales. St. Francis of Sales, protector of the arts. I was given that after I had had that hagiography on the Blessed Cordula published. Ever heard of the Blessed Cordula? Having discovered in herself an irrepressible penchant for the members of her own sex, she decided she could not take her vows. The temptations would have been too great. Her astute confessor advised her to take up a military career instead. *(Pause)* You're not listening to me, Leo. I'll move on, therefore, to the blighted hopes of the unfortunate Cordula. All you need to know is that she sacrificed her life to her virginity. Between you and me, she was a complete idiot. And now for my sash. My sash as Chef of Literary Gastronomy awarded me on the occasion of the publication of my ten thousandth review in our national rag.

FATHER: Your decorations, sir, are beautiful.

RICK: Yes, aren't they just? And my two-pointed hat. And my honorary factorum's sword. But they are small consolation to me. These decorations do not make a Shakespeare of me.

FATHER: Shakespeare?

RICK: Don't tell a soul, Leo. There are some things one only tells one's valet.

FATHER: Shakespeare?

RICK: 1564 to 1616. Stratford-upon-Avon.

FATHER: William Shakespeare?

RICK: Yes, the great Will.

FATHER: As it happens, sir. . . .

RICK: I suppose his little friends must have called him Bill.

FATHER: I have a daughter who claims she is Shakespeare.

RICK: What did you say?

FATHER: My daughter Willy-Anne insists that she's Shakespeare.

RICK: How odd. Has this sort of thing ever happened in your family before?

FATHER: Never, sir; ours is a healthy family.

RICK: And . . . upon what does she base this claim?

FATHER: Upon Bernadette Soubirous.

RICK: *(after some moments of reflection)* Try as I might, I do not see the connection.

FATHER: No, nor me, sir. And yet, that's how it is. When Bernadette Soubirous was having her visions, people stuck pins into her, and she felt nothing. Well, that's how it is with Willy-Anne when she's writing.

RICK: She has visions?

FATHER: Where else would everything she writes about come from?

RICK: I see. And . . . what does she write about?

FATHER: I don't know, sir. I don't understand any of it.

RICK: I see.

FATHER: It's beginning to worry me, sir.

RICK: She'll get over it. It's just her age.

FATHER: I'm afraid not, sir. If anything, it gets worse as she gets older. .

RICK: And....Has she thought she was Shakespeare for long?

FATHER: As soon as she could talk, sir. As soon as she could talk she told us she was Shakespeare. I didn't let it worry me at first. After all, Shakespeares were two a penny, and anyway, she was only a child—children do get these fantasies, ... but now she's of marriageable age.

RICK: Marriageable. Well, well.

FATHER: Her mother and I don't know what to do.

RICK: I can see it's a very difficult situation for you. Is she really of marriageable age?

FATHER: Just, sir. But that's the least of our problems.

RICK: It sounds to me as though she needs someone to sort her out a bit.

FATHER: Oh, yes, sir.

RICK: Someone serious.

FATHER: Oh, yes, yes.

RICK: Someone who understands women as well as literature.

FATHER: If Sir would only....

RICK: I would, my friend; I certainly would. Send her to see me tomorrow.

CATHARSIS: Must she really go and see that stuffed dummy?

NEMESIS: She must.

WALPURGIS: It's time that young lady was taught the ways of the world.

PSORIASIS: It's time she cast the dice, so that we could know what she's made of.

NEMESIS: Double or quits, win or lose everything. But it's by losing that she'll win.

* * *

RICK O'SHEA/PATRON OF THE ARTS: Write, write, write, everybody writes. Even I write.

WILLY-ANNE: Really?

RICK: Didn't you know? But it's a well-known fact! You are a little ignoramus, aren't you? How do you think I became such an important patron of the arts?

WILLY-ANNE: What are they for?

RICK: What do you mean? What are they for? What are who for?

WILLY-ANNE: Patrons of the arts?

RICK: You really don't know anything, do you? A patron of the arts is a high-ranking civil servant.

WILLY-ANNE: Oh.

RICK: A very high-ranking civil servant. You need to have a nose for it.

WILLY-ANNE: A nose?

RICK: Flair, pers-pi-ca-ci-ty . . . . A kind of sixth sense that allows you to distinguish the real artist from a potential failure, the writer of genius from the scruffy pen pusher, the darling of the muses from the humble plodder. In brief, it allows you to pick out the rrrrreal poet.

WILLY-ANNE: And you can always pick him out?

RICK: Without firing a shot, . . . thanks to my nose. The destiny of men of letters is decided by my nostrils!

CATHARSIS: This is too much. I must intervene.

WALPURGIS: Absolutely not. She must be left alone to complete her apprenticeship.

CATHARSIS: But she might lose herself.

NEMESIS: She must lose herself in order to find herself.

RICK: Mind you, I started off by studying law. Nothing quite like law as a training in style. All those condemned to death will have their heads cut off. No unnecessary words. Lesson one: When writing use the minimum possible words.

WILLY-ANNE: *(jotting it down)* . . . the minimum possible words.

CHORUS: The minimum possible words.

RICK: In an ideal situation, that would leave us with none. One must work at economy. I have in fact written far too much, but don't tell anyone, no one dares notice. About a hundred poems, a thousand articles, recipes, essays, knitting patterns, a diary. . . .

WILLY-ANNE: Do you write absolutely everything down in it?

RICK: Not on your life! Lesson two: never write everything down.

WILLY-ANNE: Never write everything down.

CHORUS: Never write everything down.

RICK: How did you first become Shakespeare?

WILLY-ANNE: I didn't become. I am.

RICK: Gulp! Since when, then?

WILLY-ANNE: As far back as I can remember.

RICK: Gulp! Explain what you mean.

WILLY-ANNE: It's just something inside me, a kind of scream, a wail, a death rattle.

RICK: That you hear all the time?

WILLY-ANNE: That wells up inside me whenever I'm suffering too much.

RICK: Have you suffered so much?

WILLY-ANNE: No more than anyone else, I suppose. Less, perhaps. But everything affects me so deeply.

RICK: Deeply? How deeply?

WILLY-ANNE: To the very center of my being.

RICK: More towards the top or the bottom?

WILLY-ANNE: I don't know.

RICK: Come, you must know. Top or bottom?

WILLY-ANNE: I don't know.

RICK: In the middle, then.

WILLY-ANNE: Yes, in the middle, in the center. In the heart. *(Pause)* And when the pain becomes unbearable, I burst.

CATHARSIS: I burst. You have nothing to do with it.

PSORIASIS: What about her body, then, her body with its life salts, its vapors, its ball of agony. Doesn't that have anything to do with it?

NEMESIS: Silence, Ladies.

RICK: Have you ever been in love?

WILLY-ANNE: My God!

RICK: In love, really in love?

WILLY-ANNE: The wound still hasn't healed.

RICK: In love, to the bitter end.

WILLY-ANNE: To the top of the Great Pyramid. To the top of the highest tower.

RICK: *(thoughtfully)* I understand. Suppose I were to stick pins in you?

WILLY-ANNE: Now is not the moment.

RICK: Suppose I were to attack you with my sword?

WILLY-ANNE: You'd have to take your medals off first.

RICK: Why? Don't you like them?

WILLY-ANNE: I'd like to see if there's anything underneath them.

RICK: There is .... There is. Feel. *(He shows his heart, then starts taking off his medals.)*

WILLY-ANNE: Quite loud. Who would have believed it?

RICK: I'm really no more than a little boy.

WILLY-ANNE: But a moment ago you were trying to give me literature lessons.

RICK: You're wrong; that was months ago.

WILLY-ANNE: Doesn't time fly.

RICK: Shall I keep my jacket on?

WILLY-ANNE: Where's your sword?

RICK: Turn the light off and I'll show you.

WILLY-ANNE: Is it more visible in the dark?

RICK: Turn the light off!

(Darkness)

RICK: Lesson three: Always get undressed in the dark. Always hide what cannot be seen.

CHORUS: Always hide what cannot be seen.

(Half light)

RICK: You're like a little wild plant that's difficult to train. You should be kept in the shade. Alone. In the warmth and security of an unflinching affection. By a mature man capable of understanding you.

FATHER: I am a wild plant difficult to train. I grow in the shade but look the sun in face. As to whether I should be alone or not, that's my business, not yours.

RICK: But I thought you loved me?

WILLY-ANNE: Naked, yes. I could love you if you were naked. But you always keep something on.

RICK: My upbringing and my position in life would never allow me to go around naked! Where would I pin my medals? Hang my sword? What are you thinking about?

WILLY-ANNE: The top of the highest tower. The top of the Great Pyramid.

RICK: Do you want me to undress completely? Do you want me to walk around in nothing but my skin?

WILLY-ANNE: What would be the point? Even your skin is a cover. You'd still be able to hide in it.

RICK: Tell me! What more do you want of me? I am at your feet. Speak! Speak! What should I do?

WILLY-ANNE: If you don't know, how do you expect me to?

RICK: Can't you see that I'm bursting at the seams? Can't you see I'm cracking up?

WILLY-ANNE: It's not enough. Not quite. Not completely.

RICK: I've taken my medals off, thrown my clothes away, lost my nose! My sword has no value any longer. What more do you want?

WILLY-ANNE: You to free me. To leave. To let me become Shakespeare once more.

RICK: But you are Shakespeare. Shakespeare. Saint-Just. Lao-Tse. Asterix. Anyone you like.

WILLY-ANNE: No. I only want to be Shakespeare. Or Bernadette Soubirous.

RICK: *(kneeling)* Willy-Anne Soubirous, love me. Bernadette Shakespeare, have pity on me.

WILLY-ANNE: Part of my soul is very close to yours, sir.

RICK: Sir? Sir? Why sir? And why are you talking about your soul? Why? It was your body that belonged to me.

WILLY-ANNE: Well, I've taken it back, and I'm going to keep it.

RICK: Lend it to me, then; only lend it to me.

WILLY-ANNE: Enough.

RICK: Well, pieces of your body, then? Your breasts, for example? Yes, your breasts. Those little breasts I stroked so often? Or your throat? That's it, your throat. And that hollow, you know, that little hollow. Or your abdomen? Oh, yes, yes, your abdomen. Let me get back into it. I'll make myself very small, very small, very small . . . .

WILLY-ANNE: Enough.

(Exit Rick O'Shea.)

(Nemesis, Catharsis, Walpurgis, Psoriasis, chanting)
> She knows what you're suffering, she'll suffer
> it too.
> She can do nothing for you, just as no one will
> be able to do anything for her.
> Each of us spins in ourselves, our own web of
> pain.
> In a love that's gone, each misses
> Not what has been taken away
> But what they had put into it.
> We find ourselves alone, as alone as a solitary
> piece of clay,
> Alone and imprisoned on the iceberg of our
> days,
> Alone and barren like a wall of stone.
> Temptation all around.
> Gyrocompass gyrating.
> The stars deceiving.
> One knows the moment has come to take the
> plunge.
> The other withdraws into his skeletal cage.
> Forever renouncing the few words he could
> say.

CATHARSIS: *(to Willy-Anne)* He said he'd undress completely. You know very well he couldn't have done it. There are certain beings who could never undress completely. They are like insects curled up in their coccoons.

WILLY-ANNE: I'm frightened. Everyone will see me; everyone will say: you know what she's like, don't you?

CATHARSIS: What she's like?

WILLY-ANNE: Different from them. Unable to fit in with their scheme of things. Loving whom I want to love, desiring whom I want to desire ....

PSORIASIS: When you know what it is, when you don't succeed, when you become delirious.

CATHARSIS: When your soul, your beautiful soul, starts to ooze out of every pore,

WALPURGIS: When, dying, you can utter no more than: more, more.

NEMESIS: What a lot it takes to make a poet!

WILLY-ANNE: I grow in the shade but look the sun in the face.

CATHARSIS: Moonless nights, moonlit nights ....

WILLY-ANNE: I'm frightened. The sea is in front of me.

CHORUS: Let's go. Let's go.

WILLY-ANNE: Loving whom I want to love, desiring whom I want to desire.

CHORUS: The sea, ... the sea. Let's go. The sea .... LET'S GO.

(In the course of the last few lines, Agatha has returned onstage.)

NEMESIS: The third time she met Agatha ....

PSORIASIS: Be quiet, this one only concerns me.

WALPURGIS: No, me!

CATHARSIS: Me.

PSORIASIS: Me!

WALPURGIS: Me!

CATHARSIS: Me!

NEMESIS: Silence, Ladies. *(Pause)* It concerns all of us. *(Pause)* Either we are completely committed or not at all.

(The sound of an engine can be heard. Agatha and Willy-Anne are in a car.)

AGATHA: Why do you keep going round and round the square?

WILLY-ANNE: I can't drive straight when I'm in love. I just keep going round and round in circles.

AGATHA: Are you really in love?

WILLY-ANNE: Very much so.

AGATHA: Me too. I can feel my Adam's apple rising.

WILLY-ANNE: I can feel my solar plexus falling.

AGATHA: 40,000 volts.

WILLY-ANNE: 212 degrees Fahrenheit.

AGATHA: Can you hear the second movement of Brahms' Sextet?

WILLY-ANNE: It will break our hearts one day.

AGATHA: No!

WILLY-ANNE: One day it will, not now, next week.

AGATHA: You'll be the one to leave me.

WILLY-ANNE: No, I won't. It will be you.

AGATHA: Are you still going round in circles?

WILLY-ANNE: I will as long as you want me to.

AGATHA: Shall I say forever?

WILLY-ANNE: It might be better if you didn't.

AGATHA: But you're still going round in circles.

WILLY-ANNE: Yes, I know, and I will until we've been around the world, around ourselves, around love.

AGATHA: But we'll never get around it.

WILLY-ANNE: I'm glad I've really met you at last, Agatha.

AGATHA: Keep me, won't you?

WILLY-ANNE: Don't leave me.

AGATHA: Can such things as this happen, then? Dreams be realized? Finding the one you had been searching for?

WILLY-ANNE: Yes. We find the one we're searching for.

AGATHA: Finding and then losing again.

WILLY-ANNE: Don't talk of losing. Not yet.

AGATHA: Where are we?

WILLY-ANNE: Here. Now.

AGATHA: I thought we were at the end of the world.

WILLY-ANNE: Even the end of the world would be here. Even the top of the Great Pyramid. The top of the highest tower. For the first time in my life I can see where I am, because you're with me.

AGATHA: We'll never be alone again, Willy-Anne.

WILLY-ANNE: Not until we've been around the world.

AGATHA: Around ourselves.

WILLY-ANNE: Around love.

AGATHA: We'll never be alone again.

> *(Nemesis, Catharsis, Walpurgis, Psoriasis, chanting)*
> Seven times they went around the world, but never around themselves and only nearly around love.
> One day they finished up by sitting down. They could see where they'd been, their footprints always intermingling—through tiredness perhaps.
> Be brave, my children, we have been counting the days you've had with one another. You will not grow old together.

AGATHA: We've managed to get through four cars, two televisions, one fridge, eight pairs of sheets, seven dozen glasses, plates, cups. Not to mention the rest.

WILLY-ANNE: We've reared three dogs, one cat, twenty-four tropical fish, and all the mice that inhabited the flat.

AGATHA: We've worked our way through nine bank accounts, all with overdrafts.

WILLY-ANNE: We've had five or six loyal friends, our share of crazes and a fair share of disappointments.

AGATHA: Thirteen years, all with their seasons.

WILLY-ANNE: The odors, colors and flavors of twenty different countries.

AGATHA: You showed me that mountains have a human face.

WILLY-ANNE: And you showed me how the sea is more than just the sea.

AGATHA: Five thousand days together. And never a dull moment.

WILLY-ANNE: Five thousand nights together when our bodies were one.

AGATHA: I slept on the right.

WILLY-ANNE: You slept on the left.

AGATHA: Left?

WILLY-ANNE: Right?

AGATHA: We'd change places from time to time.

WILLY-ANNE: Against one another, in one another.

AGATHA: Like on a tandem.

WILLY-ANNE: In you.

AGATHA: In us.

WILLY-ANNE: But I was no longer me.

AGATHA: But I became you.

(Agatha slowly leaves Willy-Anne, who tries to hold her back. This is a silent scene.)

WALPURGIS: Suddenly everything shattered!

CATHARSIS: Why did they split up? What happened?

WALPURGIS: They didn't split up. They couldn't have split up. The ground opened up between them and suddenly there was an abyss separating them that no one will ever be able to fill.

CATHARSIS: But why did they destroy one another?

CHORUS: It was no destruction. It was a construction.
One cannot build without digging right down to the foundations, without ploughing up the earth, without creating gaping holes.
The sand is left to shroud the ruins.
Waves to cover engulfed cities.
Wind and fire to reduce everything to ashes.
There's nothing to be done.
Nothing.

WILLY-ANNE: I'm in pain. I'm dying of pain. Everything is broken up inside me. There are bits scattered everywhere. How will I ever be able to find myself again? I'm dying.

CATHARSIS: Well, it's not the first time and it won't be the last. Come on, stand up.

WILLY-ANNE: We talk of suffering, but we don't know the first thing about it, really. And yet what I've experienced in life is nothing more than banal.

CATHARSIS: Nothing extraordinary whatsoever. The odd meeting. The odd affair of the heart. Come on, stand up.

WILLY-ANNE: What counts is not what I've experienced, but what I've felt.

CATHARSIS: Stand up, I said.

WILLY-ANNE: No, I want to stay lying down. I want to sleep. I want to die.

CATHARSIS: Go down to the very depths of your being. To the very center of your solitude. To your inner truth.

WILLY-ANNE: Tell me that I'll be happy again one day.

CATHARSIS: You will.

WILLY-ANNE: Tell me that I won't suffer anymore.

CATHARSIS: You'll suffer again.

WILLY-ANNE: Tell me that I'll be able to love again one day.

CATHARSIS: You will.

WILLY-ANNE: Tell me that I'll be doing extraordinary things again one day.

CATHARSIS: No more extraordinary things. No more Great Pyramids. No more high towers. No more crazy car rides around town squares. From now on, nothing more for you than a mundane existence to the depths of your innermost reality, to the corners of your true self.

(Catharsis helps Willy-Anne stand up. Willy-Anne slowly rejoins Agatha.)

WILLY-ANNE: The fourth time I met Agatha, we decided to climb to the Acropolis together.

AGATHA: I don't even know your name.

WILLY-ANNE: Shakespeare.

AGATHA: Don't tell lies.

WILLY-ANNE: My name is Shakespeare. Shakespeare is my name.

AGATHA: I suppose it could be true, Shakespeares *are* two a penny. Are you all alike?

WILLY-ANNE: Yes, inasmuch as we all think we're unique. That's why we write.

(Enter Rick O'Shea/General.)

RICK O'SHEA/GENERAL: We, General Rick O'Shea of the Literary Army, have decided, decreed, and ordered that the excesses of some linguistic revolutionaries must end. It is absolutely prohibited to say the sea lay like the folds of bright girdle. The sea is the sea and that's final. The bells of Shoreditch will never grow rich, and the city has never worn the beauty of the morning like a garment. It is forbidden to pale at the mention of the further off from England the nearer is to France, to have one eye on the pot the other up the chimney, to compare the female parts to a fig. It is forbidden, forbidden. It is obvious that there is no place for sensual delight alongside order and calm. As to luxury, we are living in a time of inflation. It is useless, therefore, to waste time remembering the house where you were born and to waste idle tears looking on the happy autumn-fields. It is useless to waste time looking for the snows of yester-year, the daughter of Elysium and Mercy, Pity, Peace and Love. It is useless if all the words that you utter and all the words that you write spread out their wings untiring and never rest in the flight! We *must* tell ourselves! We must repeat it over and over again! Reread the great authors, those who express their thoughts clearly. The sea is a vast stretch of salt water that covers two thirds of the globe. We must recognize it! We must put up notices about it! We must write it down! Good writers who are good thinkers. Or, in order to avoid a nasty shock, those who do not think at all! If in doubt, don't! Don't ever read again! Otherwise, . . . Court Martial. Bang! Bang!

(Exit.)

AGATHA: It was my dream in life to write. It was my dream in life to meet a writer. Shakespeare, for example.

WILLY-ANNE: *Je suis Shakespeare.*

AGATHA: That sounds too good to be true. Too good. You're just a hallucination. Somehow I'll have to incorporate you into my daily life.

WILLY-ANNE: It's the first time I've ever been taken for a hallucination. Look at me. Don't I look real? Am I not all that is real?

AGATHA: My daily life! A bunch of leeks, a head of celery, carrots, turnips. *(Pause)* I really like turnips.

WILLY-ANNE: A night of love, the light turned low, your hair tied back with an elastic band. *(Pause)* I really like your hair.

AGATHA: Two packets of biscuits, a pot of jam, a pound of coffee, . . . *(Pause)* Beans or ground, I wonder?

WILLY-ANNE: A mole on your right shoulder blade, a vein throbbing in the hollow of your neck. *(Pause)* Lips or hands, I wonder?

AGATHA: Two pounds of sugar, little strands of grey hair on your forehead, six cans of beer, your fingers moving all over me.

WILLY-ANNE: A bottle of wine, your body against mine, apples, oranges, don't forget the bread.

AGATHA: In bed tonight.

WILLY-ANNE: No. This afternoon. It looks as though it's raining. It always rains while we're in love. The weather's only fine when we've split up.

AGATHA: Well, for the moment it's raining.

WILLY-ANNE: What bliss!

AGATHA: Winter's going to be mild this year.

WILLY-ANNE: Well, well, well.

AGATHA: Well, well, well. That's just what my analyst said the first time I told her about you.

WILLY-ANNE: There are always three of us: you, me and your analyst.

> CATHARSIS: This is where the psychoanalyst comes in.
>
> WALPURGIS: No, no!
>
> PSORIASIS: But this is obviously the moment!
>
> NEMESIS: Sorry, it's not possible for technical reasons.
>
> CATHARSIS: All right. But she must have an answering machine?

WALPURGIS: Give me her number, will you?

NEMESIS: Silence, Ladies.

AGATHA: No, not always. She's not here at the moment.

WILLY-ANNE: Are you still happy?

AGATHA: I love . . . .

WILLY-ANNE: *(putting her finger on Agatha's lips)* Tempt not the gods. Put not your faith in the stars.

AGATHA: Who said that?

WILLY-ANNE: Shakespeare.

AGATHA: I'm always forgetting you're a writer.

WILLY-ANNE: For the moment I'm quite happy just writing on your abdomen.

(Enter the woman psychoanalyst.)

RICK O'SHEA/PSYCHOANALYST: This is an answering machine. Trish O'Shea speaking. I shall be away until the tenth of January. To make an appointment, call again on Tuesday, January tenth, between 11:15 and 12:00 noon, or on Wednesday, January eleventh, between 9:00 and 9:45, or on Thursday, January twelfth, between 9:00 and 9:45 or between 4:15 and 5:00 in the afternoon. This is the end of the recorded message.

PSORIASIS: That lady seems to know what she wants.

WALPURGIS: I'd never be able to remember what times to call her.

PSORIASIS: What could she teach us anyway?

RICK: The case of Willy-Anne S. is quite straightforward.
I'd even go as far as to say that it is the most straightforward
of cases. For reasons that could only be divulged in the
course of a long therapy session, Willy-Anne S. intends to
stay at the infancy stage that rejects penetration. *(to Willy-
Anne and Agatha)* But how, my dear young ladies, do you
make love? There aren't dozens of ways of doing it, of finding cloud nine, of ending up in seventh heaven, of attaining
the sublime! A key is made to fit a lock! It's the law of Nature, you see. Take a look at Nature and you'll see. Mo-
reover, Willy-Anne would like to give birth to Agatha while
at the same time be born of her. It's a hopeless situation.

(Exit.)

CATHARSIS: How Cornelian!

NEMESIS: That kind of epithet went out of fashion a
long time ago.

CATHARSIS: I've always spoken like that.

NEMESIS: That's no reason to carry on.

CATHARSIS: Willy-Anne is in labor, fine, giving birth
to herself; I don't mind, but I don't see that it's got
anything to do with the language she uses.

NEMESIS: You haven't understood a thing, have
you?

CATHARSIS: Is she going to express herself differently, then?

NEMESIS: She has been doing that for some time
now.

CATHARSIS: Oh, I hadn't noticed.

NEMESIS: I'm not surprised. You never got beyond the aristocratic Muse.

* * *

AGATHA: It isn't because you write, you know, that you are above doing the daily chores. I'm always sweeping masses of crumbs up from under the table where you've been eating. You spend an hour in a room, and when you leave it, it looks as though you've been holding a rummage sale in there. Your papers are always lying around the place, and you never listen to anything I say.

WILLY-ANNE: I can hear you perfectly well.

AGATHA: You can hear me, but you never listen to me.

WILLY-ANNE: I am Shakespeare.

AGATHA: Huh! Shakespeare. Let's talk about that, shall we? God knows how it was my dream in life to meet a writer. But you're no different from anybody else. Your conversations are no more than monologues, labyrinths of digressions, and totally uninteresting.

WILLY-ANNE: Yes, but you don't realize what's happening deep down.

AGATHA: Deep down!

WILLY-ANNE: O.K. Forget it.

AGATHA: Forget it! Forget it! It's too easy just to say forget it! *(Pause)* In the course of my analysis, I have killed and buried our relationship. I don't love you. I only thought I did.

WILLY-ANNE: I would never have guessed.

AGATHA: I don't love you. I don't love you. I don't love you. Anyway, our relationship is incomplete.

WILLY-ANNE: Is there something missing? Do you think there's something missing?

AGATHA: No. Not me. My analyst.

WILLY-ANNE: Your analyst! And what does she say is wrong with our relationship?

AGATHA: She says it's incomplete.

WILLY-ANNE: Yet it seems to me that together we form a whole, and that it's that that counts.

AGATHA: Be quiet. Be quiet. Be quiet.

WILLY-ANNE: And what about love in all that? What about love, eh? My stomach sinks to my boots whenever I see you. And what about desire?

   (Silence)

Why are you crying?

AGATHA: I was thinking about the Acropolis.

WILLY-ANNE: The Acropolis? Oh, yes, the Acropolis. *(Pause)* You take the number sixteen from Syntagma Square. If you're going from Omonia Square it's better to take a trolley bus, a number two or twelve. I'd planned the trip well in advance, right up to the Acropolis itself. The Propylaeum, the Caryatides. The Temple of Athena. The Parthenon. Agatha, I love you. The Acropolis, the saffron sun, the amethyst sky. We wouldn't even have noticed the thousands of tourists. I climbed up to the Acropolis three times, each time without you. How was I able to live without you? How can I carry on living without you? Acropolis. Theater of Dionysus. Dionysus. Dionysus! Theater! Agatha, if you only knew how real you are to me! You alone would I have seen. Nothing else. Except the rooftops of Athens from the Acropolis.

AGATHA: It's no good, Willy-Anne.

WILLY-ANNE: No good? No good, so soon? No good, so quickly? No good. Even though I . . . .No good, even though you . . . . No. It's not possible. Or else everything is no good, then. There should have been a way. There should always be a way. A love like ours cannot be found on every street corner, you know. The mole on your right shoulder blade. The vein throbbing in the hollow of your neck. The paving stones are worn out on the Acropolis. The marble flagstones are worn out. *(She shouts.)* What is the point of being you if one day you end up being so desperately alone?

(Some time passes.)

It is not the first time and it won't be the last. She'll come back; she's coming back. Stay where you are, Agatha! Oh, to descend inside myself, to read myself at last in the semidarkness of my solitude. Semidarkness or light? To descend inside myself. But it's so painful, I can't. Catharsis! Catharsis! Why did you make my heart so small?

CATHARSIS: It wasn't me. It was Nemesis.

NEMESIS: A thousand apologies, it was Walpurgis.

WALPURGIS: I'm very sorry, but it was Psoriasis.

PSORIASIS: There was nothing I could do about it. The heart is a hollow muscle. Uncontrollable at that, but a muscle, a muscle all the same. And hollow.

WALPURGIS: It should have been filled little by little. With compost, for example.

NEMESIS: With lime.

CATHARSIS: With cement.

PSORIASIS: Stuffed with straw.

WALPURGIS: With paper.

NEMESIS: And set alight.

CATHARSIS: Reduced to ashes.

PSORIASIS: Turned into a mortuary, a public dump.

WALPURGIS: But that's what it is, isn't it?

WILLY-ANNE: Silence, Ladies.

(Walpurgis, Psoriasis, Catharsis, Nemesis, chanting)

> Heart filled. Too filled. Badly filled. All crumpled and creased. Heart muddy, boggy, oozing ossifications, defecations, damp tins, empty bins . . . .

CATHARSIS: But, . . . but, . . . Nemesis . . . . Didn't you fill it with want?

WILLY-ANNE: That's the most beautiful present I've ever been given. To want! To want! The certainty of always having to go that bit further, always having to look elsewhere. Never having roots. God knows how I've suffered because of it!

NEMESIS: And what about simple pleasures, what do you do with them?

WILLY-ANNE: They do exist, I know. But they are not enough for me. And yet, I can find the smallest glass of water delicious .

NEMESIS: But you have been given more than a glass of water!

WILLY-ANNE: Much more! But it isn't enough.

NEMESIS: We could do better.

WILLY-ANNE: What? More acute happiness? More bitter suffering?

WALPURGIS: Come now, come now. You haven't experienced that many things. Yours has been an existence not unlike many others. Rather borderline, admittedly, but even so!

WILLY-ANNE: Mine was an existence that experienced everything.

WALPURGIS: You're not going to tell me that your love affairs ....

WILLY-ANNE: It was inside me that it all happened.

WALPURGIS: All right. All right. Meanwhile, the world went its own sweet way. The Druids picked their mistletoe, the Chinese built their great wall, Christopher Columbus's fleet forged its way across to America, man took his first steps on the moon.... And you? What were you doing, Shakespeare? Useless Shakespeare? Half-baked Shakespeare?

WILLY-ANNE: I have experienced it all, I tell you. Everything. Do you think my pathetic sufferings and meager joys are the expression of the sum total of what has been churning around inside me? I sometimes feel that I am carrying the suffering of the whole world, that I am bursting with all its joy, that I am trembling with all its agony. There is a great space inside me.

CATHARSIS: A great empty space.

WILLY-ANNE: Empty?

VOICES: A great space inside you, Willy-Anne, a great space where we can come and go, a great empty space that we fill. We who know not what to say. Speak for us. Shout instead of us. Weigh heavily with the weight of our silences. WILLY-ANNE!

WILLY-ANNE: And you tell me that I haven't experienced anything? As if my life were only me? As if the wind blew only with impunity? The soft air of a balmy evening, the cool wind of dawn. As if love were nothing more than love, as if I were nothing more than myself.

VOICES: We have searched for our father together on the ramparts of waves.
We have heard the song of the nightingale at dawn.
Was it the song of the nightingale? Oh! What a night that was to remember. What a night, without sleep.
A night as fragile as glass. We have tasted all the poisons that jealousy could offer. We have killed what we loved best in the world.
We have seen the child of our love turn away from us.

WILLY-ANNE: I am not Shakespeare.

CATHARSIS: What did she say? Did I hear her properly? Did she say she wasn't Shakespeare?

WILLY-ANNE: ...never have been Shakespeare. Never believed in it for a single moment.

CATHARSIS: It's not true!

WILLY-ANNE: *(shouting)* I am not Shakespeare!

CATHARSIS: Why claim it? Maintain it? After all, you did. One day....

WILLY-ANNE: I was pretending.

CATHARSIS: I don't understand.

WILLY-ANNE: I had to live. Believe in something.

CATHARSIS: And now? What's going to happen to you now?

WILLY-ANNE: I'll fall in love again. Write again.

CATHARSIS: But you are no longer Shakespeare?

WILLY-ANNE: The sparrow knows he is not an eagle. But he still flies. I was born to write. So I write.

> WALPURGIS: You've got to admit, the girl's got a lot of courage.

> PSORIASIS: She's healthy. It's because she's healthy.

> WALPURGIS: When the superstructure's good, everything's all right.

> PSORIASIS: Right, O.K., then. But we're not out of the woods yet.

> WALPURGIS: Deo gratias!

> CATHARSIS: But now that she's not *(whispers)* Shakespeare?

FATHER: I'd even got to the stage where I believed she was Shakespeare.

MOTHER: But of course she's Shakespeare. We know it better than she. After all, we are her parents. We made her.

FATHER: Are you sure?

MOTHER: I've never doubted it for a moment.

FATHER: Well, so much the better. At least we'll have succeeded at something in our lives.

MOTHER: We didn't do it on purpose.

FATHER: It was the fault of the daffodils.

MOTHER: Actually, I think they were lilies of the valley.

RICK/DOCTOR: Identity crisis resolved. But what a lot of other problems to sort out still. Two forty-five minute sessions a week for five or six years, at a rate of $50 a session . . .

    CATHARSIS: I beg of you, leave her with her problems, or I'll have nothing to get my teeth into . . . .

    PSORIASIS: If you do, you'll start complaining about getting too fat!

    CATHARSIS: No doubt. But Willy-Anne will help me get thin, even if she isn't Shakespeare.

RICK'S VOICE: Shakespeare or not, she's guilty. Borderline without having wanted to be. Not accepted by decent people. A misfit.

VOICES: Guilty
Borderline
Lost
Misfit

CATHARSIS: Have we managed to make something of her anyway?

NEMESIS: Have we salvaged anything?

WILLY-ANNE: I think I still have a lot left to say.

CATHARSIS: And from now on you will say it without pretense, without disguise, getting straight to the point.

RICK'S VOICE: The sea is the sea, and that is final.

(The sound of the sea can be heard.)

WILLY-ANNE: The sea is the sea but I am not Shakespeare. Faced with the empty page of my life, I can believe it. But, when the page is full, I can no longer believe it. Shall I write a line, or twenty-five tragedies? *(The sea can still be heard.)* The sea is the sea and will wash everything away. The meanest comma. Nothing will be left. Nothing. Neither Shakespeare. Nor anyone else. *(The sound of the sea is very loud, and then suddenly there is silence.)*

What are poets for, Nemesis?

NEMESIS: I've already told you: nothing.

WILLY-ANNE: Nothing *(Pause)* I'm going to take a step, and then another. Even though it is for nothing. One step, and then another. My whole life like that. For what? For whom? For nothing?

CATHARSIS: Perhaps just to find out what life is all about?

WILLY-ANNE: To find out what life is all about....

(Silence)

The world revolved before us, and it will continue to revolve after us, but while we're here, what a difference it makes!

(Curtain)

ꝿ